THE
BOARD
GAME

About *The Board Game*:

"Women must be included among the candidates presented to my boards for consideration. Period. The old excuse of 'We can't find any qualified women' is no longer acceptable—because it's no longer true!"

—Julie Hill, director of Anthem Inc.

"Until recently, thirty percent women on boards seemed like an audacious goal, but now it's becoming realistic."

—Joe Keefe, CEO of Pax World

"*The Board Game* makes a great case for women in the boardroom, opening doors for corporations to find a deep, rich, untapped talent pool of potential independent directors. Thought-provoking, and clear in its arguments, this is a must-read for those who can impact board configurations."

—James G. Ellis, dean, USC Marshall School of Business

"With the pipeline of board-ready women bursting at the seams and growing evidence that having women directors strengthens performance, 'business as usual' is at last on the verge of a power paradigm shift. *The Board Game* is a savvy insider's guide to riding the wave."

—Anne Doyle, author of *Powering Up:
How America's Women Achievers Become Leaders*

"For the first four decades of women and corporate governance, the focus was on inviting women into the boardroom. We are now on the cusp of critical corporate change where outstanding women are emerging as business leaders, rather than simply supporters of management. Today, women are opening up new vistas by building innovative businesses and crafting their own boards to guide them. Conversations with accomplished women in leadership will help them navigate their careers at corporations, in governance, and as leaders."

—Elizabeth Ghaffari, author of *Outstanding in their Field:
How Women Corporate Directors Succeed*

THE
BOARD
GAME

HOW SMART WOMEN BECOME CORPORATE DIRECTORS

BETSY BERKHEMER-CREDAIRE

President and Co-founder
Berkhemer Clayton Inc.
Retained Executive Search
Los Angeles, California
www.BerkhemerClayton.com
www.WinningTheBoardGame.com

The Board Game: How Smart Women Become Corporate Directors

By Betsy Berkhemer-Credaire

Copyright © 2013 Betsy Berkhemer-Credaire

Design by Hilary Lentini, Lentini Design

10 9 8 7 6 5 4 3

ISBN-13 978-1-883318-98-7 (print edition)
ISBN-13 978-1-62649-007-8 (EPUB edition)

LIBRARY OF CONGRESS CATALOGING-IN-PUBLICATION DATA

Berkhemer-Credaire, Betsy
The board game: how smart women become corporate directors / by Betsy Berkhemer-Credaire.
pages cm
Includes bibliographical references and index.
ISBN 978-1-883318-98-7 (pbk. : alk. paper) -- ISBN 978-1-62640-007-8 (e-pub)
1. Women executives--United States. 2. Directors of corporations--United States. 3. Board of directors--United States. I. Title.
HD6054.4.U6B47 2013
658.4'220820973--dc23
2013011553

ANGEL CITY PRESS

Published by Angel City Press
2118 Wilshire Blvd. #880, Santa Monica, California 90403
+1.310.395.9982 | www.angelcitypress.com

To order additional copies visit
www.WinningTheBoardGame.com or www.angelcitypress.com

To my voyagemate of thirty years, my husband
Cris Credaire, for his intelligence, patience, and
unflagging support of my career and my writing
this book, and for the many years of flying our Cessna
Turbo 182RG—especially from California to the Carolinas
and back. Together, we logged more than ten thousand
miles and soared over spectacular rainbows.

A STANDING OVATION
Two Remarkable Trailblazers

Shirley Hufstedler in Los Angeles, one of the first women corporate directors, is now retired from Harman International, Hewlett-Packard, and US West. Born in 1925, only five years after the U.S. ratified the Nineteenth Amendment and finally women could vote, she was one of a handful of women who went to University of New Mexico and Stanford Law School. In 1968 President Lyndon Johnson appointed her Judge, U.S. Court of Appeals for the Ninth Circuit. Although not the first woman to serve on the federal Court of Appeals, the Honorable Shirley Hufstedler was for most years of her service the only woman among one hundred judges nationwide. Appointed the first-ever Secretary of Education by President Jimmy Carter, she was considered a possible candidate for Justice of the U.S. Supreme Court at a time when she would have been the first woman appointed to the court. She became well-acquainted with Bill Hewlett when they both served on the national committees to choose Rhodes Scholars and White House Fellows. After her term as Education Secretary ended, he asked her to join the Hewlett-Packard board, where again she was the first woman. Thank you Shirley Hufstedler, for leading the way and opening the doors.

Dr. Judy B. Rosener, retired from the Paul Merage School of Business at UC Irvine, has been a beacon for working women for decades. She received her bachelor's degree at UCLA, went to California State University Fullerton for her master's, and Claremont Graduate University for her doctorate. She set the pace in 1990 in *Harvard Business Review* with her article entitled "Ways Women Lead." She co-authored *Workforce America! Managing Employee Diversity as a Vital Resource,* and in 1997, wrote the book *America's Competitive Secret: Women Managers*. Then in *Directorship* in May 2003, Judy had the audacity to proclaim, "Women on Corporate Boards Makes Good Business Sense." Outspoken, respected, and tireless, she was a regular columnist for the *Los Angeles Times*, for the *Orange County Business Journal*, and a commentator on the PBS television program *Life and Times*. She has inspired countless women—including me—to achieve their fullest potential. Thank you Judy Rosener, for your great sense of humor and for encouraging women to "Never give up!"

CONTENTS

MEET THE
Women

Directors

INTRODUCTION
Goodbye,

Monopoly.

THE BOARD GAME: HOW SMART WOMEN BECOME CORPORATE DIRECTORS ANSWERS THE QUESTIONS ASKED BY MORE AND MORE WOMEN TODAY — How do I get on a corporate board? What career choices should I make so I can ultimately serve on a corporate board? Having more women on corporate boards couldn't be more important to America today—to strengthen the business foundation of our country by making sure women have a voice in corporate boardrooms. To be more successful, the country and American corporations need gender diversity at the highest levels of decision-making.

Getting more women on more boards takes the same kind of strategies as any complex game, one well-planned move after another. And that's what this book is about: winning The Board Game. The best part is that when more women win board seats, everybody wins. It's not a game of men against women—far from it. This game puts gender aside, and puts shareholders first.

I first became concerned about how few women corporate directors there were in 1996. I invited a small group of Los Angeles-based women corporate directors whom I knew personally—Bonnie Hill, Andrea Van de Kamp, Betsy Sanders, June Lockhart, Beverly Thomas, and Vilma Martinez—to get together informally, share stories and ideas, and, perhaps most importantly, to discuss why women were in the minority as directors. The women served on Fortune 500 corporate boards in other states as well as in California, and they had incredible insight.

The conversation was eye-opening, energizing, and educational—especially for me. As a retained executive search professional, and as a business owner for four decades, I have long been active in the advancement of women in the business world—and a champion of financial independence for women. These women directors who gathered then (and still do!) are definitely examples of success in both.

We came together annually after that, and more Southern California women directors joined in. The conversation continued to be open, candid, and confidential. Exploring different topics each year, we talked about business challenges we faced, and offered one another suggestions, solutions, and sources. The women directors gained strength in numbers and, even though most were the only woman on their boards, they no longer felt alone.

At the same time in New York, Susan Stautberg also had started an informal women directors group, and Alison Winter had launched another group in Chicago. In 2003, those two dynamic women officially formed WomenCorporateDirectors, and as its co-chairs, built a global network with chapters in several major cities. They invited my group to become the official Southern California chapter. Henrietta Holsman Fore in Washington, D.C., became the global co-chair. In just ten years, WomenCorporateDirectors expanded to fifty chapters, with more than 1,800 members who serve on 2,600 corporate boards worldwide.

As you will read on the pages to come, there is a sea change underway. The business case for women on boards has been proved by independent research. Recognizing this, male business leaders are collaborating with women's organizations to promote the issue. We know now that the supply-side pipeline is full to bursting with board-ready women, many endorsed by their own CEOs as qualified candidates for outside corporate boards.

But the demand side is the problem. The number of board seats held by women at Fortune 500 corporations remains static, at only 16.6% in 2012, almost no increase over recent years. There are thousands more public and private companies in America that traditionally have had few women on their boards. The challenge is to create more demand. Proactive women's organizations, enlightened CEOs, institutional investors, and the media have come together to produce a steady drumbeat, urging corporations to increase the number of board seats for women. They are shining the spotlight on fifty of the Fortune 500 corporations that by 2013 still don't have any women directors, and on many more that have only one.

I wrote this book to move this important issue forward by increasing awareness among CEOs and corporate nominating committees about the depth and talent of board-ready women. The profiles of successful women corporate directors will help women at all stages of their careers create roadmaps to become board-ready themselves. This is just one tool to increase the number of women destined to win The Board Game.

With this book, I intend to:

- Increase awareness of research studies supporting the business case for more women on boards.
- Inform career women there has never been a better time to seek a seat on the board of directors of a public company.
- Show women how to gain board membership through wise career choices and building strategic networks.
- Spark conversations at dinner tables and boardroom tables about why there are so few women on the boards of directors of American corporations— and what can be done about it.
- Applaud the advocacy and initiatives of forward-thinking male CEOs, several women's organizations, and activist shareholders.
- Create a guide for women on how to navigate the waters, seize the opportunities, and stay alert to potential openings on corporate boards, so they will be ready to step over the threshold.

More than fifty women corporate directors are here to help. They have shared their pathways—how they managed their careers to become capable, dynamic, and creative corporate directors—so others can learn from their success and follow these women into America's boardrooms.

No matter what challenges they have faced, these women report tremendous satisfaction with their roles on boards. They bring different perspectives and useful recommendations about the issues before boards, and clearly demonstrate the value of diversity to the decision-making process. Their common goal is to recruit more women to the highest levels of American corporations.

There has never been a better time for corporate boards to bring more qualified women to the table, and for women to set their sights on the boardroom as the pinnacle of their careers. The rules of The Board Game have changed. Why shouldn't there be as many women as men on public boards of directors bringing their experience and judgment to govern companies and represent America's shareholders?

Just look at the U.S. Congress. In 2013, for the first time in history, the 113th Congress had twenty female senators, the most ever—that's twenty percent of the total one hundred. And the House of Representatives had seventy-seven congresswomen—17.7% of the 435 members. If women can be trusted to run the country, certainly they can be trusted to run America's corporations.

As they've done in the Senate, women should be able to take over at least twenty percent of the seats in boardrooms in short order. Longer term, we will see women occupying more and more board seats. I'm betting on thirty to forty percent in the next few years. And eventually, that percentage should be fifty.

The ideal minimum is three women on every corporate board, because it takes three women together to truly make a difference. Since the average board has eight to twelve people, three unified voices make a decided impact. As James Kristie, associate publisher of *Directors & Boards* Magazine, says: one woman on a board is a token, two women on a board might be heard—three women actually can make an impact.

To shift the numbers, women who already sit on corporate boards must urge their colleagues to bring on other women. Shareholders must use the power of proxy and letters to CEOs to demand that at least one woman be nominated for every slate of board candidates. Because numbers count, activist shareholders may well be the most potent force for achieving gender parity on corporate boards in a shorter time.

Research shows that corporations with women on their boards perform better than companies without. That's why investors and shareholders have a stake in this issue for business performance reasons. All investors want to make money. If more women on boards can help make that happen, shareholders should be clamoring, "Bring on more women!"

Let's all make gender diversity *and gender equality* a priority. Women *can* win this game.

Author's Note:

The Board Game was first published in May of 2013. The following October, the California State Legislature was the first in the nation to pass a Resolution urging all public corporations in California to seat one to three women on their boards of directors by December of 2016. Proposed by the National Association of Women Business Owners-California, and sponsored by Senator Hannah-Beth Jackson and Assembly member Bonnie Lowenthal, SCR 62 recommends at least three women directors on boards with nine or more seats; at least two women directors on boards with five to eight seats; and at least one woman director on boards with four or fewer seats. See California Legislature http://leginfo.legislature.ca.gov/faces/billTextClient.xhtml?bill_id=201320140SCR62

START HERE...

Chapter 1
Women Belong in
the Boardroom

WOMEN

1 Belong in the

Boardroom

IT IS JUST AS IMPORTANT FOR WOMEN TO SIT ON AMERICA'S CORPORATE BOARDS AS IT IS FOR WOMEN TO SIT ON THE SUPREME COURT, IN THE WHITE HOUSE, IN CONGRESS, AND IN CIVIC LEADERSHIP positions. It's time to bring women into the decision-making process.

One hundred forty-four years after the Declaration of Independence was signed—almost five generations later—American women won the right to vote in 1920. It took protests, hunger strikes, and women going to jail to finally prevail. Now it's been almost one hundred years since the Nineteenth Amendment was ratified. Will we need to go to similar extremes to put women into the boardrooms that control American business?

Not this time. Today there are thousands of women with stellar business careers who, with visibility, strategic networking, and smart moves, can win The Board Game. In fact, more women are planning their career strategies and making it known that they want to be directors. Ten percent of the Fortune 500 boards still have no women, and only 16.6 % of the seats are held by women. Those women are ready for more women to join them at the directors' tables. The stockholders certainly are ready. How do we create the demand? The research says it's high time for change.

"Ultimately, value creation comes from people," says Deborah Wince-Smith, president of the Council on Competitiveness, based in Washington, D.C. "Good boards are moving away from the strictly fiduciary oversight, to add focus on risk, resilience, and strategic direction, and sustain their positioning for growth over time. Women directors bring excellent business experience and different leadership styles. They are often more collaborative thinkers and more integrative in ways they solve problems. Women tend to look across the landscape to connect strategy with conceptualization."

Women, as Wince-Smith points out, bring a different perspective to the boardroom. As so many corporate directors I've interviewed have said, board-ready women now have the business acumen and years of experience needed to be excellent board members. They know that The Board Game is serious business and makes a difference not just to the American economy, but also to the global economy. The stakes are high, so corporate boards should be hustling to find women candidates—at least three per board. Or why not fifty percent?

Mark T. Bertolini, chairman, president, and CEO of Aetna, says: "Current economic and social changes confronting the U.S. economy call for a style of leadership that requires the acceptance and advancement of the idea that companies can do well by doing good, and that the power of influence provides better results than many alternative approaches. Women are proving to be particularly skilled in these areas, and will be sought after by corporations around the world. Women in leadership roles at the executive and director levels will be an essential ingredient for organizational success."

Bertolini recognizes that women bring a decision-making difference to the table—Aetna already has four women on its twelve-person board.

Women's performance as directors—grounded in business acumen and decision-making expertise rather than as tokens—amplifies the obvious: women are equal to men at running companies. That's why women are now ready to win The Board Game.

In a strategic game there is a defining moment—the instant when a confluence of external factors and good strategy determines the outcome. The Board Game is absolutely strategic, as you will learn in these pages. The object is threefold: to significantly increase the number of women serving at the highest level of in American business, to encourage boards to open seats for more women candidates, and to put *you* in one of those seats as a director.

Public awareness is growing—there is consensus that corporate boards should include more women. It is just good business. For women who want to become corporate directors, the first board seat is the hardest to win. So before you can play the game, it's important to understand why boardrooms have been dominated by men   and the factors that are converging to change the rules.

Why is there a Gender Gap in American Boardrooms?

Chief executive officers of public corporations report to their boards of directors. Independent directors are elected by shareholders as their representatives on the board. Shareholders vote to elect the board members, who are then held accountable for the company's performance and profits. Millions of women are shareholders, and hundreds of millions more are primary customers of American corporations, and yet, I repeat, only 16.6% of the board seats of Fortune 500 companies are held by women. We must ask, "Why are there so few women directors on boards?" Here's some history:

1. CEOs traditionally have surrounded themselves with board members who are experienced CEOs from other large companies. Of course. According to 2012 research by Catalyst, the nonprofit source for research about working women, there were only twenty-one women serving as CEOs of Fortune 500 companies, slightly more than four percent. So if boards limit their candidate pool to other CEOs, there's only a very small pool of women CEOs to draw from. And they are already serving on other major boards. The criteria has to expand to include women from senior executive positions, women retired from government service and women business-owners, as well as women from academia.

2. It's a given that men have historically held the reins of American industry. Based on military experience, men have structured their companies in similar hierarchies. And it's human nature that people trust those they already know

and are comfortable working with. Traditionally, men in corporate power positions have nominated new directors from their own circles of business friends—mostly men, selected from a relatively small circle of power players. They all know that serving on boards can be very lucrative—annual compensation for board service provides attractive income for directors. Early on, the same colleagues turned up as directors on other boards, and this raised a red flag of what is known as "interlocking directorates," which were banned in 1914 by the Clayton Antitrust Act. As recently as January 2012 however, the Federal Trade Commission imposed tighter scrutiny to prevent interlocking directorates from resurfacing. The FTC's action serves as a not-so-subtle reminder that boards should be on the lookout for board-ready women.

3. Board nominating committees have traditionally required that new prospective candidates have prior experience on other corporate boards, a self-limiting requirement. For years, few women served on corporate boards, so there were very few qualified women director candidates with previous corporate board experience. The boardroom became a clubby place; "no place for a woman," some male directors have even been heard to say. Women who sit on previously all-male boards have observed that male directors suffer some anxiety about initially bringing a woman into their midst. One women director explains, "You have to be pre-certified by another male director who has seen you in action and can vouch for your personality fit." That's why men tend to nominate women they have worked with on their large nonprofit boards—those are often the only women they know who have prior board experience.

In a study conducted by WomenCorporateDirectors, Harvard Business School, and Heidrick & Struggles, men and women directors were asked why the percentage of women in boardrooms was so low. Men cited "lack of women in the top-executive ranks" as the problem. Women, not surprisingly, had a slightly different view: "The candidate pool is male-dominated." Both responses are based on facts; but both situations can be changed with some concerted effort.

4. Too few women have had the experience nominating committees are looking for. The number of women in C-suite jobs (CEO, COO, CFO, CIO, CMO) always has been very low. Indeed, a 2012 study by Catalyst indicates that only 14.3% of America's top corporate jobs were held by women in 2011—that means

as few as seven hundred women had C-suite jobs in the Fortune 500. That number is perhaps even more shocking than the fact that only one out of six board seats belongs to a woman. Despite the fact that business schools are overflowing with women earning their MBAs, the top jobs are still going to men. A longitudinal look at this issue by McKinsey & Company from 1970-2000 confirmed this. Although fifty-three percent of new hires at the largest companies in the U.S. were women, only twenty-six percent of those women were promoted to executive management positions as vice presidents or higher.

16.6% of Fortune 500 board seats are **held by women**

5. For generations, women did not know that the board of directors could be their ultimate goal. Even if a woman reached the CFO level, in most cases, she didn't expect to get invited to join a corporate board. So she didn't prepare, she didn't have the networks, and she didn't have the visibility. Perhaps she took time off from her career to raise children, and thus unwittingly took herself off the executive track. Women today have many choices about how to approach work/life balance. For example, Marissa Mayer, the new CEO of Yahoo!, accepted the top job, took about two weeks off to have a baby, and then went back to work, making executive decisions right along with family decisions—she also serves on the board of Wal-Mart and large nonprofits, including the San Francisco Museum of Modern Art, the San Francisco Ballet, and the New York City Ballet.

Those are five key reasons men have dominated boards. But all that is about to change. With more women corporate executives, more women college presidents, more women business owners, and more women in visible leadership positions in major nonprofits and government service, the supply side is bursting at the seams with potential board candidates. Now the job at hand is to increase the demand side by creating or opening up more board seats.

"One of the reasons for the slow growth is the dynamic nature of the Fortune 500 itself," explains Ilene H. Lang, president and CEO of Catalyst. "Every year, large companies merge or go private. When two companies with women on their boards merge, only one board remains." But the next-largest company then brings *its* board seats into the Fortune 500, so why would this be a problem for women on boards? Women directors are not evenly distributed among the Fortune 500. The largest companies tend to have more women board members. In 2012, Catalyst reported that only 19.3% of the companies had twenty-five percent or more women directors. But the lower-ranked companies had fewer or none, so the total number of seats held by women remains relatively unchanged.

Look beyond the Fortune 500 for a moment. *Bloomberg* counts approximately fifteen thousand publicly traded companies in the U.S., of which about one-third are traded on stock exchanges and the other two-thirds are traded over-the-counter. Assuming those fifteen thousand public companies each has about ten members, there are approximately 150,000 seats. If women held just thirty percent of those seats, 45,000 women could sit on America's corporate boards. That would dramatically expand the number of women with current and prior corporate board experience, the prerequisite for larger boards. And when the numbers increase to fifty percent, we'll finally have a business world that is gender balanced, and, as research indicates, far more profitable.

Current women directors have indicated that women who already serve in the boardrooms must take a more active role. Women surveyed said that the most effective way to build more diversity on boards is for women to be appointed as lead directors, board chairs, or chairs of the nominating or governance committees. Unfortunately, the percentage of women nominating committee chairs of the Fortune 500 has decreased over several years to 14.2%, says Catalyst.

Only **14.3**% of **senior executive officers** of the Fortune 500 are women

There is already a growing demand for women directors, and a larger pool of candidates is evolving that includes entrepreneurs and women working in government agencies, whose experience will bring added value to boards all over the country. Julie Hill, director of WellPoint, says, "When my boards are looking for new directors, I require that women and minorities must be included in the lists of candidates presented to the board for consideration. Period. The old excuse of 'We can't find any qualified women' is no longer acceptable—because it's no longer true!"

Global Factors Influencing The Board Game in the USA:

Global factors in business have evolved concurrently over the last decade to produce a business environment that will welcome women to corporate boards. No single factor could change the game for women in American business. But with the convergence of all seven factors simultaneously, an historic moment has arrived. It's the perfect storm, yet this storm has a potentially excellent outcome. The seven global factors are:

- **Financial crises resulting in new government regulations**

- **Quotas in Europe mandating up to forty percent women directors**

- **Women leading countries as presidents and prime ministers**

- **Globalization and technology calling for expanded expertise on boards**

- **Institutional investors and activist shareholders demanding better business performance**

- **Directors approaching board retirement age should open seats for women**

- **Male CEOs and women's organizations collaborating for more women on boards**

In the midst of this perfect storm came the ultimate game-changer. This *Bloomberg* headline "Stocks Perform Better If Women Are On Company Boards" got people's attention. On July 31, 2012, Credit Suisse, one of the oldest and largest multinational banks in the world, released an unprecedented six-year, global research report that unequivocally confirmed the fact that women on boards make a *profitable* difference. The Credit Suisse report stated that stock in companies with a market capitalization of more than ten billion dollars—*and whose boards have women*—outperformed shares of comparable businesses with all-male boards—by a staggering twenty-six percent over a period of six years. More than two thousand companies worldwide were included in the study by the Credit Suisse Research Institute from 2006 to 2012.

In addition to the headline news, the highlights of the Credit Suisse report were:

- A greater correlation between stock performance and the presence of women on a board after the financial crisis in 2008.

- Companies with women on boards significantly outperformed others when the recession occurred.

- Companies with women on their boards tend to be a little more risk averse and have, on average, less debt—perhaps one of the reasons they outperformed so strongly in this recessionary period.

- Net income growth for companies with women on their boards has averaged fourteen percent over a six-year period, compared with ten percent for those with no women directors.

Catalyst research also demonstrates that companies with women on boards outperform those with no women directors. Catalyst first focused on the number of women on corporate boards in 1995 with its original survey of the Fortune 500. That year, women comprised only eight percent of all board seats on Fortune 500 boards of directors. The number doubled by Catalyst's December 2012 report, showing 16.6% of Fortune 500 board seats were held by women, but it was still a very small increase. Of those, 3.3% were women of color. One-tenth of the Fortune 500 still had *no* women on their boards.

The Credit Suisse research shows an incontrovertible correlation between significantly better business performance and gender diversity on boards of directors. Because shareholders demand better performance, and CEOs of course want to succeed, the demand for women on corporate boards should be growing in response to the facts. Granted, the 2012 Catalyst Census noted that only 913 of the 5,488 board seats of Fortune 500 companies were held by women. But, if thirty percent of those seats belonged to women, the number of seats would expand to 1646, and from there, getting to 2,000 seats would mean women would hold thirty-six percent of the Fortune 500 seats. From there, the increase to fifty percent doesn't seem so far-fetched, does it?

These increases are achievable, and I believe they can be accomplished. Especially now. The convergence of the following seven global factors has set the stage for more women in the boardroom. So it's important to understand them.

Financial Crises Resulting in New Government Regulations

Ironically, the failed leadership of the traditional old-boys' network is partly responsible for many of the major changes in American business. Two severe global recessions rocked the first ten years of this century. These fiscal catastrophes caused federal legislators to implement new rules for the oversight of national and global corporations. The Sarbanes-Oxley Act and the Dodd-Frank Act require many changes in corporate governance—including "finance experts" on boards, greater transparency of actions taken, and more independent directors.

5,488
= total seats
on Fortune 500
boards of directors

Independent directors are defined as board members who do not work for the corporation and have no direct ties to the CEO. Shareholders are better served when a sufficient number of outside men and women serve on the board to ensure objective oversight. According to the 2012 *Spencer Stuart Board Index*, independent directors chairing the board now has become the norm. While only eighteen companies report having a formal policy to split the chairman and CEO positions; forty-three percent of boards—up from twenty-five percent in 2002—now split those roles. That means an independent director chairs the board, rather than the CEO of the company. That's an important division of power.

913 = **Fortune 500 board seats** held by women directors

Failures of major American banks, mortgage giants, and industries—from insurance to automobile companies—created a crisis of confidence that has permeated business and society. The turmoil in the business segment of the most powerful nation on earth has forced increased government scrutiny and regulations. Unfortunately, women—who represent 50.8% of the U.S. population—are still largely excluded from decision-making in executive suites and corporate boardrooms.

However, new regulations requiring "finance experts" on boards have opened opportunities for more women CFOs to join boards, as several of our women directors have shared in this book.

Quotas in Europe Mandating up to Forty Percent Women Directors

Forward-thinking governments have legislated quotas to seat more women on boards in Belgium, Spain, the Netherlands, Norway, Iceland, and Italy. Norway first caused gasps by introducing a forty-percent quota for women on boards a decade ago—a goal that was reached in 2012. Government-mandated quotas in these European countries puts substantial pressure on the U.S. and individual states to respond in kind—*and* on companies to make sure that there is no need for the government to impose quotas. While quotas may be effective in Europe, they are not likely to be legislated in the U.S., primarily because our democracy-based, free-enterprise Establishment might not respond well to being forced to place women on boards.

Many women say they believe that male directors would discount them if they were brought on boards because of quotas, thus negatively impacting their influence. Nonetheless, many advocates of gender parity—both women and men—believe that quotas, or other strong incentives, may be needed to get the attention of nominating committees.

In 2011, France passed legislation requiring twenty percent of board seats for women by 2014, increasing to forty percent by 2017. This boosted the number of women on French boards from twelve percent to twenty-two percent in the first year. Belgium mandated a minimum one-third quota, as did Italy, where in 2012, only six percent of board seats were held by women. Spain established a forty percent goal, and the Netherlands introduced new laws, but without stiff penalties. In 2012, Germany was debating quotas.

Also in 2012, Viviane Reding, vice president of the European Commission and commissioner of its Justice, Fundamental Rights and Citizenship agency, proposed fines or sanctions against state-owned companies whose supervisory boards have less than forty percent of seats held by women by 2020. Rules vary, but opinion seems to be converging on near-term quotas of twenty-five percent to thirty percent. Enforcing the laws may be problematic.

The U.K. and Swedish governments have embraced voluntary targets. A British government report has recommended a twenty-five-percent target for women in boardroom positions at the biggest companies by 2015. Sweden is aiming for boards composed equally of men and women.

As European boards hurry to meet their gender parity goals, some are recruiting American women with expertise in specialties such as digital media, emerging markets, and accounting, explains Susan Stautberg, co-founder of WomenCorporateDirectors, a global network of 1,800 women currently serving on 2,600 corporate boards worldwide. Women with dual citizenship, language fluency and prior experience working in Europe have extra advantages.

Would mandated quotas in the U.S. help America's corporate boards improve gender balance? In a 2012 international survey of men and women on boards, conducted by WomenCorporateDirectors (WCD), Harvard Business School, and Heidrick & Struggles, fifty-one percent of the women directors who responded said quotas would be an effective tool for increasing diversity. Only twenty-five percent of the male directors agreed.

Gender-balanced boards are no longer just the right thing to do, but the smart thing. Boards with no women have been referred to for years by some investors as "male, pale, and stale." That was a phrase coined way back in 2003 by Sir Derek Higgs in his now-famous report "Review of the Role and Effectiveness of Non-Executive Directors," published in 2003 by the United Kingdom Department of Trade and Industry.

Women Leading Countries as Presidents and Prime Ministers

Another benefit of globalization for American women is the presence of so many outstanding women in positions of authority in foreign governments and businesses, where they demonstrate the capability of women at the highest levels. Interacting with these women leaders should be eye-opening and instructive to U.S. executives. On the global stage, the excellence of women's leadership has been in the spotlight, and perhaps such visibility might have been an impetus toward legislating quotas in Europe.

These exceptional women on the global stage are pillars supporting the case for a greater number of women in the boardroom. Among the most influential women in the world are: Angela Merkel, chancellor of Germany; Hillary Clinton, former U.S. secretary of state; Dilma Rousseff, president of Brazil; Sonia Gandhi, president of the Indian National Congress; Christine Lagarde, managing director, International Monetary Fund; Susan Rice, U.S. ambassador to the United Nations; Aung San Suu Kyi, chair, National League for Democracy in Burma; Mary McAleese, president of Ireland; Michelle Bachelet, president of Chile; Portia Simpson-Miller, prime minster of Jamaica; Helen Clark, prime minister of New Zealand, and Julia Gillard, prime minister of Australia.

Even though there are only twenty-one women CEOs of Fortune 500 companies in the U.S., they are well-known, highly visible, and respected. They include Virginia Rometty of IBM, Ursula Burns of Xerox, Irene Rosenfeld of Kraft Foods, Indra Nooyi of Pepsico, Meg Whitman of Hewlett-Packard, Marissa Mayer of Yahoo!, and the three CEOs profiled in this book: Maggie Wilderotter of Frontier Communications, Denise Morrison of Campbell Soup Company, and Debra Reed of Sempra Energy.

It only makes sense that women, who comprise more than half of the population, should be represented wherever major decisions are made—from marriages to corporate mergers. Clearly, if women can run countries, they can run corporations. Several women directors profiled in this book earned their credentials on the global stage, running huge government agencies and departments. More women were elected to Congress in 2012 than ever before. And more women business owners have built large, successful private companies. The combined visibility and achievements of these international women leaders have proved that not only do women have the capability to run countries and huge agencies, but the public endorses them. Shareholders *are* the public; shareholders are as ready to endorse women directors as they are to endorse women leaders.

Boards Now Calling for Digital, Human Resources, Information Systems Expertise

Globalization—for large companies and small—brings increased enterprise risk due to unregulated global supply chains, the need to understand local cultures and business practices in other countries, and the potential for international bribery scandals. Finding solutions to the complex problems facing corporations in the global marketplace requires a diversity of knowledge and experience.

The rapid evolution of technology and the voracious appetite of the 24/7 news cycle have been major drivers toward re-thinking the structure and composition of American companies. These developments require that corporations seek directors with more global experience, more diverse backgrounds and more contemporary perspectives and expertise.

53% of new hires at America's largest companies are women

Executives who have interacted with markets abroad and done business with foreign governments at the highest levels are attractive candidates for boards. Even if a company does not have operations outside the U.S., it is essential to have directors with knowledge of other countries—their cultures, consumer behavior and ways of doing business—from supply chain management to importing and exporting products and services.

Many women directors indicate that experience "on the ground" in international markets is an increasingly beneficial skill set for women—and for men—who seek board membership. Women who served as public servants in multi-billion-dollar U.S. government agencies acknowledge that they were recruited to boards because of their experience interacting with foreign authorities, in addition to their management expertise with huge staffs and budgets. As markets expand worldwide, women who volunteer for foreign-office assignments—short-term and long-term—enhance their resumes and signal their willingness to take on these challenges. Until recently, accepting an offshore promotion was not a favorable career move. Foreign assignments used to be considered remote outposts, far away from the mainstream corporate operations, and off the fast track for advancement.

With respect to laws and regulations defining the practices of American companies doing business abroad, regulatory and legal expertise is an asset for today's boards. Corporations have their own general counsel and law firms on retainer, so CEOs and board chairs saw no need to add lawyers to the board. That was then. *Now*, however, in today's highly regulated global environment, attorneys with backgrounds in international law are attractive board candidates.

Doing business globally entails a greater degree of operational complexity, which has opened new board opportunities for women who have expertise in global human resources or worldwide marketing. In the past, careers in human resources, communications, and marketing were not considered pathways to corporate boards. Such specializations tended to be discounted because they are on the expense side of management, rather than revenue-generating. Today such functional expertise is suddenly attractive to corporate boards of global companies.

21 women are CEOs of Fortune 500 companies

Robin Ferracone, author of the book *Fair Pay, Fair Play: Aligning Executive Performance in Pay*, consults with chairs of compensation committees on boards. CEO compensation is one of the primary roles of the board. She confirms that serving on the compensation committee is a challenging assignment that requires finesse and a significant commitment of time. "Corporate boards are more likely now than ever before to recruit candidates from global human resources careers. The increasingly complex problems of managing people from different cultures, who speak different languages, and have culturally specific expectations, require advanced expertise and guidance," Ferracone says. "Issues of executive compensation and succession planning can be very complex, and sometimes uncomfortable. Directors with extensive knowledge about key elements of succession planning are clearly needed, especially with more directors expected to retire in the short term."

Laurie Siegel, who retired from Tyco in 2012, is on the board of CenturyLink, where she has been instrumental to its transformation into a much larger, more complex, diversified global communications company. She began her career as a compensation specialist and brings this expertise to her board responsibilities. "Executive compensation has become controversial as a result of increased scrutiny by the government, institutional investors and the media," she explains.

"The Compensation Committee of the board is where the action is," says Susan Schnabel of Credit Suisse and board member of Neiman Marcus. Geraldine Laybourne, board member of J.C. Penney and Symantec, agrees, "Compensation has become the new Audit."

Global human resources leaders who have been recruited to corporate boards include Mirian Graddick-Weir, EVP of human resources at Merck, who serves on the board of Yum! Brands; Nancy Reardon, retired chief HR and communications officer from Campbell Soup, who serves on the board of Warnaco; and Ursula Fairbairn, retired EVP-HR from American Express, who currently serves on boards of Air Products and Chemicals and VF Corporation, and previously on the board of Sunoco.

Chief marketing officers are also now on the radar screen as board candidates, although CMOs may not have the operations experience in a line management role that boards have traditionally preferred. However, boards may lack a deep understanding of global marketing, so bringing on a director who knows how to target the growing customer base is value added—and complements the existing expertise of colleagues.

A new candidate qualification category has emerged. Digital Directors are technology-savvy candidates from online companies. Online expertise allows younger candidates to skip over about ten or twenty years of working in the career trenches to qualify for boards—because boards urgently need their digital expertise. In addition to having senior marketing and public relations staff who report to the board about digital marketing and social media, the board members want at least one of their own colleagues to help them better understand the increasing impact of these phenomena on the corporation. Board members also want to know about online risks—how to protect the company, themselves as directors, and corporate reputation.

Even though relatively early in their careers, some women senior executives leading digital companies are now on boards. Well-known examples are Facebook COO and board member Sheryl Sandberg, who is on the Walt Disney Company board, and Yahoo!'s Marissa Mayer, on the board of Wal-Mart.

Clearly, executives who are among the new leaders of the digital media world will continue to be sought after as board members because of their technology knowledge, their management success, and their image as cutting-edge, current and cool.

Institutional Investors and Activist Shareholders Demanding Better Performance

Institutional investors invest public funds long-term and own significant stock holdings in thousands of companies. Public pension funds manage the life savings of millions of working and retired government employees, so they are responsible to the citizens of their states to invest their funds in companies that perform well. State governments influence how state money is invested in corporations by having seats on the boards of their state pension funds.

Institutional investors and other activist shareholders vote their proxies—they make it known when they believe a board member may not be doing his or her job according to their policies. And they may nominate candidates for consideration whom they think would be outstanding board members, especially those who are finance experts. Some institutional investors will vote no, or withhold votes on slates of candidates, if they think persons on the slate will not be effective board members. These huge investors could have a powerful impact on gender diversity on boards.

Consider that State Treasurers Steven Grossman of Massachusetts, Rob McCord of Pennsylvania, and Denise Nappier of Connecticut have publicly stated that diversity on corporate boards is one of their key considerations for investing. Grossman said he will vote "no" on the proxies for board candidates if slates do not include women.

California State Controller John Chiang sits on the boards of California Public Employees Retirement System (CalPERS), which is the nation's largest, with a value of $236.8 billion in 2012; and the California State Teachers Retirement System (CalSTRS), the largest teacher pension fund and the second largest public pension fund in the U.S. He explains his position on board diversity this way, "In serving as trustees on the boards of our public-employee pension funds, state treasurers and controllers have a common purpose with the companies where we invest—and that common purpose is sustained and sustainable value creation. We monitor closely those companies with poor performance that don't have diverse boards, because we know from our own research that having women on boards can lead to better company performance. It is in challenging times like these that good governance matters most. I believe that corporate board members will continue to face complex challenges and trying economic times, which makes it particularly important that diverse perspectives, ideas, and solutions are at the boardroom table."

10 = **average number** of seats on U.S. public boards

In a combined effort to help companies find diverse candidates for boards, CalPERS and CalSTRS together created and co-funded the Diverse Director DataSource (3D) database. To promote 3D, they informally partnered with WomenCorporateDirectors (WCD), Catalyst, ION, other institutional investors, as well as Coca-Cola, Home Depot, Johnson & Johnson, and Prudential. This online service is a central resource for self-nominated women and minority executives to be considered as potential candidates for boards—and it may be used as a source at no charge by shareholders, nominating committees and executive search firms. The heads of corporate governance, Anne Simpson from CalPERS and Anne Sheehan from CalSTRS, were instrumental in developing the 3D Database.

"Our goal is to bring greater diversity and fresh perspectives to corporate decision-making and help corporations achieve long-term, risk-adjusted returns," said Sheehan, who is also a member of the SEC Investor Advisory Committee, which was created as a requirement of the Dodd-Frank Act.

Private institutional investors include companies such as TIAA-CREF (Teachers Insurance and Annuity Association of America—College Retirement Equities Fund) based in New York, a leading financial services provider, with $487 billion in assets under management (as of March 2012); Black Rock, T. Rowe Price, Fidelity, and Pax World that manage large retirement pension funds. These private companies have taken the lead from their public counterparts and have become more proactive in demanding more diversity on boards as a business performance issue.

Jack Ehnes, CEO of CalSTRS, says corporate boards should review their gender representation along with all aspects of diversity of thought and perspective on their boards. "We look for richness of discussion and not the typical 'group think' that led to the financial crisis," Ehnes explains.

15,000
public corporations
in the U.S. have close
to **150,000**
board seats

Even though public institutional investors do not require companies to have greater gender parity, they do strongly encourage every element of better board performance, including board composition. They make investment decisions based on key factors called Environmental, Social, and Governance (ESG). Diversity falls under their ESG guidelines. At CalSTRS, for instance, their own Principles for Responsible Investment require that environmental, social, and corporate governance (ESG) issues be addressed because these affect company performance. "That's why we incorporate ESG into investment analysis and decision-making," notes Ehnes.

To enhance business performance, the executives of CalSTRS recommend women candidates whose exceptional experience would bring added value to corporations where they invest. CalSTRS was instrumental in placing Margaret "Peggy" Foran on the Occidental Petroleum board; Geraldine Laybourne on the Move, Inc. board and Sheryl Sandberg on the Facebook board.

In 2012, Ehnes publicly stated his disappointment that when Facebook went public, it could have had a well-balanced board, an ideal model for such a contemporary company. But it did not have any women on its board. Responding to public pressure, Facebook CEO Mark Zuckerberg nominated his COO Sheryl Sandberg. She has outstanding credentials as a leader in technology and global business. But it's unfortunate that such a modern CEO as Zuckerberg needed such prodding to add a woman director.

Peggy Foran was known to CalSTRS through her work as co-chair of the Council of Institutional Investors (CII) in Washington, D.C., and later she was co-chair of the International Corporate Governance Committee for CII. CalSTRS determined that Occidental Petroleum in Los Angeles could benefit from someone with Foran's expertise, so CalSTRS recommended her to the nominating committee. She has been on Oxy's board since December of 2010.

CalSTRS had a class action suit against the company Move, Inc., and nominated a potential board candidate they knew and respected, Geraldine Laybourne, to the board because of her real estate and entrepreneurial experience.

Joe Keefe, president and CEO of Pax World Management LLC, with $2.7 billion in assets, is an institutional investor who has publicly committed to use his influence to achieve gender balance on boards. Keefe believes there's a real possibility to move the number of women directors up to thirty percent in the U.S. by 2015. "Until recently, this was considered an audacious goal but now it's becoming realistic," says Keefe, chair of the institutional investors committee of an organization called the Thirty Percent Coalition.

In June 2012, the committee sent a letter, signed by institutional investors—representing $1.2 trillion in assets under management—to CEOs and nominating chairs of forty-one U.S. companies that had no women on their boards. Keefe was a corporate signatory, along with retired Campbell Soup CEO Doug Conant, state treasurers and controllers, and heads of many women's organizations. "Sending that letter constituted a game-changing event," says Keefe. "It was the first time that leading women's organizations and institutional investors came together to press for greater gender diversity on corporate boards."

The Thirty Percent Coalition's institutional investor committee started dialogs with fifteen of the forty-one companies about how to include gender diversity policies in their board-nomination processes. The Thirty Percent Coalition then expanded its campaign in 2013 to include those companies of the Russell 1000 index with no women on their boards.

Under Keefe's leadership, Pax World is one of the leading asset managers in the rapidly growing field of sustainable investing and one of the strongest proponents for gender diversity as a criterion for investing. Keefe launched a "Say No to All-Male Boards" campaign to help move the gender needle. "I believe that quotas in Europe have helped, although quotas are not likely an approach that will work in this country," says Keefe. "However, the SEC has issued a new rule requiring companies to disclose whether they have a policy regarding board diversity and, if so, what they are doing about it—so the SEC considers this to be a business issue. More diverse groups make better decisions and senior management sees the benefits over time. Shareholders are the key to creating 'demand' for women board members because when shareholders write letters and vote against all-male slates of candidates, companies start to listen."

A Generation of Directors Approaching Board Retirement Age

The retirement age for most corporate directors is seventy-two to seventy-five years old. That means the pending retirement of a generation of baby-boomer directors who have served on boards for the last thirty years *should* produce an unprecedented wave of open seats. Some directors continue to serve beyond retirement age, however, because they are asked to stay on for their knowledge of the company's history. Others stay on too long, and are not motivated to give up their seats, since they earn good money for serving on boards. A 2012 report from GMI Ratings entitled "Entrenched Board" indicates that directors who've served together on a board for a long time may no longer be deemed to be "independent."

26% of S&P 1500 boards have NO women directors

The 2012 *Spencer Stuart Board Index* reported that nearly three-quarters of all S&P 500 boards—up from fifty-five percent in 2002—set a mandatory retirement age for directors. Of that group, twenty-two percent set the age limit at seventy-five or older, versus just two percent in 2002. That may be one reason board turnover continues to decline: S&P 500 boards elected just 291 new directors in the 2012 proxy year—the smallest intake in ten years and a twenty-seven percent drop in a single decade! This does not help create open seats.

Are there solutions? Former Xerox CEO Anne Mulcahy, now a director at Johnson & Johnson, Target, and the Washington Post Company, recommends term limits. In a *Bloomberg* article in September of 2012, she said term limits would make room for more women on U.S. boards. With term limits for directors, "The pool would inevitably be more diverse," Mulcahy says. This is another area where shareholders can exert pressure. Activist shareholders can monitor the ages of directors on boards, listed in the company's public records online—in the 10-K or proxy statement—and withhold their votes from directors who stay beyond retirement age.

Over the next five to ten years, a wave of this baby boomer generation of directors will retire due to advanced age or death, and openings should peak—all potential seats for women. Enlightened boards are preparing for this wave of retirements by doing succession planning now to ensure gender balance. Activist shareholders and women's organizations should be monitoring this expected wave and the boards that will be affected.

Male CEOs and Women's Organizations Collaborating for Change

Savvy male CEOs have begun collaborating with and supporting women's organizations that have long been advocates for change on boards. Leading this effort are WomenCorporateDirectors (WCD), the Women's Forum of New York, Catalyst, ION, 2020 Women on Boards, International Women's Forum, and the American Bar Association's DirectWomen. Databases of CEO-sponsored women candidates are a new and welcome development.

Many women's organizations have recognized and applauded supportive CEOs from General Motors, Aetna, McKesson, American Express, Macy's, Bank of

America, CalSTRS, and Pax World, to name just a few companies whose CEOs actively champion the contributions women make on boards of directors.

In 2011, the Women's Forum of New York launched the Corporate Board Initiative with its first bi-annual "Breakfast of Corporate Champions" at the New York Stock Exchange to honor companies with at least twenty percent women on boards. An important goal of this event was to increase the supply of board-ready women by aligning with the Partnership for New York City, whose longtime president and CEO is Kathryn S. Wylde, and then-co-chairs were Kenneth Chenault, CEO and chairman of American Express Company, and Terry Lundgren, CEO and chairman of Macy's, Inc.

19.3% of Fortune 500 companies have **25%** or more **women directors**

Recognizing it is important for women to be known when boards are seeking candidates, the Partnership asked its member CEOs and board chairs to sponsor women deemed board-ready. The result was the first database of women candidates recommended by chief executives who personally endorse them as board-ready.

"The database already has profiles of more than one hundred executive women from the CEOs' own companies or women they have observed in other boardrooms," said Janice Reals Ellig, immediate past-president of the Women's Forum of New York, and chair of its Corporate Board Initiative. "We offer use of the database for free to nominating committees and search firms as a source of board-ready women."

Another CEO-endorsed database, developed by Catalyst in 2012 and called the Corporate Board Resource, is open to its members only; and WCD has developed its database of members over ten years—women who are current corporate directors categorized by career background, board service, and board committee experience.

The existence of these databases gives every CEO the opportunity to formally endorse women for board seats. Historically, CEOs have informally sponsored women in their companies for outside board positions (including Debra Reed and Denise Morrison, featured in later chapters), but now CEOs have the opportunity to endorse women for board seats, and place those names on databases of these respected organizations.

Women serving on boards are actively seeking others to join them. It's getting easier to find appropriate candidates because there are more women in the C-suite to draw from—never enough, but more than ever before. And, women's organizations have mobilized in great numbers to actively sponsor more women for board seats. Women corporate directors started collaborating with each other officially in 1998, five years after Catalyst's first survey of Fortune 500 boards.

That's when Susan Stautberg, a New York-based consultant to boards, invited a group of women directors to gather around her dining room table and share their experiences. They responded enthusiastically to her invitation, an opportunity to discuss the special issues that lone women face on corporate boards—including not being listened to by the male directors, being excluded from social events, being discounted as seeing things from "a women's point of view," and even being left out of important decision-making discussions.

By December of 2012, that group expanded to become the global network called WomenCorporateDirectors (WCD), with fifty chapters around the world. Stautberg says the original goal of WCD was to create a community of trust among the pioneer female directors, where the women could candidly discuss the challenges they faced, and educate and advise each other.

Over ten years, the WCD membership grew to 1,800 women directors from both public and private boards, and its mission evolved to define best practices in corporate governance and to educate women to excel as corporate directors. WCD has become a champion for women directors and a vital source of expertise. Not only is it a trusted community for advice and experience, but the organization now proactively helps secure Board and Advisory Board positions for qualified women around the world. The Southern California group I organized in Los Angeles and Orange County in 1996 officially merged with WCD in 2006, and has grown to be one of the largest chapters.

WCD stands arm-in-arm with Catalyst and other women's organizations to advocate for increasing gender diversity on boards. WCD issued a call-to-action in 2011—a public challenge to every business leader to purposefully recruit more women for corporate boards and energize corporate shareholders to demand more diversity on their boards.

In December of 2012, WCD's Global Nominating Commission posted Best Practices for Director Selections and Development on its website as a roadmap to building diverse boards. The commission is a high-level task force of board-nominating chairs, CEOs, and WCD members to provide corporate executives, board members and search firms with databases of qualified women, research findings, and articles on leadership—to significantly increase the numbers of women on boards.

Nancy Calderon, the Global Lead Partner at KPMG, based in New York, who serves on the WCD global advisory board, explained: "At KPMG, we are strong advocates for more women directors on boards. In 2012, KPMG/U.S. added a fourth female partner to our board of directors. We believe it is critical for influential firms like ours to help move the percentage higher. It takes initiatives, like WCD's recently-formed Global Nominating Commission, to provide valuable insights and resources needed by chairs of nominating committees so they can open doors for women on boards."

Calderon continues: "And it takes leadership. Meeting Susan Stautberg was a game changer for us at KPMG. She saw the vision early on and invited us to help grow WCD in the U.S. and other countries. I was so impressed—because I personally know many outstanding women who are senior executives in our client companies who are poised to serve on corporate boards. We are confident the momentum created by WCD, ION, and other champions will achieve change.

In 2010 Stephanie Sonnabend, a WCD member in Boston, created a nationwide campaign called 2020 Women on Boards (2020WOB) to urge U.S. public corporations to increase the number of women holding directors' seats to twenty percent or more by 2020. Sonnabend is president of Sonesta International Hotels Corporation. She had been CEO and a founding-family member when Sonesta was public on the NASDAQ, before it was sold and went private in January, 2012.

The 2020WOB grassroots campaign brings together organizations and corporations to raise funds, promote awareness, and create a million-member alliance of advocates. According to Sonnabend, now co-founder and chair, "We started the 2020 campaign to address three problems: First, there had been no definition of diversity on boards. Twenty-percent is a minimum standard for diversity, which should translate to having at least two to four board members who are women or people of color. Second, there had been no goal, so we created a ten-year goal of twenty percent by 2020. Third, there had been little accountability. We created our 2020WOB.com Web site to list and categorize companies according to the number of women on their boards."

To promote education and advocacy, in December of 2012, the campaign orchestrated a nationwide series of luncheons on the once-in-a-century date of 12/12/12. They staged twenty-six events in twenty-one cities, attended by more than 1,400 people, including many women interested in serving on corporate boards. The widespread response paved the way for annual events. The campaign also encourages supporters to send two emails: one to congratulate those companies that have twenty percent or more women on boards; and the other to a company with no women on its board. "Our theory is that when hundreds of people send emails, especially shareholders and customers, companies will feel compelled to address greater diversity on their boards," explains Sonnabend. "Our goal is to create a tipping point so that diversity in the boardroom becomes a corporate imperative." 2020WOB provides a valuable online resource for shareholders to find out how many women are on the boards of the companies in which they invest.

3.3% of board seats are held by women of color

The InterOrganization Network (ION) started in December of 2003, founded by leaders of four executive women's organizations, all of whom were tracking the numbers of women directors and executive officers of public companies in their regions. They agreed to adopt a common methodology for their research, so regional results could be compared nationally. Within six months, two other organizations joined and in 2004, the first comparative report was issued. By December 2012, ION became established as a nonprofit organization with sixteen member organizations. ION, a member of the Thirty Percent Coalition, tracks and publishes statistics on gender balance nationally and in eight regions of the U.S. Its research includes Fortune 500 companies, plus hundreds of small and mid-cap public corporations that comprise the backbone of regional economies.

Their 2010-2011 report showed the New York metropolitan region had the highest percentage of women directors—17.7%. However, only 87 out of the

542 new independent directors elected to public company boards in all twelve regions nationwide were women—another missed opportunity for gender parity.

In November of 2011, ION, led by then-President Charlotte Laurent-Ottomane (now executive director) convened a summit of industry leaders including corporate executives, institutional investors, heads of women's organizations, and directors who were frustrated by the low percentage of women in corporate boardrooms. As a result, the Thirty Percent Coalition was born, representing many stakeholders who wanted to help make change happen. The mission of the Thirty Percent Coalition is to achieve a minimum of thirty percent female representation in public company boardrooms by December 2015. The Coalition defines itself as a group of industry leaders—both men and women—whose goal is to execute strategies that affect the demand-side of the equation by creating more board seats to be filled by women.

Only 8.1% of top-earner positions in the Fortune 500 are held by women

Laurent-Ottomane explains that the Thirty Percent Coalition "is a powerful example of how collaboration can be far more effective than one voice or one action. However, this is only the beginning." The Coalition is actively seeking more corporate leaders to support and endorse its mission. She believes that change will be inevitable once public company CEOs, leading institutional investors, and women's groups collaborate to execute strategies.

Women Directors Hold the Keys

Despite the slow pace of change, there *is* change in process, especially for career women who want to roll the dice in The Board Game. As American companies continue to show the stress and strain of doing business the old-fashioned way, more women directors could bring balance and broader perspective into corporate boardrooms. The future of American business will be energized and improved by more women's voices being heard at the top of

American companies as they compete in the rapidly expanding and changing global market.

"Accelerating women's advancement takes commitment fueled by urgency," says Catalyst's Ilene H. Lang. "Our research points to a solution that can narrow the gender leadership gap and supercharge the candidate pool, making corporate America more competitive in the process."

So in this atmosphere of positive change, women corporate directors themselves are working to make gender parity on boards a reality. One woman director remembers having to put her foot down to bring another woman onto a board where she had been the lone woman director for years. When a previous slate of candidates was presented to her board by a search firm, they were again all white men. She said she would compromise just one more time and vote for the best qualified man. However, she insisted that the next slate of candidates had to include women, or she would withhold her vote. Lo and behold, the next slate included women, and that board now has two women directors.

Women directors who are still the only woman on their boards say they don't feel constrained about speaking up. But most agree that having two or three women would change the dynamics in the boardroom. In the 2006 study *Critical Mass on Corporate Boards,* Vicki Kramer, Ph.D, and co-authors from the University of Western Ontario School of Business and Wellesley Centers for Women, show that three or more women on a board "can cause a fundamental change in the boardroom and enhance corporate governance." Women provide different perspectives, expand the content of discussions, raise difficult issues that pertain to multiple stakeholders (employees, consumers, community members, as well as shareholders), and use their interpersonal skills to promote collaboration and help management hear board concerns. Kramer observes that "the magic seems to occur when three or more women serve on the board together. Suddenly having women in the room becomes a normal state of affairs. Women are no longer seen as outsiders."

Referring to that same study as "The Rule of Three," James Kristie, editor and associate publisher of *Directors and Boards* magazine, says, "One woman on the board is a token; two is a presence; but it takes three to have a voice." As Kristie points out, "I thought things would have opened up with Sarbanes-Oxley, but the percentages haven't really moved. If we continue at this rate, it will be sixty to seventy years before we see any parity on boards. It was thought at one time that if we have more women on nominating committees, that would ensure more women candidates. But I don't see that happening at a speed fast enough. If CEOs talk to each other about the benefits of women on boards, that could help. And maybe even quotas here in U.S. should be given consideration."

In the 2012 WCD, Harvard Business School and Heidrick & Struggles survey about women on boards, fifty-seven percent of the women directors surveyed agreed that three or more women make a more effective board. Only sixteen percent of male directors agreed. The willingness and commitment of sitting women directors to identify openings on their boards and sponsor more women candidates for those openings is the most influential factor in improving the demand side. Male CEOs also help when they recommend their own women executives to serve on outside boards.

George Halvorson, the longtime chairman and CEO of Kaiser Permanente, the nation's largest nonprofit insurer and hospital system, is outspoken when it comes to the need for diversity at the highest levels of corporate decision-making. "The obvious value of having diverse boards of directors ought to be apparent to anyone who knows how people interact and think. A Board of Clones tends to do clone thinking and usually has a very narrow range of creativity. A board that has both genders, multiple ethnicities, and a diverse membership is far more likely to be creative, productive, and responsive to the employees and the customers of an organization. I feel sorry for any organization that does not have a significant level of diversity."

The seven global factors have converged. Halvorson's comments reflect the game-changing new thinking that's desperately needed among leaders of business in America. Research clearly demonstrates the business case for more women on boards. But board nominating committees remain resistant. While having more women on boards may not directly produce better business performance, enlightened companies with gender-balanced boards are shown to make better decisions in an increasingly complex global environment. Business leaders globally and locally are expressing the need for board diversity. Such an attitude change should lead to boards opening more seats for women. So now it's time for more women—and that means you—to get board-ready. Your next move is to build or strengthen your strategic networks.

GO IMMEDIATELY

TO

Chapter 2
Strategic Networks
and Visibility

2 STRATEGIC
Networks and

Visibility

FORMER SECRETARY OF STATE MADELEINE K. ALBRIGHT TOLD A *WALL STREET JOURNAL* REPORTER IN 2012, "We have begun to see that as women get into leadership positions, networking is very important. Women now really understand that we have to help each other."

Pathways and strategies for winning any complex game require preparation, planning, politics, and promotion. For women to successfully play The Board Game requires even more. Women must build strategic networks and become visible within those networks to be known by people who can recommend them for boards. Men have done this for years—perhaps because it is expected of them. So in addition to stellar education, proven leadership track record, and financial literacy, women must be willing to step outside their normal routines of job and family to *network*—starting early in their careers.

Building your strategic networks and becoming more visible are essential steps toward corporate boards. As Doug Conant, retired CEO of Campbell Soup Company says, "The goal of obtaining a board seat must be a career-long, purpose-driven endeavor." Campbell Soup is one of the 19.3% of Fortune 500 companies that have twenty-five percent or more women on their boards.

Like most good things in life, getting on a corporate board depends not only upon whom you know, but more importantly, who knows you. Business leaders ask for recommendations from their friends on boards, and executive search firms find candidates who are visible. Boards look for knowledgeable leaders whose professional reputation assures they can be trusted to have good judgment and be relied upon in a crisis. If you are not seen and known, you won't be found.

"Boards know they need fresh talent," says Ilene Lang of Catalyst. "And they are looking for it." CEOs are being urged to sponsor more promising women executives in their own companies for leadership development programs; for attendance at board meetings to gain insight into the dynamics of the boardroom; and for outside corporate and nonprofit boards, where they will learn about the responsibilities of governance.

Building Strategic Networks

How do you become known to corporate board members who will recommend and champion you? First and most importantly, perform well at your job. Then, build strategic networks of contacts inside and outside your company.

Build strategic networks by forging invisible concentric circles of influential business colleagues, nonprofit leaders, government friends, and stakeholders who can help you advance in your career and groom you to serve on corporate boards. In return, along the way, you can help those in your networks reach their goals. A network relationship is a two-way street based on mutual respect and reciprocal actions, and networking is a skill and an art that *can* be learned.

As you move up in your company, you are also in a position to be of service to your community—on task forces, government commissions, public-private partnerships, chambers of commerce, and other business associations. These are strategic platforms where other business leaders will see you in action, benefit from the value you bring, and gauge your ability to get along with others. Make your own strategic moves; take advantage of every opportunity to learn to be a leader. Head a task force or manage an ad hoc group. Enroll for leadership training seminars offered by your company or by universities or trade associations. This is how to create networks—of both men and women—who can help, advise, and teach you how to become a better manager or executive, and a prospective candidate for boards.

Network outside your own company as much as possible, too. Don't spend all your time in the office. Women have a tendency to do this, and their lives are further complicated by the responsibilities of marriage and family. But getting ahead on the job—and being considered for promotions on the career ladder—require that women make time to be seen and known by leaders in and out of the company.

Marilyn Alexander, a corporate director who previously held executive positions at the Walt Disney Company and Marriott Corporation says, "Use strategic networking in pursuit of corporate board positions precisely the same way you built your career—you carefully selected where you wanted to work, knowing that one good choice would lead to another. So in that same way, carefully select those organizations and places where you should go to meet the people who will help you get to corporate boards. An effective key to a successful career is to get to know business leaders in your industry—those relationships that develop through the course of business networking can lead to an invitation someday to sit on a nonprofit or corporate board. It worked for me."

Over my own forty-year career as an entrepreneur, I've profited from the benefits of networking. I have grown two successful companies by building strategic networks with a singular goal—to establish relationships with business people who could lead to client relationships. Through both direct and indirect relationships, strategic networking has led to successful connections resulting in business, involvement in nonprofit organizations, and lasting friendships. Of course, as co owner of a retained executive search firm, our strategic networks are the core of our business.

My early days in newspaper and television led to a public relations position at Disney and NBC, where I first learned the value of networks—no pun intended. From there I launched my own public relations agency to use my networks of contacts to benefit my clients. After selling the PR agency to a global firm, I launched my next enterprise—a retained executive search firm with business partner Fred Clayton (whom I met on the nonprofit board of March of Dimes/Southern California.) In 1994, Fred and I brought together our wide circles of contacts and networks to launch Berkhemer Clayton Inc., Retained Executive Search, and our company has thrived and continues to grow.

To reinforce both my public relations and executive search careers, I have attended countless events, been involved on select nonprofit boards, and gone to a minimum of two networking receptions or business programs per week where I meet potential clients or important speakers. Here's an insider's tip from the expert: The holiday season is the best networking time of the year—from Halloween to New Year's Day.

Take advantage of opportunities to meet experts in their fields. When I go to a conference, I always approach the keynote speaker to introduce myself, exchange business cards and create a meaningful reason to follow up with that speaker. I ask the speaker to connect me to her or his human resources or public relations executives with whom I can develop business. Such personal introductions are always more effective than cold calls. Once I have shaken hands and talked with an executive in person, that person becomes part of my own strategic networks. Many profitable relationships have started that way.

Nonprofit organizations are instrumental to the pathways for women to become corporate directors. Nonprofits are such an important part of the equation that I have dedicated the next chapter to the process. There are countless large and influential nonprofit organizations, local and national, from volunteer agencies that manage community and cultural institutions, to universities and health services organizations. Using online sources to plan your strategic networking is efficient and makes it easier to attend events and get involved with organizations where you reap the benefits of your own efforts.

My top picks for building strategic networks are:
- Business and Industry Connections
- Mentors and Sponsors
- Private Boards/Equity Investors
- Advisory Boards
- Executive Search Firms
- Women's Advocacy and Professional Organizations
- Nonprofit Organizations (Chapter 3)

Business and Industry Connections

Developing relationships with influential leaders in your industry can be a key factor in securing corporate board positions. Women are notably skilled in building business relationships and maintaining communication—a clear advantage in developing networks that will help you get noticed by a corporate board member who could give your name to the board nominating committee.

Professional organizations are networking goldmines, according to CEO Maggie Wilderotter, of Frontier Communications. "Getting involved with associations in your industry is critical. You'll have access to CEOs in your field or industry and the opportunity to be a voice looked to as an expert." (See her profile in Chapter 9)

Geraldine Knatz (See her profile in Chapter 7) who is the executive director of the Port of Los Angeles, built her networks strategically as a volunteer in her industry association—she became an elected officer, eventually president, of the International Association of Ports and Harbors. She credits her contacts and experience there with paving her pathway toward career promotions and corporate board service.

Sara Grootwassink Lewis, a member of the board of PS Business Parks, met the CFO of the company where she serves on the board through her lobbying efforts in Washington, D.C., on behalf of REIT, a real estate trade association where she was CFO. She subsequently sat next to him at a business dinner and they talked about the global economy, corporate capital structure, leverage, and the fiduciary duties of shareholders. A year later, he nominated her to his board. Lewis says, "You never know when your work is being observed by someone who might possibly affect your career pathway—even at dinner." (See her profile in Chapter 6.)

Betsy Sanders' story is another example of visibility and networking through business organizations, such as chambers or United Way. When Sanders was named the first woman officer at Nordstrom, vice president and general manager of the Southern California region, she was put in charge of opening the first Nordstrom store outside of Washington state. She moved to Orange County from Seattle, not knowing anyone there, and had to establish her networks from scratch. She had a natural inclination to be of service to the community, and through her commitment to the United Way board, among others, she came to the attention of Carl Karcher, who later invited her to join his board, Carl Karcher Enterprises, owner of Carl's Jr. Restaurants. "The board connections were an outcome of my commitment to service," she explains.

In addition to the experience she brought from her Nordstrom background, Sanders knew operations as well as retail customer service. Known for her exceptional performance at Nordstrom and applauded for her work on the CKE board, Sanders was propelled over the next two decades onto major corporation boards—Wal-Mart, Wolverine Worldwide (Hush Puppies), Washington Mutual, Denny's Restaurants, WellPoint (Blue Cross), Vons Supermarkets (before acquisition by Safeway), H.F. Ahmanson & Co., and Great Western. (Read more about her in Chapter 10.)

Connections with government leaders as a businesswoman can be helpful on the journey to the boardroom because government leaders make appointments to commissions, boards and other leadership roles that can provide a platform for visibility. Women directors who have served on local arts commissions, planning boards, state authorities, and other appointed roles made superb contacts and generated visibility that led to their corporate board positions.

Edith Perez, when named partner at the law firm of Latham & Watkins in Los Angeles, informed all her business and community contacts that she wanted to serve on a government commission. She was introduced by a friend to then-Los Angeles Mayor Richard Riordan who named her to a city commission, which ultimately led her to chair the Los Angeles Police Commission. That put Perez in the media spotlight, and she learned to run a huge budget and a 10,000-employee organization. That paved her pathway to a corporate board position years later. (More about Perez in Chapter 4.)

Mentors and Sponsors

Mentors are men or women who take an interest in someone's career, recognize that person's abilities and help the person to recognize opportunities for growth. Most successful women executives have benefited from counsel by mentors either inside or outside their companies. There are formal and informal mentors. Formal mentor programs are often established by companies to encourage and provide senior-level advice to up-and-coming men and women. Formal programs intentionally match professionals, like the senior engineers mentoring younger engineers; or matching through affinity groups inside the company, such as diversity, unions or special interest clubs.

Formal programs set aside specific times when mentors and mentees can spend meet and get to know each other. Such programs certainly have value and produce benefits for both sides involved. But sometimes the matches lack "chemistry," or common interests. So they languish. Perhaps the mentor does not want to feel responsible for the mentee's advancement, and the mentee might have unrealistic expectations. Both parties need to remember that mentorship means giving counsel only, not parenting.

I prefer informal mentorships—short and sweet—like inviting a senior-level person for a cup of coffee to ask his/her advice about specific career situations, or inviting that person to be a speaker at a corporate event. I like what I call "mentor moments" when you notice something a senior person does or says that you apply to your own way of doing things. Simply telling the person you have captured a "mentor moment" during the regular course of business might set up a longer conversation.

A "sponsor" is a senior person in the company who identifies someone as a high-potential individual, and champions that person for strategic responsibilities and promotions. The sponsor sees that the executive has the potential to advance the department or the team and alerts her to opportunities she might not have been aware of. A person who is perceived by the bosses as someone who gets things done will likely attract the attention of a mentor or sponsor to assist her continued development and leadership training.

Operations experience is a significant requirement for corporate board service. A career in corporate finance is an attractive calling card—you don't have to be a CFO to serve on a board. Financial literacy is often sufficient when combined with results-oriented operations or exceptional marketing experience. Your mentor or sponsor can help you get such cross-discipline opportunities.

Linda Griego, who serves on several boards, became the CEO of a huge public/private partnership, ReBuild LA, which gave her access to influential business leaders on the board. "One of the board members, Roy Anderson, who has since passed away, was my champion," she said. "When he retired from the board of First Interstate Bank, he recommended me to replace him. It truly was an honor to be considered. He gave me my first big break toward board service."

Debbie Reed's sponsor was her CEO at the public energy utility in San Diego where she worked her way up the corporate ladder, having started as an intern there. Today she is chairman and CEO of the corporate holding company, Sempra Energy. She says her CEO actively saw to it that she got well-rounded experience on the job and groomed her to be a CFO. He asked her to sit in on board meetings and suggested her as a candidate for outside corporate boards.

Ilene H. Lang, president and CEO of Catalyst, says that mentoring, although helpful for women's career advancement, is not sufficient. Women need sponsors. She asserts women who have sponsors during their careers have a better chance of winning a corporate board seat in the long run.

"Good sponsors can supercharge a woman's career by providing her with access to essential networks, bringing her achievements to the attention of other senior-level executives, and recommending her for key assignments," Lang says. "Often, when opportunities for promotion arise, women—who can do eighty percent of the task but are not sure about the remaining twenty percent—hold back. A sponsor would encourage the woman to take on that stretch assignment," Lang explains.

The Catalyst Corporate Board Resource allows member-company CEOs to sponsor top women executives for board positions, based on a Catalyst report that demonstrates how sponsorship can offer high performers greater access to advancement and the opportunity to excel.

Anne Doyle is former director of North America communications for Ford Motor Company. In her book *Powering Up! How America's Women Achievers Become Leaders,* she defines a sponsor as someone who has the positional power to leverage on behalf of the woman being sponsored. A sponsor opens doors for leadership opportunities, inside and outside the company. A sponsor can be of either gender, but Doyle believes the majority of power players, who have the clout to be effective sponsors, are still primarily men.

Historically, executive men have sponsored other male rising stars, who have demonstrated high potential, and positioned them for greater responsibilities— in the same way that professional sports teams scout for and cultivate outstanding athletes for their pipelines. High-potential women must be given the same advantage—they too should be strategically developed for positions on the leadership team. Unfortunately, as experienced board member Betsy Sanders observes, "Women are promoted on performance, and men are promoted on potential."

"Men are often willing to mentor and guide women—as long as the man remains in the authority position," Doyle explains. "Talent, drive, ambition, skill, and passion for the job—even with the help of executive coaches—might not be enough for high-achieving women to break through to upper echelon positions. You need powerful advocates who are willing and able to use their 'political capital' and influence on your behalf."

It's important to develop advocates, both men and women, Doyle acknowledges. "If you don't already have trusted male allies you can count on in your company—who will counsel you, tell you the truth, engage you in healthy debate and back you up when you need a sponsor—make it a priority to develop them," she urges. "Women are still so rare in senior-most executive positions that there are few female allies to be strategic confidantes when the going gets tough, which it always does. That's why trusted male allies who can provide professional and personal support are essential, in addition to women mentors."

Doyle's book quotes Xerox CEO Ursula Burns, who speaks openly about the executives who groomed and sponsored her throughout her career. "Such relationships are not easy for women to find. Start with men who realize that their efforts have been advanced by your great work—even if you had to bring your achievements to their attention originally. Then, when the time is right, ask them for their help. Be very clear about your goals." Burns makes the point that it is critical that women who want to move up in their companies let these executives know that "when they have the opportunity, you would greatly appreciate their support."

Private Corporate Boards and Private Equity

Experience on private company boards prepares prospective directors for public boards. Some women directors tell me they actually prefer serving on private company boards rather than public. There are literally thousands of successful private companies in the U.S. (including Mars Inc., Publix Super Markets, Ernst & Young, Enterprise Rent-A-Car) where the stock is privately held, not publicly traded. Board members have the same basic responsibilities—fiduciary oversight to make certain the company is well run. But they are accountable to a majority investor or to private owners, rather than public shareholders.

Cesca Luzuriaga, former CFO of Mattel and a board member of OfficeMax, currently sits on the board of SCAN, a nonprofit Medicare Advantage insurance company for senior citizens, which she says operates "very much like a public board." She advises women seeking public board placement to start with small, private boards or public boards in the lower Fortune 1000 or 2000, and work up to the larger boards. It's a sure way to learn board dynamics, committee structure, and fiduciary responsibilities of less complex companies.

Luzuriaga says she also prefers private companies for board training, rather than nonprofit boards, although she agrees that valuable contacts are made on nonprofit boards. Nonprofit board training, by definition, doesn't focus on operations that create a profit and pay dividends to shareholders. Some private companies are family-held, Luzuriaga cautions, which can present issues if the majority of board members have family connections. Part of the candidate's necessary due diligence should include researching the personalities and agendas of who's on the board and whether it's a private or public company.

Gabrielle Greene, a venture capitalist, sits on the Whole Foods board, her first public board. She had been on a number of private boards and several nonprofit boards over a span of fifteen years. So when she was asked to serve on Whole Foods she already had a good deal of governance experience, as well as financial expertise.

Greene notes, "I made fabulous contacts on boards of the Boston Partnership and the Boston Children's Museum, but I would add that my board experience on five or six private companies was more relevant than my nonprofit-board experience from a functional point of view." Her experience was diverse enough that she became a highly desirable director candidate. "When private companies are preparing to go public, the checklist requires having at least one outside director. That's when I have been invited to join most of my boards, primarily because I put out the word to attorneys and investors to let them know I was interested in serving on boards," she explains.

Greene recommends that women with financial background introduce themselves to venture capitalists. "There are many conferences in the venture capital and private equity world where they are looking to round out their boards, especially with women who have the experience they seek. It's typical to bring in one independent director. So VC gatherings are really a good way to make valuable connections."

Several other directors also earned their board experience through private equity, where they were responsible for investing their firm's money in a new venture and were then appointed to its board. These women gained valuable experience by representing the largest shareholder on the boards they helped create. Private equity consists of investors and funds that invest directly in private companies, or conduct buyouts of public companies that become private. Private equity money is often used to fund new companies, technologies, make acquisitions, or to provide working capital.

Susan Schnabel, a managing director at Credit Suisse and co-head of DLJ Merchant Banking Partners in Los Angeles, started as an investment banker before making the switch to private equity. As a result, she has served on twenty-five boards—mostly private. She was thirty-one years old when she served on her first. Schnabel and her partners often control the companies they invest in, approve who serves on the boards, and appoint their own company representatives as directors. This is ideal board experience for future public board members, especially since many private companies subsequently go public.

Because of her deep experience on boards and her financial acumen, Schnabel has chaired virtually *every* type of board committee over the course of her career. She is the lead director on STR Holdings, a public company in which Credit Suisse was an investor. The lead director represents all the other independent directors and closely counsels the chair of the board. "The lead director is like the 'quarterback' of the board," she says.

"Since there is a shortage of women CEOs to serve on boards, I believe there is a clear window of opportunity for women who are finance experts and CFOs to be recruited for boards. By mid-career for women, it's an ideal first step to get on a private board to learn about governance," says Schnabel, who also serves on the board of the now privately held Neiman Marcus.

Other women directors began their board careers by investing their own money in start-up companies. Carolyn Chin, now CEO of her own company, CeBIZ in Florida, started investing in start-ups in San Francisco. A banker by training, she built strong networks of business connections early on in her career. One of her contacts approached her about a local consortium that wanted to start a bank. Her goal was to serve on corporate boards, so she said she would personally invest in the bank, *if* she could have a seat on its board. Within a few years, she was named chair of that local bank board, which has led to many other directorships.

Advisory Boards

Corporations, public and private, often establish an advisory group of community, customers and professional people to give the company valuable feedback about a wide range of issues—generally related to marketing, sales and supplier diversity. Banks are required by law to have community advisory boards representing their customers. Serving on an advisory board for a corporation enables advisors to interact with the company leaders.

An advisory board does not have the fiduciary responsibility of the board of directors. It meets regularly under the auspices of the corporation. Members are nominally compensated for their time and reimbursed for travel expenses. The advisory board does not give input about finances, legal, or management matters as boards of directors do, and it does not represent financial interests of shareholders.

CEOs or directors will often meet with their company's advisory boards to hear the feedback, an important opportunity for the CEO, especially, to get to know these advisors. Sometimes there are receptions at the board of directors meetings—where the directors can get to know the community advisors. Being an advisory board member may not be a direct ticket to joining the board of directors, but it's a unique opportunity for the company leaders to see advisors in action. And who knows—a positive impression could lead to an invitation to the board of directors someday.

Developing advisory boards is the business created by Susan Stautberg in New York, called PartnerCom. Also the founder of WomenCorporateDirectors, Stautberg says she has often encountered intense male bias merely suggesting women for advisory boards. She cites the following case to underscore how shortsighted this attitude can be.

A few years ago, Stautberg recommended a woman she knew to serve on the advisory board of a large institution with international business activities in which this candidate had a successful track record. The organization first turned down the candidate, sight unseen, saying they hadn't heard of her. But at Stautberg's urging, they agreed to meet her.

"Once Christine attended the first meeting, they loved her. They just didn't want women. Period. But she proved them wrong." That woman was none other than Christine Lagarde, who is now managing director of the International Monetary Fund (IMF), and has been listed many times in *Fortune's* Ten Most Powerful Women in the World.

Carolyn Chin agrees that advisory boards provide good contacts for women interested in corporate directorships. She was first asked to sit on an advisory board for the *San Francisco Chronicle* whose executives she knew through her position at Citibank. As a direct result, Chin was later asked to sit on her first board of directors for a tech start-up called CommTouch, where she later became CEO and board chair.

I serve on the consumer advisory panel of Southern California Edison, the utility that provides electricity to much of Southern California. The SCE advisory group meets quarterly to advise and review marketing, consumer education, and outreach strategies to serve its customer base of eleven million Southern Californians living in 749 communities. SCE selected me for my perspective as a small business owner and as a statewide board member and past president of the National Association of Women Business Owners in California (NAWBO-CA). SCE asks the group for feedback about its marketing to the greater community and about doing business with suppliers who are minority and women-owned companies. I provide my opinions and take back educational information to the women business owners throughout the state. This has allowed me to build business relationships with the senior executives of Edison, and get to know the SCE board members.

Executive Search Firms with Corporate Board Practices

As a search firm owner myself, I can advise that retained executive search firms should be on your list for strategic networking. Even if a firm doesn't yet consider an executive to be qualified to be a corporate director, she may be a candidate for other senior executive searches it handles. Once someone is a candidate for an executive position, that person is already known by the firm as a potential for its board-seat pipeline, or as someone to be monitored during her career over the years ahead.

At Berkhemer Clayton, we constantly add profiles of board-ready women and ethnic minority executives to our files, because we are often engaged by corporations that want to bring greater diversity to their boards and their senior management. Well-known global firms with specialty practices handling corporate boards include Heidrick & Struggles, Spencer Stuart, Korn/Ferry, and Russell Reynolds.

So here's this insider's opinion about how to meet consultants from executive search firms: Direct phone calls are not the best approach. Emails are okay. Do research to get to know the partners and consultants who specialize in corporate board placements in industries where your experience is a fit. Find out what high-level community networking groups they belong to that you can also join. Meet them through speaking engagements, chambers of commerce or nonprofit fund-raising events. Engage them in conversations. Ask their counsel about how your experience could add value as a board member for a public or private company.

In return, do search firms a favor by being a valuable resource. Whenever executive search consultants call for recommendations of candidates for other searches—for positions at any level—take the time to help them. Even if the position they are currently calling about is not right for you, be thoughtful about your recommendations. Make sure you only provide names of executives you think would really be well-suited to the search they are handling. This win/win exchange will reinforce your relationship, and you may ask them to remember you for future corporate board positions.

Walgreen's board member Jan Babiak, previously a partner at Ernst & Young in London, says that in Europe, all searches are handled by executive search firms. To be considered for boards in Europe, networking with search firms is essential. And thanks to the quotas in Europe—some corporations there want to find women board members who live and work in the U.S. However, for corporations in the U.S., search firms are not always involved. Corporate board members, nominating committees, and corporate secretaries often do their own outreach to find candidates.

When Suzanne Nora Johnson retired as a top executive at Goldman Sachs, she received many calls from executive search firms and corporations asking her to serve on their boards. "Search firms were quite relevant in terms of the process, but most of my board situations came from relationships with directors who served on those boards," says Johnson. "If your name gets referred by someone reliable, the search firm takes notice and can be very helpful."

Women directors acknowledge that big search firms tend to recommend women who are already well-known for being on other boards. Nevertheless, women who want to serve should include search firms in their networking. Many women say they were recruited for their second or third board by search firms, after performing well on their first. Please note that client corporations often instruct search firms to present only candidates who have had previous corporate board experience. The unintended consequence of this requirement is that it limits the pool, and does not allow consideration of otherwise-qualified candidates.

However, some good news in 2012. The *Spencer Stuart U.S. Board Index* reported that thirty percent of the new independent directors chosen for the boards of companies in the S&P 500 were newcomers to public board service.

Bonnie Hill was recruited by a search firm for her first public board, the Niagara Mohawk Power Corp. Even though she had never served on a board, her work experience and visibility trumped the need for previous board experience. The company was looking for someone with a background in consumer or environmental affairs. "I had both," she recalls. "And I had just left an appointment as a special advisor to President George H.W. Bush." Clearly, Hill's public role serving the White House made her a highly visible candidate. (See her profile in Chapter 4.)

Women's Advocacy and Professional Organizations

Women are a powerful force when joined together with a common goal. I always remember Gloria Steinem's response when asked how feminism could spread to a country like India: "All women need is a small room to get together in, and great things will happen."

Women's groups and professional organizations provide an ideal setting for women to connect with other women who have the same dedication to a specific purpose. An historic example is when the advocates for women came together with the National Organization for Women (NOW) to level the playing field for women athletes and scholars. They were able to win the Title IX Legislation in 1972 that bans gender discrimination in schools—both in academics and athletics.

Influential groups advocate for getting more women on corporate boards. WomenCorporateDirectors (WCD) is a membership organization of women who have served a minimum of two terms on a public board. From its beginning around Susan Stautberg's dining room table, WCD has become a global network comprised of more than 1,800 members serving on 2,600 boards in fifty chapters around the world. And that only took ten years!

ION stands for InterOrganization Network, comprised of sixteen women's business organizations around the country. A number of like-minded organizations are "friends" of ION, including other women's organizations, corporate executives, universities, and companies. Toni Wolfman is a past president of ION and has chaired ION's research committee for many years. She is also founder and co-chair of the Boston chapter of WCD.

ION, Catalyst, and 2020 Women on Boards provide connections and events for strategic involvement and visibility as women look for avenues to contribute their time or dollars, in order to build networks of influential people involved in board development.

The National Association of Women Business Owners in California (NAWBO-CA) is actively promoting and training women business owners to serve on public, private, and nonprofit boards. As an entrepreneur myself, I believe women business owners are key contributors to the economy, who could bring hands-on operations experience as CEOs to corporate boardrooms. A non-partisan nationwide association of women business owners, NAWBO informs women business owners about building their companies and taking active roles as business leaders in their communities. NAWBO also advocates for women's business issues when laws and regulations are considered by federal and state governments.

Employer-based women's leadership groups, executive women's networks, and political affinity groups with executive women members—all can lead to making helpful contacts. Women can find mentors, information, education, and opportunities for service and leadership. Professional women's associations—groups of lawyers, physicians, accountants, and engineers—are excellent places to network and make contacts. The other advantage of these groups is making good friends who share common goals, concerns ,and attitudes.

Avery Dennison sent its then-employee Margaret Dano to attend the Harvard International Women's Forum, which she looks back on as "four weeks of building bridges, networking, and getting to know successful career women." Among them was an executive at Catalyst. Dano told her she would like to sit on a corporate board, and sometime later the Catalyst contact recommended her for her first board. Dano has now served on a total of six. For each nomination, references from her strategic networks were invaluable. She had been active in the Los Angeles Alzheimer's Association, as well, where the director has been a helpful reference. "For every one of the six boards I have served, someone from my networks has recommended me," adds Dano.

When WellPoint (Blue Cross of California) was looking for its first woman member, Julie Hill was recommended by Jane Hurd, a partner at Korn/Ferry, whom she knew from her women's networks. Hill remained on the merged board of WellPoint, Inc., which was formed in 2004 when WellPoint Health Networks Inc. and Anthem, Inc. merged to become the nation's leading health benefits company.

"Take current women board members to lunch or coffee!" Hill says. "Just as you network with people who have the corporate jobs you aspire to, introduce yourself and get to know women who actually serve on boards. Seek out women who serve on the board of the company where you work, or whom you know from business or nonprofit connections. Research others. It's all part of building your strategic networks."

Participate in proactive women's organizations (see in Resource Guide for details):

- Contribute and subscribe to Catalyst
- Join an ION member organization
- Join and sponsor the Thirty Percent Coalition
- Join 2020 Women on Boards
- Join NAWBO if you are a woman business owner
- Join a professional business women's organization

Pump Up Your Visibility

"Women always ask me how to get on a corporate board," says Andrea Rich, who has served since 1998 on the board of Mattel, the largest toy company in the world. Dr. Rich had been the executive vice chancellor and COO at UCLA for many years, then became president of the Los Angeles County Museum of Art. "It's the question I am most often asked, yet my answer is always the same—I don't know. That's because every person is different. It's a combination of serendipity, visibility and being known for a lifelong career of achievement. It doesn't happen overnight."

Rich is right. Visibility matters, and maintaining your visibility is essential to eventually being invited to sit on a board. The keys to achieving that powerful visibility are:

- Define and become known for the experience you have that can add value to boards.
- Confidently express your goals to serve on boards to all friends and business contacts.
- Use networking tactics in this chapter to impress influential people who can play a role in realizing your goal.

According to the longitudinal study from 1970 to 2009, called "Women Matter" by McKinsey, fifty-three percent of all new hires at the country's two hundred largest corporations were women. Thirty-seven percent of the women hired were promoted. Only twenty-six percent of those women became vice presidents or senior vice presidents. That means, sixty-two percent of the women hired over this time period were stuck in staff jobs, while sixty-five percent of line jobs were held by men, who were only forty-seven percent of new hires. Remarkably, two-thirds of the men hired got line-management jobs, but almost sixty-five percent of the women hired over the same thirty-year period remained in staff jobs—clearly not the pathway to the C-suite.

This helps explain why the number of women CEOs in Fortune 500 companies appears stuck at about twenty-one out of five hundred. The numbers immediately below CEO are similarly discouraging. Catalyst cited in its 2012 report that in 2011, women held only 8.1% of top-earner positions, despite the fact that research shows fifty percent of women in middle management are interested in leadership positions.

What happens to women? There are countless reasons cited—from taking years out of their careers to raise families, to subtle discrimination at the workplace, to simply not tooting one's own horn effectively. As a former public relations agency owner, I offer this singular, critical suggestion for becoming more visible:

When you do a good job on an assignment, make sure you let your bosses know so you can be recognized for your intelligence and leadership.

Calling attention to yourself may feel awkward at first, but it's critical to your success. Don't think of it as bragging—it's communicating how your achievements are helping the company and your team succeed. Of course, you always include your team-members and give them credit for success.

It's no secret that women in general are reluctant to shine the spotlight on themselves. Women are conditioned to believe they will be noticed just because they do excellent work. But that rarely happens. However, you can bet the man in the neighboring cubicle probably tells his superiors about his accomplishments. Board women I know were unanimous that women should always be alert for opportunities to be noticed and credited for a job well done. Obviously, they caution against coming across as arrogant or pushy. There's a delicate balance that can be learned with practice.

Many women have to fight against the urge to toil at their desks for eighty hours a week, doing everything they can to win a merit badge—just like Girl

Scouts. Women have to fight against entrenched assumptions. The McKinsey research reported that many men still believe women are less ambitious and less focused on careers than men.

Visibility and experience add up to leadership. Getting to the top requires putting your hat in the ring for promotions and for tough assignments. Know that you are capable, have faith in yourself and your ability to assemble a strong team. Ask for advice from people you trust, if you need reinforcements. Men don't hesitate to ask for help. Smart women tell me they often learn more from their failures than their successes. My advice is, don't ever let fear of failure hold you back. It's likely you'll do a terrific job, and your boss will know you took on the challenge. Getting a tough job done with an efficient use of resources, handling a crisis with composure, or building an effective team that trusts your leadership enough to follow you into the fire—these are sure ways to make a good impression.

"Women who advance often raise their hands for the 'ugly jobs' in line management, where they take on the challenge and prove themselves in a visible way," Beth Mooney, CEO of KeyCorp, based in Cleveland, Ohio, told the *Wall Street Journal* in May 2012. "People appreciate those who step up." Mooney started as a secretary and became the first woman CEO of a top-20 bank in the U.S. The KeyCorp board is 36% women—five women out of fourteen directors!

If you are early in your career, your first step toward getting noticed is to speak up about things you've done that exceed others' expectations—maybe you've stayed late to help meet a deadline, or you've gone the extra mile for the company's volunteer-service initiative. The next step is when you volunteer for projects that are "not your job"—such as offering to research how your department could implement an efficient new system or helping out a colleague with a huge assignment.

If you think you're qualified, nominate yourself for a promotion. Many people agree with me that by the time a woman *thinks* she's "ready," she was probably ready a year earlier. Women who have mentors or sponsors in their companies are much more likely to raise their hands because their own readiness has been validated, bolstering their confidence.

Several women directors in the following pages told me they were keynote speakers at industry conferences, events where the people who eventually recommended them for board seats were in the audience. Once you strategically raise your profile in your industry, seek out opportunities to speak. If speaking in front of an audience isn't your favorite thing to do, find a professional coach—or join Toastmasters, the group that trains up-and-coming executives who need practice with public speaking and networking.

An excellent avenue for networking and building strategic networks is through nonprofit organizations—the next chapter is dedicated to inside tips about how to get involved and get noticed. Do good volunteer work along your pathway to corporate boards, no matter what your career might be.

GO IMMEDIATELY

TO

Chapter 3
Read About Nonprofit
Connections

3 HERE'S THE CLUE— Nonprofit

Board Service

Here's the clue to winning The Board Game long-term: Most women directors were recommended for their first corporate boards by directors who saw them in action on *nonprofit* boards.

This is important for you to know when mapping out a strategic pathway to corporate boards. And it's good news for nonprofit organizations seeking enthusiastic new board members. When corporate board nominating committees review candidate profiles, the questions asked around the table include: "Who knows this person?" "What board experience does she have?" "Have you seen her in a leadership role?" "If she has no public board experience, has she been successful on large nonprofit boards?" "Has she managed large budgets and staff?"

The fact that the overwhelming majority of women corporate board members in this book were recommended by fellow board members from large nonprofits confirms what many of us already knew intuitively. Men who serve on public company boards also serve on nonprofit boards. So it's logical—when they are asked to suggest possible women candidates with previous board experience, their nonprofit boards may be the *only* places they have actually seen women in action as board members.

Boards of directors of *non*profit organizations have the same governance and fiduciary responsibilities as boards of *for*-profit corporations. Both are legal entities under state law, with different federal and state tax requirements. In preparation for future corporate board participation, members of nonprofit boards learn the dynamics and responsibilities of governance on a smaller scale, and with lower potential risk. Even though it's a volunteer commitment, serving on a nonprofit board is far more than having one's name on the stationery and a picture on the website. Active involvement makes a positive impression on fellow board members.

In a 2011 article in *Directors & Boards*, several women directors talked about their experience with nonprofits. "Serving on high-quality, not-for-profit boards is a good way to get experience and exposure before you make a move to a corporate board," says Lulu Wang, who serves on the board of MetLife in New York, and is founder and CEO of Tupelo Capital Management. Wang serves on the nonprofit boards of the Metropolitan Museum of Art, the Columbia Business School, Asia Society, and Rockefeller University (which she characterizes as "a brain trust with more Nobel laureates than most countries"). She refers to these as "high-octane" nonprofits, and urges women to look to similar organizations to get board experience, preferably "on the investment, finance or audit committees."

Wang has observed that women often assume leadership positions when they are on nonprofit boards, which requires a great deal of time. Her personal experience has shown her that those leadership roles leave less time for corporate boards, so she has taken on only one for-profit board at a time. "When I was approached by a search firm about my first public corporate board opportunity, it was a busy time in my life," recalls Wang. "The letter sat in my inbox until a fellow board member from a nonprofit board called to follow up. I explained I had been busy and had not had a chance to focus on this invitation, but would certainly do so, now that he had encouraged me. I believe that another nonprofit board colleague also supported my nomination. So I think I'm a good example of how nonprofit board service can lead to corporate board positions."

LULU C. WANG
New York City

Current Boards/Select Nonprofits:
MetLife Insurance Company
Columbia Business School
Metropolitan Museum of Art
Rockefeller University
Asia Society

Career History:
Tupelo Capital Management: LLC, Founder and CEO (current)
Jennison Associates Capital Corporation: Director and EVP
AXA Financial; SVP and Managing Director, Equitable Capital
   Management

Education:
MBA, Columbia University
BA, Wellesley College

The odds are good that a woman's first invitation to join a board will come from a nonprofit board colleague's recommendation the way Wang's did. Nonprofit board membership creates an enriching experience from doing good work for a favorite cause, and fellow board members recognize good work and authenticity. The opportunity to serve a nonprofit creates a pathway that can be orchestrated strategically to eventually lead to a seat on a corporate board.

Evaluate Large Nonprofits in Your Networks

Large nonprofit boards range from regional hospitals and health systems to universities, cultural centers, community service organizations such as United Way and other community foundations. Ilene H. Lang of Catalyst cites nonprofit medical centers and hospital boards as key venues where many women corporate directors have developed business relationships and contacts that led to their first or second corporate board nominations. If you currently serve on nonprofit boards, find out if your fellow board members serve on corporate boards, or if friends in their networks do. And use this nonprofit board experience to your advantage. Let other board members know you want to serve on corporate boards in the future.

Caring about the specific work of a chosen community organization is crucial for success on that board. To become a vital part of the governing board requires substantial volunteer time—that's why it should be a cause you truly care about. Don't jump on a nonprofit board with the idea that it will be a stepping stone. You will be evaluated for your dedication, concern and action. If you are not sincere, other board members will recognize any lack of authenticity immediately. Sincerity pays off—for you as well as the nonprofit.

Says Lydia Kennard, a board member of URS Corporation, "It took well over a decade to get on my first corporate board. I started serving on nonprofit boards in my early thirties and then got on my first publicly traded corporate board in my mid-forties. It was a long journey, but along the way I was preparing myself in terms of relationships and developing expertise to be a strong candidate."

Women corporate directors I've interviewed have all expressed how well their nonprofit boards prepared them for future service on corporate boards. They developed insights about how boards function most effectively—through mutual respect and collegiality, solution-driven discussion, teamwork, and clear lines of communication among themselves and with management. These lessons directly relate to corporate boards—working with committee structure, dealing with management and financial issues, and decision-making by consensus.

Learn Dynamics of the Boardroom

For those who are not yet on nonprofit boards, here's what can be learned about the similar responsibilities shared by both nonprofit and corporate boards:
- What it means to be an advisor to the CEO from a board perspective, allowing management of well-run nonprofits to operate day-to-day matters without undue interference from the board.
- The role of the board of directors in decision-making, fiduciary responsibility and strategy.
- Committee structure, board etiquette, and dynamics.

Getting along with people on nonprofit boards is important. Nominating committees seek out strong leaders who work well with a variety of personalities and styles. They check out a prospective candidate's reputation through news media, online, and among acquaintances—long before the person may be aware she is being considered. A candidate's previous achievements on nonprofit boards will also be reviewed by corporate boards as part of the selection process.

One of the pioneers among women corporate directors is Andrea Van de Kamp. Her nonprofit board connection was the key to her first public board, the Jenny Craig Corporation. "I had volunteered on the Los Angeles Music Center Foundation board with the man who recommended me to Jenny Craig. He said he had been impressed with my management ability and financial expertise on that board."

Van de Kamp says, "Even though you are a volunteer on a nonprofit board, you demonstrate leadership when you are a successful part of the team. When you introduce your ideas in a constructive manner and express your point of view in ways that are solution-driven, you demonstrate your competency to serve on a corporate board." Nonprofit boards offer low-risk opportunities to try out innovative concepts, learn and practice new management skills, and find out how to get things done within the board dynamic. Producing win/win outcomes for the community is especially gratifying to women.

Several women directors have expressed to me that the committee system of nonprofit boards allowed them to stretch their skills outside their comfort zones and expand their primary expertise. It's an ideal place to learn about overseeing finances of complex organizations and how to read and prepare annual reports. A well-rounded portfolio of skills is essential for future corporate directorships. If opportunities for growth and learning new skills are not available at your own company, look for training through nonprofits, university extension courses or business seminars.

Relationships with fellow nonprofit board members are based on trust and reliability, just as on a corporate board. When choosing nonprofit organizations where you might want to volunteer, choose strategically. Select a highly respected organization whose mission you care deeply about. Research the backgrounds and networks of the directors to see if they are admired and respected, and on what corporate boards they serve.

Volunteer for leadership roles within the nonprofit while continuing to perform well at your own job. Early in their careers, people may not realize the competitive edge and visibility that such volunteer service provides—both outside and inside their own companies. For those who are just out of college, it's never too early to start. For those already at mid-career, begin immediately to accrue the benefits of valuable contacts and expanded networks. There's still time to ramp up.

Choose a Nonprofit Whose Cause Is Important to You

Most people who volunteer for nonprofit organizations have a personal interest in the substance of the work—health services, children's causes, environmental issues, for instance. A deep personal commitment to the mission usually generates outstanding performance that can lead to a seat on the board.

Eileen Kamerick, who sits on the board of Associated Bancorp, tells a story about a friend of hers who served on an influential nonprofit medical center board. Two of her friend's fellow board members were so impressed by her volunteer efforts to successfully achieve a very difficult merger of two hospitals, that each man nominated her for his own public company board. For her friend, one nonprofit led to two corporate boards.

During my own career as an entrepreneur, I have volunteered over the years to help organizations related to women's health and financial literacy for women and girls. I moved up quickly from community volunteer to serve on the boards of key nonprofit organizations. I did so to help advance those causes, long before I realized the strategic advantage. Over the years, I made valuable business relationships—as well as lasting friendships—with other board members.

Even if you don't end up on a corporate board, the business connections made through nonprofits are advantageous to your career. When I was about thirty and the owner of a growing public relations agency, I was asked to serve on the board of the March of Dimes of Southern California. I had no idea how valuable that experience would become. But I said yes, because the mission—women's reproductive health—appealed to me.

Among the business contacts I made on the March of Dimes board were my future (now current) business partner of twenty years, Fred Clayton; the publisher of the Spanish-language newspaper *La Opinión* and CEO of ImpreMedia, Monica Lozano; the future (and now-retired) CEO of Aetna Insurance, Ron Williams; Tracey Doi, the future CFO of Toyota USA, and other corporate executives, some of whom became my firm's clients in later years.

One of the most effective ways to become visible on a nonprofit board is by raising money. You can solicit contributions from corporate leaders, business contacts and colleagues; find new board members who are rising stars at their companies; and build strategic alliances with other nonprofits or corporations for mutual benefit. Achieving such milestones builds credibility. Notice how men in corporate leadership positions raise money for causes—they support their friends' nonprofits and their friends return the favor. This is a technique that women have not yet mastered. But it has worked for men to advance their careers and become visible. I can assure you, it works equally well for women.

Bring Money to the Nonprofits—Yes, You Can Do It!

It just takes practice. "Give or Get" is the informal phrase that nonprofits use regarding the fund-raising responsibility of board members. Each nonprofit expects board members to personally "give" a tax-deductible donation every year from $500 to $2500, or more. Large nonprofits can require $10,000 or more, which is often paid by the board member's corporate foundation. Don't let such numbers deter you.

If you are not able to "give," then "get" by securing contributions from corporations, foundations, or other individuals. Another way to give is to provide in-kind services. Many business owners who become board members donate their own professional skills to help their nonprofit boards. A nonprofit organization has to document the value of in-kind contributions of board members on its tax returns, thus professional services donated are given a true value received.

Foundation boards give grants to worthy causes. Rather than raising money, foundations give money away. Excellent experience can be gained, without the additional pressure of having to raise money for a nonprofit organization. Appointment to a foundation board usually comes through business or industry contacts or service on other large nonprofit boards. Large private foundations are run like businesses, and board members have the fiduciary responsibility to manage the endowment for growth and maintain strict accounting of grants and expenses in order to keep their special tax status granted by the IRS.

Over my career, I also dedicated my volunteer time on boards of the UCLA Medical Center, the National Association of Women Business Owners (NAWBO) of California, and Southern California Leadership Network (SCLN), a region-wide, five-county leadership training program under the aegis of the Los Angeles Chamber of Commerce. Through my involvement on these nonprofit boards, I have generated visibility and built relationships with corporate sponsors and fellow board members. Along the way, I learned I could raise money (which I had never done before), manage budgets, lead strategic planning, and manage issues related to the reputation of the organization, and in some cases, resolve crises. Such success in raising money helped to build my confidence. I learned that just asking often makes it happen.

My leadership skills and board management acumen were honed through serving on these nonprofit boards. There's no compensation for volunteer service—just the rewards of gratitude and generating business contacts. Most nonprofit boards are unpaid positions. An exception to that rule is that some large foundations provide annual compensation to their board members.

United Way has a nationwide network of chapters where prominent businesspeople serve on the boards, as do the Boys & Girls Clubs, Big Sisters/Big Brothers, and Girl Scouts and Boy Scouts in large cities. There are literally thousands of nonprofit organizations in major cities throughout the country that welcome outstanding volunteers in these challenging times.

Becoming a Board Candidate

The selection process for a nonprofit board is similar to a corporate board—you must first be known to the current board members. The process usually starts when volunteering at the rank and file level, taking on a difficult task, and doing it well. Volunteering for nonprofit boards does require hard work. And word of an outstanding performer travels upward fast. You can shoot to the top quickly, based on your performance, primarily fund-raising.

Your company most likely sponsors specific nonprofit organizations in the community, so let your own executives know of your desire to volunteer, and ask for their counsel and recommendations. This will improve your own visibility and recognition among them, as an ambitious employee, looking for meaningful ways to learn, grow and represent the company in the community. If you have focused solely on your own career, juggling work and family life, perhaps there has not been enough time to add a nonprofit board commitment. Once the children are older, and you are confident in your job, time can be carved out for a nonprofit board.

See if your industry or professional associates will recommend you for a nonprofit board. Whatever strategy you choose, let other business and professional colleagues know of your interest. Describe the value you would bring to any board— because not all your contacts may be familiar with your background. Marie Knowles was executive VP and chief financial officer for ARCO, one of the largest corporations in Los Angeles. Actively involved in the community, ARCO required its senior executives to volunteer in community organizations and helped match them with nonprofit causes of interest to the company. Knowles was matched for her first board with the LA Chamber Orchestra because she loved music and played the harpsichord. That was the start of her nonprofit involvement, and she expanded to larger boards during her career at ARCO. (See her profile in Chapter 4.)

Responsibilities of Nonprofit Board Members

Here are the responsibilities individual board members should be prepared to take on at a nonprofit organizations, according to BoardSource, a national advisory organization for nonprofits. These requirements are the same for corporate boards:
- Attend all board and committee meetings, functions and events.
- Be informed about mission, services, policies and programs.
- Review agenda and materials prior to board meetings.
- Serve on task forces and take on special projects.
- "Give" a personal financial contribution, or/and "get" additional monies from other sources.
- Recruit senior-level candidates to the board.
- Follow conflict-of-interest policies.
- Don't make special requests of the staff.
- Be aware of your fiduciary responsibilities, understand the financial statements and budgets, and read the tax returns.
- Always be ethical and true to the mission of the organization.

You can see why corporate boards want candidates who have previous experience being on a board of directors, even a nonprofit. Corporate directors don't have time to educate new members about board dynamics and responsibilities. They need women and men who have already gained this valuable experience earlier in their careers and can add value immediately. They want to hear good reports about the candidate's performance on nonprofit boards. If your performance was not notable, chances are slim that it will help you lad a seat on a corporate board.

All boards of directors—both corporate and nonprofit—are required by law, to meet certain standards of conduct and commitment in the discharge of their duties. These standards are often described as the duties of care, loyalty and obedience. Here are the formal definitions, also from BoardSource:

- The Duty of Care describes competence and common sense in decision-making as a steward of the organization.
- The Duty of Loyalty is a standard of faithfulness, allegiance, without benefit of personal gain, always acting in best interest of the organization, and without conflicts of interest.
- The Duty of Obedience means dedication to the mission, acting always within the rules and policies of the organization, following state and federal laws, and ensuring that funds donated are managed to fulfill the mission.

For Women in Developing and Established Career Stages

Choose the one or two nonprofit causes that are most meaningful to you. Use your personal and professional connections to secure introductions to people on those nonprofit boards. Volunteer to be your company's representative on boards of nonprofits that the company sponsors.

- Select a nonprofit with the largest endowment or annual revenues, so you can learn about financial responsibility and how to manage large budgets. But make sure the nonprofit has sufficient staff—so that board members are not involved in day-to-day operations.
- The tried-and-true way to rise in an organization is to help raise funds—the main concern of nonprofits and business alike. Raising money through contributions from your business connections, developing ways to generate income, or volunteering to lead a capital campaign will advance the nonprofit cause, and your cause, too. Corporate boards need people who are financially savvy—so a track record of raising significant dollars for your nonprofit is the best impression you can make.
- Volunteer for tough assignments—anything related to finance—and do a good job. But take on a nonprofit project, only if you can commit the time required. This will unchain you from your desk so you can make connections

and build relationships essential for your future career growth. Once you have learned new concepts and new management techniques from your nonprofit board service, take these back for use at your own company.

Converting nonprofit access into business relationships requires taking responsibility for the success of the nonprofit organization and lending your expertise and insight into furthering, and perhaps broadening, the mission. In other words, you are remembered and visible when you have been an active, productive agent of change.

Looking Forward...

These next chapters explore the career pathways taken by women who have won The Board Game—through public service, corporate finance, banking and investment, technology and engineering, academia, and entrepreneurial endeavors. Some pathways are straight forward, others are unexpected. But the common theme is that most have volunteered their time and talents in nonprofit organizations. The organization benefits, the woman executive benefits—it's a win/win strategy for building credentials and visibility along your pathway.

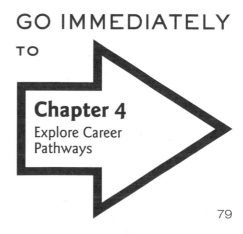

GO IMMEDIATELY

TO

Chapter 4
Explore Career
Pathways

PATHWAYS
4 Through Public

Service and Law

ACAREER AS A GOVERNMENT LEADER OR IN-HOUSE CORPORATE GENERAL COUNSEL GARNERS PUBLIC VISIBILITY and recognition for outstanding management performance on the job—key factors for attracting the attention of corporate board nominating committees. Women who take on the challenges of public service careers deserve applause for all the work they do to serve, from fundraising to intense media scrutiny to balancing public life with family priorities. One benefit of a public service career is that it can offer a long leap toward corporate board service after politics.

The public servants you meet in these pages have worked at local, state, national, and international levels—on legislative bodies, commissions, and cabinet posts—some overseeing huge international agencies for the U.S. and the United Nations. Many are lawyers who decided early in their careers they would rather make laws than practice law.

For women attorneys who want to become corporate directors, a career as a partner at a law firm is not necessarily the ideal pathway. However, many directors with law degrees worked in a law firm as their first career step. Due to potential conflicts of interest, most law firms do not allow their attorneys to serve on corporate boards. Some law graduates advance directly from law school to the public sector; others leave law firms to become general counsels inside the C-suite of corporations to gain essential business experience which can lead to board service.

Serving the public at the national, state, or local level is not exactly like running a shareholder-owned corporation. Though government officers and leaders are not responsible to shareholders, they are accountable to those who put them in power—either through appointments or the ballot box. Many also manage multi-billion-dollar budgets and huge staffs—so their management experience is clearly demonstrated, and their track records are public.

The great advantage of public service is, of course, visibility. In our democracy, the news media play an ever-present role, responsible for monitoring and covering the constant goings-on of government—the people, the process, the successes, and the scandals. Public officials continually demonstrate their ethics, trustworthiness, and values—important considerations when boards are looking for experienced candidates.

Another advantage: the women profiled in this chapter also became known to business leaders through the media and through the industries they oversaw, partnered with, and regulated. Businesspeople who see public servants in action already have impressions of their strengths as leaders, problem-solvers, and personalities. As we mentioned in Chapter 2, a board candidate's public image is a critical factor for consideration and selection.

HENRIETTA HOLSMAN FORE

Henrietta Fore serves on the boards of ExxonMobil and Theravance, and co-chairs the global network of WomenCorporateDirectors (WCD). She is a business owner, not an attorney, who became highly visible through her appointed roles in Washington, D.C., as head of United States Agency for International Development (USAID) and director of U.S. Foreign Assistance; previously as chief operating officer of the U.S. State Department, and originally, head of the U.S. Mint. She owns Holsman International, a manufacturing, consulting, and investment company that includes Stockton Wire Products (her family business in California, Arizona, and Nevada), as well as Vicenza, a manufacturer of home hardware, and Green Express Direct, a distributor of water- and energy-saving products.

HENRIETTA HOLSMAN FORE
Summerlin, Nevada; Washington, D.C.

Current Boards/Select Nonprofits:
Exxon Mobil Corporation
Theravance, Inc.
Asia Society: Global Co-chair

Past Boards:
Dexter Corporation
HSB Group, Inc.
Overseas Private Investment Corporation
Millennium Challenge Corporation

Career History:
Holsman International: Chairman and CEO (current)
Stockton Wire Products: Chairman (current)
WomenCorporateDirectors, Global Co-chair (current)
U.S. Agency for International Development: Administrator
U.S. Department of State: Director of U.S. Foreign Assistance;
    Undersecretary for Management
U.S. Department of Treasury: 37th Director of the U.S. Mint

Education:
MS, Public Administration, University of Northern Colorado
BA, History, Wellesley College

In 2001, Fore took leave from her company when she was appointed by then-President George W. Bush as the thirty-seventh director of the United States Mint, under the Department of the Treasury. She was later appointed to the State Department, where she was the under secretary of state for management, overseeing a budget of $3.6 billion, with 7,200 employees and 30,000 contractors located in 172 countries. These positions demonstrated her ability to manage huge multinational organizations—giving her the CEO experience that attracted the attention of corporate boards.

Fore capped her government career as the first woman to serve as the administrator of USAID and director of U.S. foreign assistance, at a rank equivalent to deputy secretary of state, with an annual budget of $39.5 billion in foreign assistance. The State Department is similar in size to a Fortune 100 public company. So, the size and scope of her responsibilities were comparable to those of CEOs of the largest companies in America. Similar experience in any large government agency can be valuable to a corporate board.

"When I was young, I dreamed of having my own international business," says Fore. "Little did I guess how my career would evolve. As the years passed, and I traveled the world serving my country, I wanted to make the world a better place. I found that many people will help along the way, if you just keep after those dreams. You can go anywhere you want to go."

Born and raised in Chicago, Fore graduated from Wellesley College and was just beginning her career journey when, at age twenty-seven, she was unexpectedly called to run her family's business, Stockton Wire Products, after its general manager died of a heart attack. "My father called after the GM's sudden death, to say he did not know anyone under the age of sixty, and asked if I would help. Of course I said yes—I would come for two weeks, help hire a new manager, and then return to my work. As it turned out, I stayed for twelve years, grew the business, its product lines, its machinery, its profitability, made acquisitions and divestitures, and learned to understand my father through business eyes."

Under her leadership, the company expanded beyond its origins as a manufacturer and distributor of steel and wire products. Fore had become the consummate small business entrepreneur. She knew operations and finance, but she wanted to learn more about the interaction of all types and sizes of businesses and their social impact. She pursued a goal of corporate board service by taking the Board of Directors course at the Stanford Graduate School of Business, learning more about the governance of public corporations. She says the experience is essential—especially for private company owners.

She had previously been appointed by then-President George Herbert Walker Bush at the U.S. Agency for International Development from 1989 to 1993, first as assistant administrator for private enterprise in the U.S. Agency for International Development and then assistant administrator for Asia. In the interim between her two government service roles, Fore contacted Catalyst about potential corporate board service. Catalyst recommended her for her first public boards, Dexter Corporation and Hartford Steam Boiler Group, Inc., both in Hartford, Connecticut.

"I found corporate board work really engaging—I loved it," Fore says. "And I found that my nonprofit board experience had been important training, especially for learning about governance. I believe it is essential to bring business 'results' to the missions of nonprofits." In addition to her visibility at USAID, she came to know corporate directors while serving on the boards of nonprofits, such as the Committee for Encouraging Corporate Philanthropy, the Center for Strategic and International Studies, and Aspen Institute.

"For any woman interested in corporate board service, visibility is an important side benefit of volunteering on nonprofit boards," Fore asserts. "Other nonprofit board members will want to serve with you on their public corporate boards once they see your dedication to service, your similar values, and your approach to problem solving."

Fore was called back into public service at the Department of Treasury, Department of State, and again at USAID. In 2005 she received the Department of the Treasury's highest honor, the Alexander Hamilton Award; and the secretary of state's highest honor, the Distinguished Service Award, in 2009.

When public service career concluded, she had served on two public corporate boards, in government at the highest levels, and run her own business. Her next public board was Theravance, a biopharmaceutical company based in Northern California. She had previously served on another board with one of its board members, who invited her as a candidate, and she enjoys the biopharma industry.

In 2011, ExxonMobil, the largest company in the world, invited her to join its board. During her public service career, when she was exposed to the inner workings of international business, Fore had witnessed and respected the work of ExxonMobil in the developing world. She also had served on two large nonprofit boards with two directors from the ExxonMobil board, so they had seen her in action. Since Fore joined the ExxonMobil board, Ursula Burns, CEO of Xerox, has been recruited.

Fore urges any future board candidate to choose boards based on her interests and ability to contribute, not simply for career advancement. She says, "The term is to 'serve' on a corporate board. Always keep that in mind. You must contribute good judgment, good counsel, and good value to the shareholders. You will learn much along the way and will be proud of your corporation, and that is enough reward for any director."

Fore's other recommendation is to learn about the stock market. "Personal experience with investing is essential for everyone sitting on boards. Corporate performance, prospects, leadership, and reputation are reflected in the stock price. A director must understand how the stock market operates."

Based on her extensive experience, Fore says she believes one reason the percentage of board seats occupied by women is stuck at 16.6% is that nominating committees and executive search firms tend to use the same traditional matrix of skills: a list of boxes to check about a person's experience. Such checklists often overlook or undervalue the experience of someone like Fore, who led and managed extremely large enterprises in the public sector, any one of which was comparable to running a large public company. "However, there is no 'box' to check for such equivalent experience," she says.

Another major drawback of the "checklist matrix" is that no boxes adequately represent the value of successful entrepreneurs, a category where leadership and operations experience can add value to boards. As Fore points out, "Successful entrepreneurs are nimble, creative, productive, and adaptive—all qualities that public companies really need in today's fast-changing, global environment. Entrepreneurs know everything about a business—manufacturing, human resources, marketing, profit and loss, strategy, and finance."

"As a board candidate, if you are a business-owner, a president, but not a CFO, talk about your financial skills. Entrepreneurs and investors have to understand and use a variety of financial statements about their own companies. Make sure you convey that you have this knowledge in your interviews," she advises.

Fore says that regulatory and international experience will be increasingly valuable to boards. "Most companies are looking for growth in developing-country markets. Board members who know international markets, global policy makers, laws and local regulations in other countries will help corporations make smart decisions."

BONNIE G. HILL

Bonnie Hill has served on eleven well-known public boards, including Yum! Brands, The Home Depot and The Hershey Company. Her career included corporate and academia, but it was her public service that was her pathway to corporate boards. While a secretary at Mills College in Oakland, California, she became a part-time student at age thirty. By the time she graduated two and a half years later, she had become a lecturer there, assistant dean of students, and interim head of the Ethnic Studies department. She moved into business when she was recruited by Kaiser Aluminum and Chemical Corporation as vice president in charge of Kaiser Center, a high-rise real estate development in downtown Oakland.

Hill's public service pathway was not planned. She was among a group of business leaders who went to Washington, D.C. with the Oakland Chamber of Commerce to meet legislators. During the trip, she was invited to dinner with two key members of then-President Ronald Reagan's staff. The next day, after a private tour of the White House, where she met Press Secretary Jim Brady, President Reagan and Brady were shot by a would-be assassin. Hill phoned staff members to check on the President's status. They stayed in touch after that fateful day, and two years later she received a call from Presidential Personnel at the White House with an offer to serve on the U.S. Postal Rate Commission, where she later became vice chair, and she subsequently was appointed assistant secretary of the U.S. Department of Education.

When President George H.W. Bush followed President Reagan into the White House, Hill was appointed to be Special Advisor to the President for Consumer Affairs and Chair of the Consumer Affairs Advisory Committee of the Securities and Exchange Commission, where she launched the first national symposium on minority consumer issues, including privacy and the accuracy of computer information. She also led the U.S. Delegation to the Organization for Economic Cooperation and Development on Consumer Policy. After spending six years in the federal government, Hill became CEO of the nonprofit Earth Conservation Corps, recruiting young people from urban neighborhoods and teaching them how to plant trees and turn unused city land into neighborhood gardens.

A public service appointment came once again—this time for a position in California Governor Pete Wilson's cabinet as secretary of the California State and

Consumer Services Agency, with a two-billion-dollar budget and 14,000 employees. In this role, Hill continued to advocate for consumer protection and the prevention of the misuse of personal information. She re-organized the Department of General Services, one of the eleven departments she supervised.

BONNIE G. HILL
Beverly Hills

Current Boards/Select Nonprofits:
The Home Depot, Inc.
Yum! Brands
AK Steel Holding Corporation
California Water Service Group
RAND Corporation

Past Boards:
Financial Industry Regulatory Authority
NASD Regulation, Inc.
Albertsons
The Hershey Company
ChoicePoint

Career History:
B. Hill Enterprises, LLC: President (current)
Icon Blue, Inc.: Co-founder (current)
The Times-Mirror Foundation: President and CEO
Los Angeles Times: SVP, Communications and Public Affairs
University of Virginia: Dean of the McIntire School of Commerce
State of California: Secretary, Consumer Services Agency
U.S. Dept. of Education: Assistant Secretary under President
    Ronald Reagan
Special Advisor for Consumer Affairs to President George H.W. Bush
Securities and Exchange Commission: Consumer Affairs Advisory
    Committee Chair
Kaiser Aluminum and Chemical Corporation: VP and General Manager
    of wholly-owned subsidiary Kaiser Center Inc.
Marcus Foster Educational Institute: President and CEO

Education:
Ed.D, Education, University of California, Berkeley
MS, Educational Psychology, California State University, Hayward
BA, Psychology, Mills College

In 1991, Hill's national visibility as a leader in consumer and environmental issues brought her to the attention of a search firm that was looking for a board member for Niagara Mohawk in upstate New York. After meeting with her in Washington, D.C., Niagara Mohawk's CEO invited Hill to join the board, on which she served for six years until the company was acquired by London-based National Grid Transco. She was invited to serve on the National Grid board, and did so for nearly two years. Before the transition to National Grid, Hill was asked to serve on the board of The Hershey Company, then Louisiana Pacific. Thereafter, the board invitations came frequently.

Hill's career took another short turn back to education in 1993, when she was named dean of the McIntire School of Commerce at the University of Virginia (UVA). When the search firm called to tell her that the school was looking for a nontraditional candidate, she said, "I may be nontraditional in terms of my background—but have you seen a picture of me? I will fax it to you, and if you are still interested, please feel free to call back."

Hill said she was afraid that being an African American might negatively affect the Southern school's ability to raise money, but the university search committee comprised of faculty, alumni, and students judged her to be the best person for the job. Her daughter had loved attending UVA, and Hill decided to take the job because of her abiding commitment to youth and to education. She became one of only seven women deans of 245 graduate business schools in the country.

In 1997, she moved back to California to join her husband, whom she had met in Sacramento and married in Virginia. Hill was recruited by Times Mirror, the parent company of the *Los Angeles Times*, to become CEO of its foundation, as well as the SVP of Communications and Public Affairs at the newspaper.

Hill offers valuable advice to women: "While I did not know this when I was recruited for board work, I have since learned that it helps to have established a reputation as a leader, whether in the corporate sector, academia, or public sector. I did not plan my career, but today it helps if women plan their careers with opportunities to expand their own leadership ability and acquire true expertise. As others begin to recognize your expertise and leadership, they become strong advocates, helping you become known to search firms and sitting board members."

She also notes that "The academic platform—university presidents or deans of business schools—can also be a good career pathway for board recruiting. I think two or three of my boards came about when I was dean of the McIntire School at UVA."

Hill says there are great opportunities for women to become board members. In her twenty-year board experience, diversity has always been an important factor. "Both men and women want more diversity on boards," she says. "Diversity of gender, thought, ethnicity, and experience. When I served on the Albertsons board, half of the members were women and it was a great experience."

Hill recommends that women board members encourage women executives at their companies and coach them. She believes that leadership development is an important part of board service, and she often meets informally with high-potential employees in informal settings.

Hill urges board members to get to know the high-potential members of the management team, and emphasizes that directors should frequently invite those individuals to make presentations to the board. Many CEOs are now encouraging members of their team to seek board positions, and have asked their board members to assist. This is a trend Bonnie Hill sees as a means to increase the number of women in boardrooms.

SUSAN C. SCHWAB

Susan Schwab says "visibility and a public profile can be a critical factor for being chosen to sit on corporate boards." Since Trade Ambassador Schwab has spent much of her distinguished career in the government sector (plus fourteen years in academia and two in private industry), that has been her own personal experience.

"I went into government service right out of graduate school as an agricultural trade negotiator," says Schwab. Next she worked on Capitol Hill from 1981 to 1989, and then as the assistant secretary of commerce, and head of the U.S. & Foreign Commercial Service from 1989 to 1993 under President George H.W. Bush. She subsequently became the U.S. Trade Representative from 2006 to 2009.

When she was assistant secretary of commerce, Schwab ran the export promotion arm of the government with 1300 employees in two hundred offices in seventy countries and most U.S. states, with a budget of more than a hundred million dollars. During her tenure, its budget grew from $95 million to $115 million, so she had operating experience on a scale commensurate with the COOs of some large companies.

After she retired from government service, she was invited to join the boards of FedEx, Boeing, and Caterpillar. Her international trade knowledge was her key "added value" that attracted corporate boards. Schwab's first board service, in the late 1990s, was with Calpine, an energy company then headquartered in Northern California. A former colleague from the Department of Commerce had told the search firm retained by Calpine about her because they were looking for someone with international trade experience.

SUSAN C. SCHWAB
Annapolis, Maryland

Current Boards:
Boeing Company
Caterpillar, Inc
FedEx Corporation

Past Boards:
Calpine
Adams Express Company
Petroleum & Resources Corporation

Career History:
University of Maryland, College Park: Professor, School of
    Public Policy (current)
Mayer Brown, LLP: Strategic Advisor (current)
Office of the United States Trade Representative: U.S. Trade
    Representative; Deputy U.S. Trade Representative
University System of Maryland Foundation, Inc.: President & CEO;
    Vice Chancellor for Advancement
U.S. Department of Treasury, Consultant
University of Maryland, College Park: Dean, School of Public Policy
Motorola Inc.: Director, Corporate Business Development
U.S. Department of Commerce: Assistant Secretary of Commerce
    and Director General, U.S. and Foreign Commercial Service
Office of Senator John C. Danforth: Legislative Director; Chief
    Economist; Legislative Assistant
U.S. Embassy, Tokyo: Trade Policy Officer
Office of the Special Representative for Trade Negotiations:
    Agricultural Trade Negotiator

Education:
Ph.D, Public Administration and International Business, The George
    Washington University
MA, Development Policy, Stanford University
BA, Political Economy, Williams College

Schwab had worked briefly in the private sector as director of corporate business development at Motorola in the early 1990s, and later in academia. Schwab served as dean of the School of Public Policy at the University of Maryland and later as president and CEO of the University System of Maryland Foundation, Inc.

Schwab offers that it's essential to determine your strengths in making a decision to go on a board, then find where you would be a good fit. Since she is adamant that being known to board members is extremely helpful to being recruited, she states, "Unless someone on the board knows a candidate, or knows someone who knows that candidate, it's not likely to happen. You have to be well networked and visibly connected, within a few degrees of separation."

Today, she has a "portfolio" career that includes teaching part-time at the University of Maryland and advising clients at the law firm, Mayer Brown, but she makes sure she sets aside enough time to do justice to her corporate board responsibilities.

LINDA M. GRIEGO

Linda Griego, Los Angeles city government appointee and entrepreneur, became well-known through her public service roles, the news media, and running her own successful business. Griego serves on the board of CBS Corporation, AECOM Technology Corporation, American Funds, and the David and Lucile Packard Foundation. She is a successful entrepreneur as president and CEO of Griego Enterprises, Inc., a business management company. She also owns Oso Ranch and Lodge in New Mexico, and co-owns Zapgo Entertainment Group, which develops television programming for the Latino market.

In 1988, after renovating an historic downtown firehouse in downtown Los Angeles, Griego built her iconic restaurant, Engine Co. No. 28, in the building. She remained founder and managing general partner of Engine Co. 28 from 1988 through 2010, when the restaurant was sold.

The late Mayor Tom Bradley appointed Griego to deputy mayor of L.A. in 1991. She took on this added responsibility at City Hall because she had encountered so many city-permitting obstacles while she was renovating the circa-1912 building and constructing the restaurant. "It took fifty-three building variances! The mayor wanted me to help him streamline the building permitting process and make the city more inviting for small businesses, so I wanted to help."

LINDA M. GRIEGO
Los Angeles

Current Boards/Select Nonprofits:
CBS Corporation
AECOM Technology Corporation
American Funds
David and Lucile Packard Foundation

Past Boards/Select Nonprofits:
Federal Reserve Bank of San Francisco
Blockbuster Video
Granite Construction Incorporated
City National Bank
Southwest Water Company
Tokai Bank
Robert Wood Johnson Foundation

Career History:
Griego Enterprises, Inc.: President and CEO (current)
Zapgo Entertainment Group LLC: President (current)
Engine Co. No. 28 Restaurant: Founder, Managing Partner
Los Angeles Community Development Bank: Interim President and
    CEO
Rebuild L.A.: President and CEO
City of Los Angeles: Deputy Mayor

Education:
BA, History, UCLA

She served as deputy mayor until 1993. Then in 1994, she replaced Peter Ueberroth as head of Rebuild LA (RLA). RLA had been established by Mayor Bradley and then-Governor Pete Wilson in 1992 following the civil uprisings in Los Angeles. She was charged with completing the five-year economic recovery effort because many inner-city neighborhoods were still devastated, many businesses had moved out of the city, and tourism was down.

At RLA, she led a powerful board of Los Angeles business people. "In that role, I became highly visible in the media as the spokesperson for RLA. We were in the press practically every day," she said. Through her dedication and commitment to such visible civic and nonprofit efforts, Griego forged many long-lasting relationships with prominent businesspeople in California. One of those was Roy Anderson, a Los Angeles corporate leader, who recruited her to take his place when he stepped down from the board of First Interstate Bank. That was her first public corporate board.

Strategic alliances that she developed at RLA generated relationships with executives who subsequently recommended her for the public corporate boards of Blockbuster, Inc., and Granite Construction. She later served on the Southwest Water Company board until it was acquired in 2010. When CBS acquired Blockbuster, Griego was invited to remain on the board of CBS Corporation.

After RLA, she went on to become interim president and chief executive officer of the Los Angeles Community Development Bank, a $430 million federally funded empowerment-zone bank. In 1995, President Bill Clinton appointed her to NAFTA's Community Adjustment and Investment Program Advisory Committee for the North American Development Bank, a position she held for five years. Griego was also a director of the Los Angeles branch of the Federal Reserve Bank of San Francisco from 1998 until 2003. Her next bank board came through another mentor, Thomas Phelps of the Manatt Phelps law firm, who recruited her to serve on the Tokai Bank board. She has also served on the advisory board of U.S. Bank and on the board of directors of City National Bank.

Griego credits her twelve years of service on the board of the nonprofit Robert Wood Johnson Foundation with her ability to understand board dynamics and how to perform as a director. "I never actively sought opportunities to sit on corporate boards," Linda says. "But I was always looking for ways to expand my knowledge and my skills." She highly recommends major nonprofit boards— those that are run like a business—and government commissions as a great pathway to corporate boards.

"Getting early experience on boards is crucial, starting with major nonprofit organizations, as well as government commissions," advises Griego. "The key is not just serving on those volunteer boards, but how active and visible you are, particularly in the audit and finance arena. Chairing committees and being a part of the leadership is required for consideration on a corporate board. I got that experience at the Robert Wood Johnson Foundation."

LYNN SCHENK

Lynn Schenk says it's difficult for lawyers to get on corporate boards, because nominating committee members often believe that legal talent can be hired and boards don't need that skill set. "But legal training gives you the ability to analyze almost any issue," she counters. "That thinking process can be applied to every challenge."

LYNN SCHENK
San Diego

Current Boards/Select Nonprofits:
Sempra Energy
Biogen Idec Inc.
California High-Speed Rail Authority

Past Boards:
Long Beach Bank
CalFed Bank
The Women's Bank
IDEC Pharmaceuticals
Toy Biz Inc.

Career History:
Attorney (current)
Chief of Staff to California Governor Gray Davis
U.S. Congress: Representative for the 49th District of California
State of California: Secretary of Business, Transportation,
    and Housing
White House Fellow to Vice Presidents Nelson Rockefeller and
    Walter Mondale
San Diego Gas & Electric: Attorney
California State Attorney General's Office: Deputy Attorney General

Education:
JD, University of San Diego
BA, Political Science, UCLA

Schenk recalls her most memorable challenge in the 1970s: women could not get credit in their own names. A male co-signer was necessary for approval. "It didn't matter if the man was a husband, boyfriend, or elderly, non-working father," she says. Also some banks had a policy of not allowing a married couple's checks to be printed with the wife's own name if different from her husband's name. In response, Schenk and a group of women in San Diego formed the first state-chartered Women's Bank. She served as chair of the organizational executive committee and then on the board of directors. A movement was started, with women's banks springing up in New York and Los Angeles. They flourished until the traditional banks realized this was an untapped market and acquired them.

Continuing to be active in the national fight for women's equality both professionally and in private life, Schenk joined with others across the state to form California Women Lawyers. In San Diego, she co-founded the Lawyers Club, a feminist bar association now with more than one thousand members. Shortly thereafter, she was appointed as a White House Fellow by President Gerald Ford, serving both Vice Presidents Nelson Rockefeller and Walter Mondale as a special assistant.

Schenk returned to California to become deputy attorney general, and later joined the in-house counsel staff of San Diego Gas & Electric. She was the first woman in that utility's law department and one of the first women in the country to work in a utility's law office.

Governor Jerry Brown appointed her to his administration in 1978. In 1980, she was the youngest person in his cabinet and the first woman to be named secretary of the California Business, Transportation, and Housing Agency, then the largest and most powerful agency in state government. Schenk was responsible for more than fifteen departments in the state government.

After her term ended, she was asked to join the board of Long Beach Bank. She learned the ropes of how boards worked by serving on the audit and nominating committees of the bank. But public service called again, and Schenk was elected to the U.S. Congress, where she served on the powerful Energy and Commerce Committee. She became involved with biotechnology, high technology, high-speed rail, and energy.

After serving in Congress, Schenk was appointed to various positions in the California state government under California Governor Gray Davis, including chief of staff, from 1998 until Davis was recalled in 2003. She returned to San Diego and was invited onto several corporate boards and agreed to become a director of

CalFed Bank, one of the largest and oldest savings banks in the country. She also joined the board of IDEC Pharmaceuticals, a San Diego biotech which subsequently merged with Cambridge, Massachusetts-based Biogen. She was retained as a board member of the merged companies, Biogen Idec, a Fortune 500 Company. With three women on its board, Biogen Idec demonstrates the viability of the major assertion in this book: its stock price tripled over fifteen years, which Schenk says demonstrates that progressive companies like Biogen Idec with women on their boards perform better than companies without women board members.

Visibility and consistent networking were also important to her election to the Sempra Energy board. Schenk maintained her contacts over the years. A former colleague at San Diego Gas & Electric became its CEO, and another friend was on the board. So she was known to at least two of the board members. There is now one other woman on the board, the current CEO, Debbie Reed.

"I believe, my insight about how regulators and those on the other side of the table think—what their pressures are—brings great value to our discussions and decisions at the board level," says Schenk.

Schenk says she is hopeful more board seats will open up for women: "I think we are on the cusp of dramatic change. However, women must step forward, and make sure they are visible."

AULANA L. PETERS

A board member of 3M, Northrop Grumman, and Deere & Company, Aulana Peters was the third woman appointed to the bipartisan Securities & Exchange Commission (SEC). She was appointed by President Ronald Reagan to the SEC in 1984, The Commission has five members, which usually works out to two seats for each political party, with the chair coming from the President's party. "They were looking for a Democrat, and found me through political and business circles," she says.

At the time, Peters was a partner at the renowned law firm Gibson, Dunn & Crutcher in Los Angeles, and took leave to work and live in Washington, D.C. She stepped down from the SEC after serving four years of her five-year term. Her first corporate board was IDS Mutual Funds in 1990, now known as American Express Mutual Funds. She was introduced to IDS by two of its board members, who also served on the Public Oversight Board of the American Institute of Certified Public Accountants (AICPA), whom she had met while at the SEC.

AULANA L. PETERS
Los Angeles

Current Boards/Select Nonprofits:
3M Corporation
Deere & Company
Northrop Grumman Corporation
The Mayo Clinic

Past Boards:
Merrill Lynch & Co., Inc.
Mobil Corporation
New York Stock Exchange

Career History:
Gibson, Dunn & Crutcher: Partner (retired)
Securities and Exchange Commission: Commissioner

Education:
JD, University of Southern California
BS, Philosophy, College of New Rochelle

A fellow board member at IDS was the retired CEO of 3M, who recommended her for the board of 3M, her second board, where she still serves. Next came Northrop Grumman, through a recommendation by the dean of the business school at University of Southern California where she had served on the advisory board of the USC Leventhal School of Accounting.

That same year, Peters joined the board of Mobil Corporation, where she served for ten years until Mobil merged with Exxon. She had met and worked with the CEO of Mobil on the 3M board, where they served concurrently for years.

In 1996, she was recommended to the Merrill Lynch board by its then-CEO, who had served with her on the board of directors of the New York Stock Exchange. She remembers this observation he made about her: "You ask probing questions, but you do it nicely."

Peters retired from Gibson Dunn in December 2000, and was recruited back into public service as a member of Public Oversight Board of the AICPA. She was recommended by the vice chair of Merrill Lynch to the CEO and Nominating Committee of Deere & Company for consideration as a board member. She joined the John Deere board after stepping down from the POB in April 2002.

Peters' story is inspiring for women seeking unique career pathways to boards—her undergraduate degree was not in finance or business, but in philosophy, from the College of New Rochelle, New York. She chose law as her career path and earned her Juris Doctorate from the University of Southern California.

She became well-versed in accounting and auditing issues while she was a litigator at Gibson Dunn, working with many corporate clients, then in public service with the SEC, and then on the board of the AICPA and its Blue Ribbon Panel on Audit Effectiveness. She also serves as a public trustee of the nonprofit Mayo Clinic.

Peters recommends keeping track of friends and business contacts who can recommend you for boards. "Take personal inventory of whom you know and who knows you and has worked with you throughout your career," she advises. "It is helpful to reach out to people within your circle who serve on boards and know people serving on boards. Remember that recommendations are usually based on the reputation you have earned from performing well. Lastly, sponsor very bright women to serve on corporate boards. As more women sponsor and support each other for corporate boards, both companies and shareholders will benefit."

MADELEINE A. KLEINER

Madeleine "Madi" Kleiner started as an attorney with a law firm and transitioned to the business world. She had been among the first female associates to become a partner at Gibson, Dunn & Crutcher. Following in the footsteps of Aulana Peters, she also became an advocate at the law firm for recruiting women and minorities. Then she was one of the first women to become general counsel for large public companies, when she was hired by H.F. Ahmanson (Home Savings) as general counsel, and later, by Hilton Hotels Corporation.

"Especially if you are in a law firm, it's very difficult to get a corporate board position," she explains. "You have to identify yourself as a business person. I was fortunate that my CEOs (at Home Savings and Hilton) allowed me to participate in strategic planning, buying and selling companies, and mergers and acquisitions. I also had a lot of interaction with various boards and general counsels throughout my career as outside counsel. Future boards were mostly interested in my work in mergers and acquisitions as a lawyer and general counsel."

MADELEINE A. KLEINER
Sherman Oaks, California

Current Boards:
Northrop Grumman Corporation
Jack in the Box Inc.

Past Boards:
The Hotchkiss & Wiley Family of Merrill Lynch
Mutual Funds

Career History:
Hilton Hotels Corporation: EVP and General Counsel (retired)
H.F. Ahmanson & Company and Home Savings of America: Senior
EVP, Chief Administrative Officer, and General Counsel
Gibson, Dunn & Crutcher: Partner
Clerk to the Honorable William P. Gray, U.S. District Court for the
Central District of California

Education:
JD, Yale Law School
BS, Cornell University

Kleiner credits Aulana Peters for sponsoring her and introducing her to her first corporate board. Peters was already serving on the board of Merrill Lynch when she recommended Kleiner for one of the Merrill Lynch Mutual Fund boards. She brought added value because of her experience working with mutual funds at Home Savings. When Ahmanson was acquired, Kleiner left the company and took time off. But she was soon back in business as general counsel for the Hilton Hotels Corporation.

Peters had been serving as the only woman on the board of directors of the aerospace giant Northrop Grumman. Advocating for more women and people of color to join the board, Peters recommended Kleiner to the CEO.

In addition to her potent introduction by Peters, Kleiner had stellar references even though she had never been a director of a public company before.

Supporting her nomination were her former CEO of Hilton and a former director. She had acquired valuable experience as general counsel at both Home Savings and Hilton Hotels Corporation, so her credentials were stellar. "When I met the CEO, Ron Sugar, we hit it off, but I still needed my networks to support me," Kleiner recalls.

Kleiner's pathway to her next board—Jack in the Box—also came through her networks. When she was at Hilton, she had engaged a former colleague from Gibson Dunn to do ethics training, and she had kept in touch with him. Years later, he went to work for Jack in the Box as general counsel and asked her if she was interested in joining its board. They were looking for a woman and a lawyer. Wendy Webb, also profiled in this book, was the nominating committee chair, and Kleiner had worked with Steve Bollenbach, former CEO of Hilton, at Disney. Kleiner's legal career had created trusted networks of colleagues who could recommend her for board service.

As with Kleiner and Peters, women today are in a position to champion and sponsor rising-star women to be recognized for their outstanding work. "I think as more women move into the C-suite, more women will become directors," acknowledges Kleiner. "That's when we can really leverage more women onto boards because more top executive women will know one another, will have experience working together for the CEOs of public companies, and will rely on each other's judgment."

EDITH R. PEREZ

Edith Perez, an attorney who became a public servant, was a mergers-and-acquisitions lawyer and partner in 1993 at a premier international business law firm when women partners were still rare. Perez's clients were mostly Fortune 500 companies, including financial institutions and large real estate developers, and she also had valuable international experience from working in Rio de Janeiro and Mexico City.

When she became a partner at Latham & Watkins, she told many of her colleagues that she was looking for an appointment to a civic commission. One of them recommended her to then-Mayor Richard Riordan, who appointed her to the Recreation and Parks Commission in Los Angeles.

When Mayor Riordan was looking for a new member of the Police Commission, the president of the Recreation and Parks Commission suggested Perez because of the expertise and leadership she had demonstrated as a commissioner. The world of policing was not friendly to women at the time, but Perez's legal training, business acumen, and bilingual skills made her an ideal choice.

EDITH R. PEREZ
Los Angeles

Current Corporate Boards:
Con-way Inc.

Past Board History:
Los Angeles Police Commission, President
Los Angeles Recreation and Parks Commission,
Vice President

Career History:
Consultant (Current)
Latham & Watkins LLP, Partner
Latham & Watkins LLP, Associate

Education:
JD, University of California, Berkeley
BA, Political Science/Public Service and Spanish, University
of California, Davis

Perez quickly found herself in the hot seat. She was named to the Los Angeles Police Commission soon after the April 1992 Los Angeles civil uprising. She was in the spotlight for local, national and global news media which was focused for months on Los Angeles as a proving ground for diversity issues.

After the Christopher Commission finished its investigation of what came to be known as the "L.A. riots," the Police Commission had oversight of the LAPD reforms, its annual budget of two billion dollars, and a staff of eighty. Perez had become president of the Commission, and her very visible leadership and calmness under intense pressure paved her pathway to corporate boards.

In 2010, she retired from Latham, so was available to sit on a public company board, Con-way snapped her up. She was recommended by a man with whom she had served on a foundation board for twelve years. Her leadership on the Police Commission, as well as her strong legal background, impressed the Con-way board members, so Perez was invited to join the board, as its only woman.

"I really appreciated the opportunity to serve the City of Los Angeles at a time of great crisis," Perez explains. "The experience leading the Los Angeles Police Commission, as well as my legal training, prepared me well for the work of serving on corporate boards, which also requires strategic thinking, collaboration, collegiality and sometimes, courage."

LYDIA H. KENNARD

Lydia Kennard served twice as the executive director of Los Angeles World Airports (LAWA), an organization with a budget of almost a billion dollars, more than three thousand employees—equivalent to a large private company. Because of her experience running a complex and highly visible airport system, Kennard was recruited by UNOVA Corporation for its board of directors. She was recommended by a colleague who knew the board was in need of a director who understood a specific technology UNOVA wanted to sell to airports.

LYDIA H. KENNARD
Glendale, California

Current Boards/Select Nonprofits:
URS Corporation
KDG Construction Consulting
ProLogis, Inc.
Intermec, Inc.
Unihealth Foundation

Past Boards:
AMB Property, Inc.
IndyMac Bancorp Inc.
RAND Corporation
UNOVA Corporation

Career History:
Airport Property Ventures, LLC: Principal (current)
KDG Construction Consulting: President & CEO (current)
Los Angeles World Airports: Executive Director
    (two appointed terms)
McKenna & Fitting: Associate Attorney

Education:
JD, Harvard Law School
MCP, Massachusetts Institute of Technology
BA, Urban Planning and Management, Stanford University

However, getting on boards didn't happen overnight. "It took well over a decade. I was in my early thirties when I joined nonprofit boards. And in my mid-forties when named to my first publicly traded board. All that time, I was preparing myself in terms of relationships and professional expertise. I didn't have family members or business friends who served on corporate boards, but I somehow knew early on that if I wanted to become a viable board candidate, I would have to prepare."

Kennard had a strategic plan. She graduated from Stanford with a BA in Urban Planning and Management, then earned her master's degree in City Planning from MIT, and her JD from Harvard Law School.

"Even though I had the education as a lawyer with a master's degree, I don't think I would have been considered had I not had operating experience managing the aviation system owned by the City of Los Angeles, which included LAX and Ontario Airports," Kennard recalls.

After joining Los Angeles World Airports (LAWA) in 1994, Kennard rose to the top position, which she held until 2003. She returned to LAWA in 2005 to serve again as Executive Director until 2007. She has served on numerous public boards, including AMB Property Corporation, Prologis, Inc., Intermec, Inc., and URS Corporation.

Kennard now is a principal of Airport Property Ventures, Inc., an airport management and development company. She is also President and CEO of KDG Construction Consulting, a construction management company which primarily serves public and institutional clients.

In addition to her professional activities, Kennard has been active in community and civic affairs, including serving as a member of the California Air Resources Board and the Los Angeles City Planning Commission. She is also a trustee of the University of Southern California.

KATHLEEN L. CASEY

Kathleen Casey, an accomplished Washington, D.C., attorney, held senior positions with two of the most important financial-sector policy-making bodies in the federal government. In 2006, after working in the U.S. Senate for more than thirteen years, she was appointed by President George W. Bush, and confirmed by the Senate, as the eighty-eighth Commissioner (and only the eighth woman) of the Securities & Exchange Commission.

KATHLEEN L. CASEY
Arlington, Virginia

Current Boards:
Library of Congress Trust Fund Board
Alternative Investment Management Association
    Council

Past Boards:
FX Alliance, Inc.

Career History:
Patomak Global Partners: Senior Advisor (current)
Georgetown University McDonough School of Business, Center for
    Financial Markets and Policy: Distinguished Policy Fellow (current)
U.S. Securities and Exchange Commission: Commissioner)
U.S. Senate: Staff Director and Counsel, Banking, Housing,
    and Urban Affairs Committee
U.S. Senator Richard Shelby: Chief of Staff and Legislative Director
U.S. Senate: Staff Director, Subcommittee on Financial Institutions
    and Regulatory Relief, Senate Banking, Housing and Urban
    Affairs Committee

Education:
JD, George Mason University
BA, International Politics, Pennsylvania State University

Casey's Washington career began right out of George Mason University law school—when she got a job working for U.S. Senator Richard Shelby from Alabama. "I was always interested in politics and policy, and when an opportunity arose to work on a Senator's staff, I jumped at it."

Later, when Senator Shelby became chairman of the Senate Committee on Banking, Housing, and Urban Affairs, one of the thirteen standing committees in the Senate, he promoted Casey to staff director and counsel. "It was a career-building experience to run a committee and work on important legislation affecting financial markets, international trade and investment, and housing policy." Casey explains.

"I gained greater understanding and insights into the operations of the banking and finance sectors." The committee's legislative and oversight jurisdiction also included the SEC and its regulatory supervision of all securities exchanges, securities broker-dealers, investment advisors, and mutual funds. She was one of two women commissioners when she was appointed, and one of three when she completed her five-year term in 2011.

"To do the job effectively, I had to actively engage with diverse stakeholders in the Senate, Congress and the White House," she says. "It was a very visible role—especially visible for a woman."

The public officials and private sector leaders who interacted with her on legislative issues saw her in action and witnessed her day-to-day command of complicated matters. The SEC is responsible for the administration and enforcement of the U.S. securities laws and oversight of the U.S. capital markets.

"The onset of the financial crisis in 2008 made it an especially challenging time, but it also highlighted the powerful roles of many women in leadership positions, such as the chairmen of the SEC and FDIC," adds Casey.

Because of their deep understanding of governance issues and their familiarity with the regulatory environment, former members of the SEC are sought after to serve on corporate boards. Since leaving the SEC, Casey has served on the boards of directors of publicly traded companies and nonprofit organizations. Her first public company board position came through a colleague who recommended her to the board of FX Alliance, an independent electronic foreign exchange trading platform in New York, that was looking to add an independent director. She served on that board until the company was acquired by Thomson Reuters.

Increased demand for independent directors, coupled with her professional reputation and peer network established through her many years of public service, have been the keys to Casey's advancement toward corporate boards.

Casey says she believes there is momentum now for more women to serve on boards. "It just makes good business sense to have women in decision-making roles on boards of directors," she says. "As women continue to be chosen more frequently for board service, they will open even more doors for a new generation of women directors."

MARGARET M. FORAN

Margaret "Peggy" Foran is an attorney who chose business rather than public service as her career pathway, but her career exemplifies the versatility of a law degree. "One of my passions is communicating legalese in plain English, so I have had many opportunities to make presentations on corporate governance to institutional investors, and I learned about investor relations along the way."

MARGARET M. FORAN
New York City

Current Boards:
Occidental Petroleum

Past Boards:
The MONY Group, Inc.
Encysive Pharmaceuticals, Inc.

Career History:
Prudential Financial, Inc.: Chief Governance Officer, VP,
and Corporate Secretary (current)
Sara Lee Corporation: EVP, General Counsel,
and Corporate Secretary
Pfizer Inc.: SVP, Corporate Governance and
Associate General Counsel
J.P. Morgan: VP and Assistant General Counsel

Education:
JD, University of Notre Dame
BA, University of Notre Dame

Foran spent her legal career as an executive in Fortune 500 companies, including Pfizer, Inc., Sara Lee Corporation, and Prudential Financial, Inc. where she is chief governance officer, vice president and corporate secretary. She serves on the board of Occidental Petroleum.

Throughout her career, search firms were often in touch, seeking recommendations for executives and board candidates. "It's important to build those relationships with search firms," Foran advises. "It gives you a chance to recommend people, including exceptional women, and the firms appreciate your making suggestions."

One such relationship paid off with an invitation to her first board, The MONY Group, Inc. The partner at the search firm for MONY knew that Foran had experience with institutional investors, in addition to expertise in governance and compensation. "I didn't know any of the MONY board members," she said, "but the other woman on the board, Jane Pfeiffer, was a Trustee of Notre Dame, where I went to college and law school. So I think that helped, and Jane became a great mentor to me."

Foran became a member of the Council of Institutional Investors, a nonprofit, nonpartisan association of pension and employee benefit funds, foundations and endowments with assets of three trillion dollars. Its mission is to educate about corporate governance, shareholders rights and investment issues.

Among the many contacts she made at the Council were Jack Ehnes, CEO at CalSTRS, and Anne Simpson, director of corporate governance at CalPERS, both huge pension funds for California teachers and public employees, respectively. "Anne, Jack, and other investors taught me a great deal about governance," recalls Foran.

She must have impressed them as well, because CalSTRS senior staff submitted her name along with others to the board of Los Angeles-based Occidental Petroleum. Foran was selected. CalSTRS recommends candidates for consideration when it believes an area of governance needs attention. "They saw me in action at the Council, and knew the values I stand for," she adds.

Foran had several energy companies as clients early in her career, but the added value she brought to Occidental was her business and investor relations experience, as well as her governance skills. After she joined, the board steered Occidental through various issues, including changes in the longtime CEO's position, and advising his successor.

Despite knowing the changes that lay ahead for Occidental when she was nominated, Foran had done her due diligence and was confident the performance of both the company and its executive team was outstanding. So she didn't hesitate to accept the invitation to join the board.

Foran credits her career success to maintaining her visibility. She developed extensive networks through her participation in many civic and professional associations serving as vice-chair of the Better Business Bureau of New York, on the advisory board of the National Association of Corporate Directors (NACD), and as a member of the American Bar Association's Business Council, among others.

One of five girls in a family of six children, Foran has always been committed to helping others become successful—especially women. "We need more women on boards," she says, so she calls on her colleagues to mentor and sponsor other women so they can get there.

DIANA M. BONTÁ

Dr. Diana M. Bontá, president and CEO of the California Wellness Foundation, is a director of American States Water Company, and two major national foundations. She began her career path in nursing at Bronx Community College and the State University of New York (SUNY) at Buffalo, followed by graduate degrees in Public Health from UCLA, where she is now an adjunct professor.

DIANA M. BONTÁ
Los Angeles

Current Boards/Select Nonprofits:
American States Water Company
The Annie E. Casey Foundation
The Archstone Foundation

Past Boards:
City of Los Angeles Fire Commission
Charles R. Drew University of Medicine & Science
The Health Professions Education Foundation
California Women's Law Center

Career History:
California Wellness Foundation: President and CEO (current)
Kaiser Foundation Health Plan, Inc.: VP, Public Affairs Southern California
California Department of Health Services: Director
City of Long Beach, California: Director, Department of Health
and HumanServices

Education:
DrPH, Public Health, UCLA
MPH, Public Health, UCLA
BS, Nursing, SUNY Buffalo
AAS, Nursing, Bronx Community College

In her previous role as vice president of public affairs at Kaiser Foundation Health Plan and Hospitals for the Southern California region, Bontá had been a highly visible advocate for public health, making local and national presentations to government and industry on the increasingly complex health care issues.

In 1999, then-California Governor Gray Davis appointed her to be the first Latina director of the Department of Health Services. Bontá developed the first major initiative to collaborate with Mexico to reduce the incidence of disease on both sides of the border. She led California's public health response post 9/11, and led the response to emerging diseases such as West Nile Virus and SARS. She also advised the director of the National Center for Disease Control and Prevention.

Recognized often for her nonprofit work in public health, Bontá serves on two significant foundation boards: the Annie E. Casey Foundation, a four-billion-dollar foundation that focuses on redevelopment and real estate to build better futures for disadvantaged children in the U.S; and the Archstone Foundation in Long Beach, California. Bontá was recommended to the Annie E. Casey board by friends who were aware of her interest in serving on boards.

Diana learned about finance and investments serving on these two foundation boards, and as the CEO of the California Wellness Foundation, which is one of the largest foundations in California. The board of American States Water Company recruited her for her expertise in public health and her understanding of the regulatory environment, rather than for her finance expertise. Her pathway to the American States Water board also came through nonprofit service where she knew a friend—a colleague overseeing the Los Angeles Human Relations Commission—who recommended her to the firm handling the board search.

Bontá has also been highly visible for her work for public health advocacy—volunteering on the corporate board of advisors for the National Council of La Raza, the U.S.-Mexico Border Health Commission, and the National AIDS Fund. She was chair of the board of the American Public Health Association, and has been recognized by *Hispanic Magazine* among the one hundred leading Latinas in the U.S., and by *Hispanic Business* Magazine as a distinguished woman in government. She also served as a City of Los Angeles fire commissioner.

GAYLE WILSON

In 1999, at the close of Governor Pete Wilson's second term, Gayle Wilson was invited onto the ARCO board by Kent Kresa, chair of the nominating committee. ARCO was a global oil company based in Los Angeles, later acquired by BP. She had been quite visible in California as first lady, but Kresa also had seen her in action as a fellow board member of California Institute of Technology.

GAYLE WILSON
Los Angeles

Current Boards/Select Nonprofits:
California Institute of Technology
Gilead Sciences, Inc.
Ralph M. Parsons Foundation
COSMOS (State Summer School for Math
and Science)

Past Boards:
ARCO
CHELA Financial
College Access Foundation
Society for Science and the Public

Career History:
State of California: First Lady

Education:
BS, Biology, Stanford University

"Even though at first I knew little about the oil industry, I made the effort to educate myself by visiting ARCO refineries and by meeting one-on-one with management to learn about the key drivers of the industry," Wilson explains. "In addition, I knew several of the board members, and I had public service and nonprofit board experience."

With her degree in biology from Stanford, Wilson was attracted to the work of Gilead Sciences, a California pharmaceutical company developing medications for HIV/AIDS, hepatitis C, and more. One evening at a dinner, she mentioned her interest to former Secretary of State George Shultz, who was on Gilead's board. As a result of his sponsorship, she was invited to become Gilead's first woman director. Since then, she has been joined by another woman from public service, former Secretary of Housing and Urban Development Carla Hills.

Wilson has no illusions about the importance of having been married to a former governor of California, especially when board opportunities came up. "There's no doubt in my mind that people thought of me for boards because I had been first lady of California. The position has a high profile and gets a certain amount of public attention."

Wilson was not educated in finance, but she had a lot of experience in nonprofit board leadership, coupled with her board service for ARCO. "There were more than enough finance experts on those boards," she said. But she learned a lot about finance when she joined the board of CHELA Financial, Inc., one of the nation's leading providers of education financing solutions. Now restructured, CHELA became the College Access Foundation, one of California's largest foundations, providing scholarships, grants, and other forms of financial aid to help improve access to higher education for disadvantaged students. "The student loan business was highly regulated and involved a lot of finance—a stretch for me," she said.

The foundation encouraged all board members to take advantage of board training courses every year, so Wilson went to the Stanford Director's College, and took advantage of other local training courses given in Southern California by the National Association of Corporate Directors (NACD). She says such training helped her to stay current with trends and issues affecting boards. "I advise anyone going on her first board to attend several board education courses. At a minimum, you come back with good ideas for your board."

Wilson notes that former officeholders and their spouses are often good candidates for boards, depending upon their career experience. "Because of their high profile, and the fact that they are so closely scrutinized by the public and the media, business people know about them. They are vetted in the public eye, so to speak. Those who are known to be responsible, reliable, honest, ethical, and demonstrate good judgment are in demand."

A champion for women and a strong advocate for women on boards, Gayle organized the first Governor's Conference for Women when her husband was governor. The conference expanded over the years to attract 25,000 women every October to the Long Beach Convention Center. Speakers have included women justices of the U.S. Supreme Court, senators, Nobel Prize winners, and journalists of international renown. The event was continued by her successors, First Lady Sharon Davis, and expanded by First Lady Maria Shriver.

"If you really want to get on a corporate board, ask someone to sponsor you," Wilson says. "A lot of times, women aren't automatically thought of as candidates for board positions. Women should share their interest in serving on corporate boards with people who are in positions to make it happen."

GO IMMEDIATELY

TO

Chapter 5
Pathways through Finance

PATHWAYS
5 Through

Finance

MANY WOMEN CORPORATE DIRECTORS WHO WERE FIRST THROUGH THE BOARDROOM DOORS TOOK THE CFO CAREER pathway. Long before the Sarbanes-Oxley Act required that boards must have directors who qualify by SEC standards as "finance experts," corporate boards needed directors with financial expertise to help ensure that companies are profitable, with the goal of increasing shareholder value.

Of course, at the top of the ladder in corporate finance, women CFOs still remain seriously outnumbered. The women you meet in this chapter had to be extremely well-qualified to reach the C-suite in their companies.

By 2013, only eighteen women were CFOs in the Fortune 500—only 3.6%. So, women CFOs of large corporations are very visible—a helpful factor for board recruitment—in addition to having exceptional track records in finance.

As CFOs, they are not only comfortable with numbers, they are comfortable in a male-dominated milieu. Being the first (and often, the only) woman on the board has been a familiar situation to them. Most women CFOs learned how to speak up and be noticed when they were in school and college. Many of the women featured here told me they were one woman among many men throughout their college educations.

For most board searches, nominating committees are looking for experience working for well-known companies like IBM, Mattel, and Disney. Working as CFO for a big-brand Fortune 500 company is an asset. Your resume stands out and carries a lot of weight with executive search firms and board nominating committees.

In this chapter, women corporate directors offer sage advice that's helpful to women in all career pathways, not just to other women CFOs.

MARILYN A. ALEXANDER

Marilyn Alexander, former financial executive at Marriott, CFO of Disneyland Resort, and marketing executive at Walt Disney World Resort, says her CFO, marketing, and brand-name company experience was her pathway to the corporate boards of Equity Office Properties Trust (her first), New Century Financial Corporation, as well as her current boards: DCT Industrial Trust, Inc. (where she is audit chair) and Tutor Perini Corporation.

Despite her impressive credentials, Alexander observes that there is serendipity in being recruited for a board. "Part of your strategy should simply be to get prepared with as much relevant professional education and experience as possible, so when the opportunity comes, you are ready to take the leap," she adds.

"When I was building my finance career at Marriott, a trusted female HR leader talked to me when I was about thirty-seven, and suggested that I prepare myself to be on corporate boards one day. It was a conversation in passing—we didn't talk about what specific training I needed to prepare. But it planted a seed, and my career progression happened to coincide with regulatory changes that required more independent directors and identification of financial experts on audit committees. It was good timing for me, and in general, the new regulations possibly opened more opportunities for women."

Alexander was first approached to serve on a corporate board by a board member at Chapman University, where she served on the finance committee and Board of Governors. At the time, she was working for Disney, which does not allow its executives to serve on outside corporate boards, so she declined. But Alexander recommends that boards of universities are ideal places to make strategic corporate connections and learn how boards function.

MARILYN A. ALEXANDER
Laguna Beach, California

Current Boards:
Torchmark Corporation
Tutor Perini Corporation
DCT Industrial Trust, Inc.

Past Boards:
Equity Office Properties
New Century Financial Corporation
PIMCO Funds (3)

Career History:
Alexander & Friedman LLC: President (current)
The Disneyland Resort: SVP and CFO
The Walt Disney World Resort: VP, Destination Marketing
Walt Disney World: VP, Finance
Marriott Corporation: VP, Financial Planning and Analysis
Cresap, McCormick and Paget (division of Towers Perrin):
    Managing Consultant

Education:
MBA, Wharton Graduate School, University of Pennsylvania
BA, Philosophy, Georgetown University

"When I interviewed for the board of Equity Office Properties, the search committee focused on my experience serving on the finance committee at Chapman, because university boards operate very professionally, like corporate boards. I encourage women to serve on nonprofit boards, especially university boards. Even if you are too early in your career to be invited to the overall board of a nonprofit, start volunteering on committees so you can move up to the big board. I think the best strategy is to get on the most prestigious board you can, and one where you truly care about the mission of the organization, in order to make strong contacts. All the while of course, you will be doing great work that's meaningful to your community and your cause."

"Like most women who are building their careers, I didn't really have much time for networking while I was a corporate executive, often working six- and seven-day weeks. Any extra time I had, I wanted to spend with my husband," Alexander says.

Her first corporate board opportunity came through a consultant at an executive search firm who previously had placed her in a corporate position. She maintained good relationships with search firms, and often hired them to find executives for her staff. The board of Equity Office Properties in Chicago, a real estate investment trust, was looking for a woman with financial and hospitality credentials for the board. Two years later, in 2007, the company was purchased through a very profitable buyout, just before the financial and real estate markets hit extraordinarily hard times.

Alexander says, "Women need to have all the credentials—education and professional experience—that the guys have." To be considered for directorships, a potential candidate needs strong financial credentials. That doesn't mean everyone has to be a finance executive: financial credibility can be gained through corporate P&L experience or education, or both.

Alexander's additional advice to young women: "Take the opportunity to gain significant international experience; take a meaningful assignment in a foreign country (or more than one). Get experience in a big, brand-name company. Be knowledgeable about the numbers, get operational P&L experience and an MBA degree. If you have a finance or accounting background, do whatever it takes early on to get your CPA license. Boards look for C-level executives of major divisions or of the company overall, so reach for the highest level position you can in your career."

FRANCESCA RUIZ DE LUZURIAGA

Francesca Ruiz de Luzuriaga has been a board member of OfficeMax since 1998, and most recently joined the board of SCAN Health Plan, a Medicare Advantage not-for-profit insurance plan for seniors. She spent most of her career at Mattel, one of the world's largest toy manufacturers, where she started as a financial analyst after working at Xerox. She worked her way up the ladder at Mattel to become chief financial officer from 1995 to 1997, then became executive vice president, Worldwide Business Planning and Resources from 1997 to 1999, and then chief operating officer of Mattel Interactive. Since retiring from Mattel in 2000, Luzuriaga has been an independent business development consultant. From 2002 until 2005, she served as a board member of Providian Financial Corporation.

FRANCESCA RUIZ DE LUZURIAGA
Rancho Mirage, California

Current Boards:
OfficeMax, Inc.
SCAN Health Plan

Past Boards:
Boise Cascade
Providian Financial Corporation
Mossimo

Career History:
Business Development Consultant (current)
Mattel, Inc.: COO, Mattel Interactive; EVP, Worldwide Business
    Planning and Resources; CFO; EVP, Finance
Xerox Corp.: Finance

Education:
MBA, University of Southern California
BA, Asian Studies, Pomona College

She honed her reputation as a change agent while at Mattel in the early 1980s, as part of a team that helped the company sell properties it owned that were not focused on the toy business, including a circus, a movie production company, and an aquarium manufacturer. Later she helped redesign Mattel's international distribution system. Her work caught the attention of the CEO of Boise Cascade, then in the paper and wood products industry. The CEO was looking to transform his company.

"Boise Cascade was then in paper/wood products, but the firm was not large enough to be a leader in that industry," recalls Luzuriaga. "The CEO recruited people from a broad base of industries and talents to transform the company. Together, we did it—with total branding and business makeover— today that company is OfficeMax."

"I do think it's easier for a woman or man to become a board member if they have a finance background, especially if they are not CEOs. My avenue to boards was definitely through my professional contacts." As she points out, "CFOs have broad experience working with corporate lawyers, auditors, and investment bankers who come to know your capabilities and reputation, and can recommend you to their wide circle of corporate board members."

Prior to Boise Cascade, Luzuriaga's first public board was Mossimo, a casual clothing company. She was identified for this start-up board by a colleague who was an investment banker and knew of her performance results at Mattel. Luzuriaga stayed on that board until the call came from Boise Cascade. Mattel, like many other companies, had a rule that its executives could sit on only one outside board, so she left Mossimo to join the board of Boise Cascade.

Providian Financial, a credit card bank, presented another turnaround challenge. Again, Luzuriaga was the right fit for the board and Providian's new CEO recruited her. Providian was interested in both her finance and operations experience. "They were looking for a director to chair the Audit Committee, and since I am a financial expert, I could do that." The company could not compete with huge banks, so the board decided to look for a buyer. "When I joined the board, the stock was at $5 a share. We sold it at $17."

Luzuriaga was born in the U.S., after her father emigrated from the Philippines. She credits her diverse background as an asset she brings to boards. Her achievements as a woman and financial expertise also give her the confidence to actively provide thoughts and ideas to her boards.

DENISE K. FLETCHER

Denise Fletcher was the first woman corporate officer and first woman treasurer of The New York Times Company, and may have been the first woman treasurer of any Fortune 500 company. This gained her the visibility that established her early career direction toward corporate board service.

During her tenure, The New York Times Company retained a major consulting firm. Fletcher and the woman principal on the team happened to reside in the same town outside New York, and they became friends. The consultant's husband was on the board of Software Etc. Stores, Inc., and he recommended Fletcher for that board—her first corporate board. So her professional and social networks were the keys to her first board seat.

DENISE FLETCHER
New York City

Current Boards/Select Nonprofits:
Unisys Corporation
Inovalon, Inc.
Mazars Group, France
Ovarian Cancer National Alliance

Past Boards:
Sempra Energy
Orbitz Worldwide, Inc.
Software Etc. Stores, Inc.
Hospital Group, UK
Girl Scouts of the USA

Career History:
Orienta-Royal, LLC: CEO (current)
Vulcan Inc.: EVP, Finance
DaVita, Inc.: SVP and CFO
MasterCard International: EVP and CFO
Bowne & Co.: SVP and CFO
The New York Times Company: Treasurer
Getty Oil: Assistant Treasurer, Eastern Operations

Education:
MCP (Master of City Planning), Harvard University
BA, Sociology, Wellesley College

Fletcher built an impressive career as a senior corporate operating and financial officer with a wide range of industry experience, including CFO of MasterCard, CFO of Bowne & Company (then the world's largest financial printer that acquired approximately twenty companies during her tenure); EVP of Finance at Vulcan, Inc. (Microsoft co-founder, Paul Allen's investment company), and CFO and Special Advisor to the Chairman and CEO of DaVita, Inc. She gained valuable operations experience when she ran MasterCard's Settlement Operations and Vulcan's Aviation operations, while overseeing its large real estate operations.

While she was working at MasterCard, Fletcher was recruited to the board of Unisys, her second board, by Sheila Wellington, then president of Catalyst. She still serves on that board.

After France established its 40% quota for women on corporate boards, Fletcher was contacted by a search firm on behalf of Mazars Group, a global accounting firm based in Paris that specializes in audit, accountancy, tax, legal, and advisory services, with 13,000 employees in sixty-nine countries. Mazars is a private company, where Fletcher and a man are its first independent directors. She is the second woman on the board, and chairs the compensation committee. Fletcher grew up in Turkey and learned to speak fluent French, Turkish, and English. She believes that French companies are open to recruiting American women as board members, but those American women must speak fluent French. Her introduction to Mazars came through a search firm consultant who knew that she spoke French.

"Even when board placements are handled by search firms, it's often someone you know personally who recommends you," Fletcher says. "That was the case with the Sempra Board in San Diego."

Fletcher was on the short list of candidates a search firm presented to Sempra Energy. The CEO recognized her name as a former colleague of his wife at The New York Times Co. Fletcher believes that this personal connection enhanced her chances for selection.

The recruiter who recommended her to Sempra also recommended her to Orbitz. Recently she joined the board of Inovalon, recommended by a trusted contact of the CEO with whom she had worked earlier in her career. She chairs the Audit Committee.

Media visibility was invaluable to Fletcher along her pathway. She was named one of the "Women at the Top" by *Industry Week* Magazine; "Women Ready to Run Corporate America" by *Working Woman* and one of "Women Leaders in the Financial Industry."

A graduate of Wellesley College, Fletcher earned her Master of City Planning degree from Harvard, and served on the Alumni Executive Council of the Kennedy School at Harvard. She is a member of the Council on Foreign Relations and the Economic Club of New York, and previously served on the national board of Girl Scouts USA. Fletcher is currently a national board member of the Ovarian Cancer National Alliance.

MELISSA LORA

Melissa Lora combined finance and real estate studies to shape her degree from California State University at Long Beach—a fortunate combination for her twenty-five-year career in finance, development, and operations at Taco Bell Corp. and her board service at KB Home.

Currently CFO of Taco Bell, she also serves as chief development officer, managing new unit and asset growth nationwide. Adding operations experience to her financial and real estate acumen, Lora spent several years as regional VP and general manager for Taco Bell in the Northeast region. She played a significant role in Taco Bell's refranchising efforts, and led the company's focus on building financial capability for its franchises.

MELISSA LORA
Newport Beach, California

Current Boards:
KB Home

Past Boards/Select Nonprofits:
Discovery Science Center

Career History:
Taco Bell Corp.: CFO (current); Regional VP and General Manager

Education:
MBA, Finance, University of Southern California, Marshall School
of Business
BS, Finance with a concentration in Real Estate, California State
University, Long Beach

She was recommended to the board of KB Home by Vilma Martinez, current U.S. ambassador to Argentina, who was a veteran corporate board member before her appointment to the U.S. State Department.

Lora had an interest in serving on outside boards, "so I initiated 'sponsorship' from the chairman and CEO of our parent company, to ask for his permission." She advises all women executives to secure permission from their own companies early in the board search process. "You should know what your company's policies are about serving on outside boards."

She also talked to the general counsel of the parent company, who gave her wise advice, as did other members of the KB Home board. "It helped that Taco Bell is a learning organization, valuing outside information and experiences that are useful to our own business and leadership development."

She was an attractive candidate for KB Home because she was not only a CFO, but had operations experience as a divisional general manager as well as responsibility for Taco Bell's expansion. "Certainly my financial qualifications were attractive to KB, but I think my operating experience counted a lot."

Lora also served on the nonprofit board of the Discovery Science Center in Santa Ana, California, an experience that helped her understand board dynamics and served in her favor for nomination to KB Home.

One valuable key to board appointments is to secure sponsorship inside and outside your company, by proactively networking in the right places. Make your goals known and develop your game plan.

"When you are looking to join outside boards, sit down with your own company's senior officers to ask their counsel and leverage their networks," Lora advises.

Lora has been on the KB Home board since 2004 and serves with one other woman, Barbara Alexander. Lora chairs the Audit Committee and serves on Nominating and Governance Committees.

CAROL B. TOMÉ

Carol Tomé, EVP and CFO of The Home Depot in Atlanta, advises women who want to serve on boards to "build your networks throughout your career." Tomé is chair of the Metro Atlanta Chamber of Commerce and on the Board of the Trustees for the Atlanta Botanical Garden. Her nonprofit work helped her to build business and civic relationships, notably with the mayor of Atlanta.

She serves on the board of UPS, and her nomination came about through business relationships and her community involvement. Tomé's boss, the CEO of The Home Depot, enthusiastically endorsed her. Before she started the interview process, she realized she was already known to two other current board members—Ann Livermore from Hewlett Packard, whom she had met at a *Fortune* women's conference, and Jim Kelly, with whom she had been a speaker on a panel with Reverend Jesse Jackson. Although she didn't ask them to, those board members supported her nomination.

CAROL B. TOMÉ
Atlanta

Current Boards/Select Nonprofits:
United Parcel Service, Inc.
Federal Reserve Bank of Atlanta
Metro Atlanta Chamber of Commerce
Atlanta Botanical Garden

Career History:
The Home Depot, Inc.: CFO and EVP, Corporate Services (current);
    SVP, Finance and Accounting; VP, Finance and Accounting;
    VP and Treasurer
Riverwood International Corporation: VP and Treasurer
Johns Manville: Director of Banking

Education:
MBA, Finance, University of Denver
BS, Communications, University of Wyoming

She also chairs the board of the Federal Reserve Bank of Atlanta. A member of the Federal Reserve board was the CEO of UPS who recommended Tomé for this role.

A woman executive about to retire recently asked her how to get on corporate boards. Tomé replied, "Tell me about your networks, your business relationships?" Unfortunately, the woman executive had not developed any networks or visibility while she was working full-time. "The sad truth is, in my opinion, she will not be invited to go on any board because she had not developed any contacts over the years," Tomé says.

"Community involvement is hard work, especially when balancing your full-time job and your family—it's tough. But you learn a lot. It's extraordinarily rewarding, and you make invaluable business connections—and it is those people who nominate you."

Tomé has been at The Home Depot since 1995. She began her career as a commercial lender with United Bank of Denver (now Wells Fargo), then spent several years in finance for the Johns-Manville Corporation. *Fortune* three times has named her one of the "50 Most Powerful Women In Business." She earned her BA in Communications from University of Wyoming and her MBA from University of Denver.

"Once you get on a board and do a good job, other boardroom doors will open for you."

KATHLEEN W. HYLE

Kathleen Hyle attributes her first job as a treasury analyst for Black & Decker Corporation to what she calls "dumb luck" since, when she was hired for the job, she had no idea what a treasury analyst did.

KATHLEEN W. HYLE
Baltimore

Current Boards:
AmerisourceBergen Corporation
Bunge Limited
ADT Corporation

Past Boards:
UniStar Nuclear Energy, JV
MXenergy Holdings, Inc.

Career History:
Constellation Energy Group: SVP (retired); COO, Constellation Energy
    Resources; CFO, Constellation Energy Nuclear Group: SVP
    Finance, IT, Risk, and Operations, Constellation NewEnergy
ANC Rental Corp.: CFO
AutoNation, Inc.: VP and Treasurer
Black & Decker Corporation: VP and Treasurer

Education:
BA, Accounting, Loyola College

"I was the only analyst in Treasury at Black & Decker, so the only limit on my activities was my willingness to work. I had lots of freedom and was able to make recommendations to the executives about changes—way outside my comfort zone—which they approved." Those changes included introducing computers and systems for finance and operations of Black & Decker (now Stanley Black & Decker), a manufacturer, designer, and importer of power tools, hardware, and home improvement products. Over sixteen years, Hyle worked her way up to corporate treasurer at Black & Decker.

When a former boss called to ask if she wanted to be treasurer of a new company called Republic Industries, the forerunner of the automotive retailer AutoNation, she said yes because it was a chance to learn and grow, even though it was a lateral move. "There were lots of 'good old boys' there, and I had zero credibility with them, coming in at the executive level," she recalls. "So it was very high-stress, but it turned out to be a key move. I acquired a whole new set of skills by working to develop relationships in that atmosphere."

AutoNation spun off ANC Rental Corporation, parent of Alamo Rent-A-Car and National Car Rental, and Hyle had the opportunity to go with ANC as its CFO. After the rental car industry consolidated and 9/11 caused an economic downturn, the company was highly leveraged and had to file bankruptcy, a process she had not experienced before.

Hyle was recruited for another lateral move to a merchant energy company, Constellation Energy in her hometown, Baltimore. When she left after nine years, she was senior vice president and COO of Constellation Energy, a $14 billion Fortune 500 company.

Because of the senior executive finance positions Hyle had held, she was called by a search firm for the board of AmerisourceBergen, an $80 billion pharmaceutical distribution company. The firm was looking for a woman who was an SEC financial expert, someone who had run a business and lived within a 200-mile radius of its Chesterbrook, Pennsylvania headquarters. She must have been a good fit: she got the seat on AmerisourceBergen's board. Today she is on the Executive Committee, and chairs the Audit and Corporate Responsibility Committees.

"These were challenging times to be in the energy business," she says, "liquidity crises, the recession, acquisitions, but we came through them all, and then Constellation was purchased by Exelon Corporation."

When Exelon took over Constellation, Hyle was out of a job. "I was too young to retire from the business world," she says. "So I developed a game plan to get on more boards. I packaged my resume with a one-page marketing bio and cover letter, and emailed it to as many search firms with board practices as I could find."

"I got quite a lot of responses, and set up face-to-face appointments with those who would meet me. I flew all over the country for those meetings. Less than a year later, I was on the ADT Corporation board and Bunge Ltd., a $60 billion international agricultural trading and logistics business."

Her board connections also helped secure the ADT appointment. She had asked the retiring CEO of AmerisourceBergen to be a reference. He was on the Tyco board, and when Tyco spun off ADT, he recommended Hyle for the board of that company.

For the moment, Hyle is satisfied with serving on three boards in order to do the best job she can on each, while also serving on nonprofit boards.

DONNA A. JAMES

Donna James is currently serving on the boards of Time Warner Cable, Marathon Petroleum, and Limited Brands. She forged her own success from humble beginnings as a young, single African-American mother with a love for math and science. At North Carolina A&T State University in Greensboro, North Carolina, she decided to major in accounting vs. engineering because they offered her a larger scholarship for accounting. So she became a CPA.

In 1981 James was recruited by Nationwide Insurance in Columbus, Ohio, to be a one-woman finance and accounting department for its new HMO subsidiary. She rose rapidly through management positions in annuities, pensions, and mutual fund operations, as well as accounting and compliance. "We had a new CEO in 1991, who was committed to leadership development," says James. "So he selected me as one of two executives to work closely with him for two years."

Such experience paved the way to her future boards. She learned all the Nationwide businesses, met many business contacts outside the company, and interacted often with the Nationwide board, but she was not happy with her next assignment. Her boss wanted James to take over Human Resources. "I thought this is where you send the women and people of color," she said. She resisted working in HR, but had to say yes. As the CEO gently reminded her, "You serve at the pleasure of the CEO."

DONNA A. JAMES
Columbus, Ohio

Current Boards:
Marathon Petroleum Corporation
Time Warner Cable
Limited Brands Inc.

Past Boards:
Coca-Cola Enterprises
CNO Financial
Intimate Brands

Career History:
Lardon & Associates, LLC: Managing Director (current)
Nationwide Insurance and Financial Services: President, Strategic
    Investments; EVP and Chief Administrative Officer; Co-President,
    Shared Services; SVP, Global Human Resources

Education:
BS, Accounting, North Carolina Agricultural and Technical State
    University
CPA (non-practicing)

After heading HR, James went on to become chief administrative officer and executive vice president of Nationwide. "I'm glad I got sidetracked. The HR experience combined with business operations made me a much more well-rounded executive," she said. "Especially for corporate board service later."

Her CEO knew what he was doing. He needed James at the helm of HR, because he was about to take the life insurance company public and knew the HR task was going to play a critical role in performance management. She eventually made it clear that her career goal was to be president of a company. She achieved her goal, became president of Nationwide Strategic Investments, and oversaw the mortgage company, health plan businesses, Global Holdings, a new business innovation unit, and Nationwide Mutual Capital before she retired in 2006.

While still in her early forties, James thought ahead to the possibility of corporate directorships. Her first board came through her nonprofit work, which had always been a priority for this busy executive. As volunteer chair of the YWCA in Columbus, she led a major fundraising campaign chaired by Abigail Wexner, the wife of Leslie Wexner, chairman and CEO of Limited Brands. In 2000, James was asked to serve on the board of the public company subsidiary, Intimate Brands.

"The YWCA fundraising campaign was complex and ambitious, and we were successful. I think boards are looking for good business judgment, good ideas, the ability to collaborate, and the willingness to push back constructively," she says.

James had to demonstrate her independence as a director protecting the shareholders in an unexpected manner. Shortly after she joined the board, The Limited decided to re-acquire Intimate Brands. She was quickly appointed by the independent directors to chair the special committee representing minority shareholder interests. "It was serious, no-joke work," she adds.

Ironically, several years later, James was invited to join the Limited Brands board, and she still serves on the board as chair of the Audit Committee. Her next board was Coca-Cola Enterprises, the largest bottling and distribution company in the U.S., separate from the Coca-Cola Company. She was recruited by a search firm she knew from her HR job at Nationwide. Coca-Cola Enterprises was looking for financial expertise and diversity—women and people of color. At the time she had just been selected to appear on the cover of *Black Enterprise* magazine as one of the "75 Most Powerful Blacks in Corporate America."

"It is all about relationships and reaching C-suite levels of responsibility and creating a network," James says. " I think women underestimate the importance of serving in significant community and nonprofit organizations. It's important to build your network beyond your professional contacts."

A search firm also recruited her for the Conseco Insurance Board. James advises women who ask her about board service, "Always take the calls from search firms. Get to know them. Even if you're not interested in the position they are calling about, let them know that you are interested in sitting on corporate boards, find out who in their company leads the board practice, and get to know them."

Conseco had recently emerged from bankruptcy, and James joined just as the recession was beginning. The board along with management was charged with keeping the company afloat. Although she says she is no longer on the board, she is pleased that it continues to be a successful company today. Yes, initially she hesitated, because her due diligence indicated it would be a challenge. But she thought she could help support turning the company around.

James joined the Time Warner Cable (TWC) board just as it was spun off from Time Warner, Inc. "I guess I've made something of a specialty of spin-offs," she says. "I am really attuned to the nuances of separation and continued success." A colleague from another board recommended her to the TWC board, where she chairs the Audit Committee.

Most recently, James was asked to join the board of Marathon Petroleum, another spin-off from Marathon Oil. Proving that you never know where a contact will lead, the CEO of Marathon Petroleum remembered a speech she gave years before at Tiffin University, where he was chairman of the Tiffin trustees, and because of her business expertise with retail companies and downstream retail operations, she was invited to serve on the board of Marathon Petroleum.

James remains active on behalf of development opportunities for minorities, women, children, and the arts. She was appointed by President Obama to the National Women's Business Council, which she chairs.

WENDY MARKUS WEBB

Wendy Webb was not a CFO, but her career path was in the C-suite through investor relations and strategic communications, working with CFOs and CEOs and boards of directors. Growing up, she never heard that girls who were good in art and English, were not supposed to be good in math, too. In high school, Wendy enjoyed calculus and biology as much as English literature.

So while at Smith College, she applied to Harvard Business School. She was accepted with a deferred admission date and went to work on Wall Street first. Her only jobs had been as a tennis instructor and a sports reporter for a local newspaper. She wanted to learn more about business in the real world.

Webb got into the investment banking training program at Lehman Brothers (now Barclays) in New York—just as an interim job, but found to her surprise that she really loved corporate finance. After finishing her MBA at Harvard, she joined PaineWebber (now UBS) for another four years as an investment banker.

Webb was recruited to The Walt Disney Company where she rose rapidly through the ranks of Treasury, then was asked to lead Disney's Investor Relations effort—at age 33. She mastered the economic models of all of Disney's many global businesses and was responsible for Disney's global strategic financial communications during an eventful fifteen-year period of Disney's history.

WENDY MARKUS WEBB
Malibu, California

Current Boards:
Jack in the Box Inc.

Career History:
Tennenbaum Capital Partners: Managing Director
    and TCP Capital Corp,
    Chief IRO (current)
Ticketmaster Entertainment: Chief Communications
    & Investor Relations Officer
The Walt Disney Company Foundation: Executive Director;
    SVP, Investor Relations & Shareholder Services
PaineWebber: Investment Banker
Lehman Brothers Holdings Inc.: Investment Banker

Education:
MBA, Harvard Business School
BA, English Literature, Smith College

Her grasp of both communications and financial analysis was recognized by *Investor Relations* magazine that nominated her team for the best Overall Investor Relations for mega cap companies, and by *Institutional Investor*, which awarded Disney's IR program as highest in effectiveness.

By her eighteenth year at Disney, and after introducing the new CEO Robert Iger to Wall Street and key institutional investors, Webb was ready for a new challenge. "My investor relations team had won many awards and was in terrific shape. We had grown the effort to national recognition and best practices. I was ready for a next step in my career." Revamping and modernizing The Walt Disney Company Foundation was that next step. Established in the 1950s, the foundation was in need of modernizing its legal structure, and updating its programs. Webb took over enthusiastically.

Two years later, Jack in the Box was looking for a new director who could serve as a financial expert, and who also was a professional with deep investor communications and shareholder relations experience, as well as someone with familiarity with global consumer brands.

Webb had always been active as an alumna of Smith College, her alma mater. An executive search firm principal had served on the Smith College Board of Trustees with Webb five years earlier. She had seen Webb in action, thought she would make a good corporate board member, and knew she had the right qualifications. So her fellow Smith trustee recommended Webb to a partner at the executive search firm hired by Jack in the Box.

Webb had to make a choice. Disney does not allow its corporate executives to sit on corporate boards. "I was forty-nine years old. I hadn't been a line executive or a corporate CEO, and I knew this was a rare opportunity to be invited to a large corporate board," Webb said. At the same time, she was being courted to join the corporate executive team at Ticketmaster, which was about to undergo an IPO—something she knew how to do, so she decided to leave Disney and work for Ticketmaster. That same year in 2008, she joined the board of Jack in the Box, where she is currently a member of the Audit Committee and chairs the Nominating and Governance Committee.

As chief communications and investor relations officer, Webb guided Ticketmaster through its IPO. Upon its subsequent merger with Live Nation, she then joined Tennenbaum Capital Partners in 2010 as managing director, and has since added the role of chief investor relations officer of that firm's publicly traded business development corporation, TCP Capital Corp.

Her performance at a high-profile public company, combined with her dedication and service to Smith College, helped her win a seat at the board table. But she also attributes her success to a mix of being an engaged contributor with being at the right place at the right time. "With hard work," she says, "I believe we make our own good luck."

EILEEN A. KAMERICK

Eileen Kamerick, currently a board member of Associated Banc-Corp, Westell Technologies and certain Legg Mason closed end funds, advises that women interested in board service take courses in board education and training at graduate business schools. Kamerick took courses at the Center for Executive Women at Northwestern University. "There was intense and sophisticated discussion of the role of boards of directors, and the qualifications and temperament necessary for board membership," she says. "The women who attended were fantastic—dynamic and energetic—from a wide range of professions and industries."

EILEEN A. KAMERICK
Chicago

Current Boards:
Associated Banc-Corp
Westell Technologies, Inc.

Past Boards:
ServiceMaster
Information Resources, Inc.
Stelmar Shipping Ltd.
SymphonyIRI Group, Inc.

Career History:
Press Ganey Associates: CFO (current)
Houlihan Lokey: CFO and Managing Director
Tecta America Corporation: SVP; CFO; Chief Legal Officer
Heidrick & Struggles International, Inc.: EVP; CFO; CAO
Bcom3: EVP and CFO
BP Amoco: CFO Americas; Amoco: VP and Treasurer
Skadden, Arps, Slate, Meagher & Flom: Associate

Education:
MBA, University of Chicago Booth School of Business
JD, University of Chicago Law School
AB, English, Boston College

A unique combination of CFO and general counsel, Kamerick is currently the CFO for Press Ganey Associates, a leading health care analytics and informatics company, majority-owned by Vestar Capital. Previously, she was CFO and managing director of Houlihan Lokey, a global investment bank in Los Angeles, which provides M&A, capital markets, financial restructuring, and advisory services. She has served both as CFO and as general counsel in leadership roles with Amoco America, and Heidrick & Struggles International.

"The increasing workload of board committees is one of the factors that has helped women gain entry to boards," she observes. "At one time, people who were financially knowledgeable, but not considered financial experts, served on audit committees. That is increasingly rare as the SEC now requires audit committee members to have specific financial expertise and experience. Dissecting and analyzing accounting issues has been made more complicated by new legislation and disclosure demands. So this need for financial experts has opened the boardroom door for women CFOs and former accounting firm partners."

"Another trend is the intense focus on Compensation Committees," Kamerick explains. "With the increasing scrutiny of compensation policies by institutional investors, activist shareholders and the Dodd-Frank legislation, there is a growing demand for directors with this specific technical expertise. Nominating committees on boards need to weigh the need for compensation expertise against the need to find directors who can focus at a high level on strategy, succession, and performance management. Certainly it would be ideal to find directors who can do both—and I am confident women exist who can."

An executive search firm recruited Kamerick to her first public board, SymphonyIRI Group, an enterprise software company. Her second board, Stelmar Shipping, came through accounting firm contacts, and personal contacts supported her nomination for two other boards. These companies went private, so Kamerick no longer serves on their boards.

Very active on the nonprofit board of Boys and Girls Clubs in Chicago for many years, Kamerick has made several board contacts through her volunteer nonprofit commitments. She also taught corporate governance at Northwestern University and the University of Iowa.

Kamerick graduated Phi Beta Kappa from Boston College in 1980 and earned both her JD and MBA from the University of Chicago. She completed postgraduate work at Exeter College, Oxford University.

JAN BABIAK

Jan Babiak spent twenty-eight years with Ernst & Young (EY), one of the Big Four assurance, tax, and consulting firms. She was a CPA who became an information technology and global security expert early in the 1980s. By 1990, she had moved to London with EY, where she lived for twenty years, and founded practices focused on technology and security across Northern Europe, Middle East, India, and Africa, and climate change and sustainability globally. Eventually deciding that she wanted more choices in her work, she retired from EY to pursue a board portfolio, and she and her husband relocated to Nashville, where she co-chairs the Tennessee chapter of WomenCorporateDirectors.

JAN BABIAK
Nashville

Current Boards:
Walgreens
Bank of Montreal

Past Boards:
Logica plc

Career History:
Ernst & Young: Managing Partner (retired)

Education:
MBA, Baldwin Wallace University in Ohio
BBA (Bachelor of Business Administration), Accounting, University of
Oklahoma

Babiak serves on the boards of Walgreens, the largest drugstore chain in America, and the Bank of Montreal, one of the fifty largest global banks and twenty-fifth largest in North America. Previously, her first board was Logica plc, in London, a $6 billion consulting and outsourcing company with offices in forty countries, where she served as audit committee chair until the company was sold in 2010. She says all her boards came through search firms with which she was actively engaged over the years, noting that most board searches in Europe are handled by search firms.

Before the Enron scandal and downfall of Arthur Andersen, Babiak secured permission from EY in the UK to serve on corporate boards. She let her search networks know—but she was told directly by those in the board practices in those days that she did not fit the profile—more than one search partner told her that their clients only asked for circa fifty-five-year-old Anglo men. Around that time, changes in the regulatory environment precluded public board service for sitting managing partners of the big accounting firms, so she put on hold her plans to become a director.

Babiak says she has always been a long-range planner, from what she calls her "humble beginnings" in Oklahoma. At age seven, she began her first foray into business—she bought packets of flower seeds for a nickel apiece, and sold each for ten cents. She ordered them from a company advertising on the back of a friend's comic book. She reinvested her profits to buy more packets. Her motivation was to pay for elementary school pictures that her family couldn't afford, as it was too embarrassing to be the only student without photos.

She expanded by offering to plant the seeds for the buyers. "Pretty soon, the trailer park where we lived was blooming with flowers," she recalls. Her business morphed into a gardening service, so she hired three other children as her "employees." Babiak made the sales, ensured her team showed up, and delivered a quality job. Showing her mind for business early on, she took a ten-percent commission.

Her big dream on the long-range plan she wrote at age eight was to go to college as her ticket out of poverty. The eldest of four children, she worked hard to graduate from the University of Oklahoma debt-free, earned her degree in Business Administration, and married her college sweetheart.

After college, she started her career with EY in Oklahoma City. She transferred to EY's then-global headquarters in Cleveland, where she managed the integration of systems technology into the firm's global audit methodology—while she earned her MBA in night school. Her leadership and expertise in IT and environmental issues are just part of her "added value" for corporate board service.

"I'm the Jerry McGuire of sustainability," she laughs. "I can 'show you the money'—how reducing carbon emissions is profitable for business, whatever you believe about the future of the planet." In 2005, she co-wrote a book on board level oversight of IT security *Defending the Digital Frontier: Practical Security for Management*—from a management perspective, how to hire the right people, support policies, build security into infrastructure, etc.

Still planning ahead, throughout her career at EY, Babiak knew she wanted to eventually serve on boards. She had hired hundreds of executives over the years, so she developed many friends at search firms. With each firm she hired to do an executive search for EY, she asked to be introduced to the firm's leader of the board practice.

Once she decided to leave EY, she let all her search firm contacts know she wanted to serve on corporate boards.

Retirement for the Big Four accounting firms is usually mandated at age sixty, but there are no pension plans in Britain in the big firms, so partners have no financial ties holding them to the company. She had a grandmother who lived to one hundred and an aunt who lived to ninety-eight, so she was concerned about saving for her potentially long life.

She decided to retire from EY early, at age fifty-one, and get started on her next career, sooner rather than later. Once she announced her retirement, she was courted by the board of Logica—and she joined its board officially on January 1, 2010, the day after she retired.

In mid-2011, she was called to join the board of Walgreens after a search firm partner in London told a US colleague about her. Walgreens was looking for candidates who understood IT, had lived and managed business abroad, had security and audit experience, and knew both US Generally Accepted Accounting Principals and European IFRS—International Financial Reporting Standards—ideally someone currently living in the U.S.—a unique combination. The search process took until early 2012. Also in 2012, she was recruited to the board of Bank of Montreal, again through a search firm.

Babiak advises women to be strategic about board service. She says that many very talented and qualified women (and men) are so eager to be on a board that they say yes to the first opportunity—or accept too many at once. "This can be a problem, because you can only serve on a limited number of boards at the same time—if you want to do a good job," she adds. "If you take on a board that might not be the best fit for you, then when the really great board you really want comes along, you won't be able to accept."

Also she urges women to design their resumes to emphasize the experience that brings value to corporate boards. As an example, she says a friend simply described herself as a Big-Four audit partner in a region. But Babiak advised the friend to say she had been instrumental in six of the largest mergers in corporate history—even if professional ethics did not allow her to mention the client company's names. Certainly a board is going to be much more interested in achievements than in knowing you were just an "audit partner."

Babiak has been tireless in her dedication to bringing other women onto corporate boards. She has given her avocation a name—Project Starfish. It's her own effort to get other women onto corporate boards. She maintains a database of 150 board-qualified women and, as she puts it, "a few good men." As needed, she helps improve resumes and highlight their "added-value" elements.

When search firms call her with board opportunities that she is unable to consider herself, Jan offers to help the firm find another qualified candidate, especially women. In 2012 alone, *seven women joined corporate boards*, thanks to Jan's personal proactive efforts!

Jan Babiak is living proof that building strategic networks is essential to getting on your first board *and* subsequent boards.

LAURIE A. SIEGEL

Laurie Siegel, retired SVP of HR and Internal Communications at Tyco International, has had a career unlike other financial professionals in this chapter. Following her MBA from Harvard, she focused on compensation when she joined Strategic Compensation Associates (SCA). As a principal, she led presentations to boards of directors at her client companies about compensation issues. All her work at SCA was at the board level, because, even then, boards were under scrutiny for compensation practices.

Siegel continued that focus when hired by Avon Products as director of global compensation until she was recruited by Honeywell International in 1994. Her role there expanded beyond compensation into broader management of all human resources.

Her accomplishments in HR management attracted the attention of Tyco, which recruited her in 2003. "It was a challenging time when the company had to be reorganized from the ground up, while under significant public scrutiny," she says about being the chief HR officer there.

At Tyco, she was instrumental in putting together a new board with new governance standards—"which resulted in Tyco's board and procedures being viewed a best practice," she said. She developed new strategies for leadership development, staffing, compensation, benefits, and internal communications, reflecting the company's new direction under CEO Ed Breen.

LAURIE A. SIEGEL
Morristown, New Jersey

Current Boards:
CenturyLink, Inc.

Past Boards:
Embarq Corporation
Hayes Lemmerz International, Inc.

Career History:
Tyco International Ltd.: SVP of Human Resources (retired)
Honeywell International: VP, Human Resources
Avon Products, Inc,: Director of Global Compensation
Strategic Compensation Associates: Principal

Education:
MBA, Harvard University
MA, City Planning, Harvard University
BA, Liberal Arts, University of Michigan

Prior to her retirement in 2012, she reported directly to the CEO as the chief human resources officer (CHRO). She says that increasingly, HR executives have been elevated to the C-suite in most Fortune 500 companies, reflecting the organizational complexities of globalization, workforce management, compensation, and succession strategies.

"Boards are not typically very comfortable with succession planning, despite the fact that it is one of the most important things boards do. Succession planning needs to be an on-going activity, not just a once-a-year agenda item," Siegel says.

"The HR voice on the board probes the issue of capability to execute, driving a line of questions that pushes beyond assumptions." She also believes that HR leaders can help the board assess its own performance—an aspect of board duty that directors are required to do—and help to counsel, coach and assess the CEO. An HR leader on the board can also help define expectations for the executive team and contribute to thinking about performance measurement and management.

Her first public board was Hayes Lemmerz, a company in the automotive industry—she had been recommended by her former CFO at Honeywell. They specifically wanted a woman, and Siegel had some experience with the automotive divisions of Honeywell. She left that board after a few years, because her duties at Tyco were so demanding, she felt she could no longer give it sufficient time.

Advantageous for HR executives are their working relationships established with the search firms they hire to find executives and board members for the companies where they work. As the lead executive in charge of hiring for very large companies over the years, Siegel developed strong professional relationships with search firms.

Her next board recommendation came through a search firm, for the board of Embarq, a new company with a new CEO, who wanted HR experience on his board. The recruiter had previously worked with Siegel in forming the new Tyco board and knew she met the criteria for Embarq. Not long after she joined the board, the CEO was hired away by Sprint, and Siegel chaired the board search committee to find his replacement. Already her HR expertise was put to good use.

"When I have been approached to join boards, it's been because a CEO or other board member saw added value in what an HR leader could bring. In general, boards are already populated with directors who know business strategy, financial matters, and risk management. But they may not have expertise in succession planning, leadership assessment nor executive compensation," she explains.

When she was recruited to the board of CenturyLink in 2009, where she chairs the Compensation Committee, Siegel says her expertise was immediately helpful in dealing with three large acquisitions over two years which more than doubled the size of the company. "This exponential growth has caused a huge cultural change from a telecommunications company to a diversified communications company," she explains. "CenturyLink is now a global and more complex company. The board has had to help the culture evolve in order to deliver on the strategic promise of the acquisition."

Siegel believes board training is imperative in a rapidly changing environment.

To keep updated on issues faced by the chairs of compensation committees, she is a member of the Compensation Committee Leadership network run by Tapestry, which facilitates board training and networking among directors of companies. And she belongs to the HR Policy Association's Center on Executive Compensation in Washington, D.C.

"Women are well-represented among HR professionals," she says. "So as more corporations see the added value of having HR expertise among their directors, an HR career is more likely than ever before to be a good pathway for women to get on boards."

LISBETH R. MCNABB

Lisbeth McNabb is one of the new breed called "digital director" because of her years in digital technology, but she's also a CFO with a successful track record in digital and high-growth divisions of traditional brands. She serves on the boards of two NASDAQ companies, Nexstar Broadcasting and Tandy Brands, Inc., an accessories apparel company.

Match.com was her proving ground, where she was CFO and chief revenue officer, working for Barry Diller's digital media conglomerate IAC/InterActiveCorp. An entrepreneur at heart, McNabb currently consults with large and high-growth companies about transforming their digital strategies, including clients ClubCorp, Sittercity.com, American Airlines, and LegacyBuilder. She was previously CEO and founder of w2wlink.com, a professional women's content and online community business.

Based in Dallas, McNabb co-chairs the WomenCorporateDirectors (WCD) chapter. She is a member of TeXchange, a technology entrepreneur community in Texas where startup founders, business executives, and investors meet; and the Entrepreneurs Foundation of Texas.

McNabb was recommended for her first board (Nexstar, a television holding company) by a male colleague at PricewaterhouseCoopers, who ran alumni and boardroom group networks—he has been a mentor to her since she worked at Frito-Lay. His client had called PwC in hopes of finding qualified candidates who could serve on the audit committee, and he introduced two women candidates. At the time, she was CFO at Match.com.

LISBETH R. MCNABB
Dallas

Current Boards/Select Nonprofits:
Nexstar Broadcasting
Tandy Brands, Inc.

Career History:
w2wlink: Founder/CEO
Match.com: CFO and Chief Revenue Officer
Sodexo, Inc.: Senior Vice President of Finance and Planning
PepsiCo Frito-Lay: Innovation and Business Planning Director,
    and Co-General Manager Business Unit
American Airlines: Marketing and Planning Manager
JPMorgan Chase: Banking Officer

Education:
MBA, Southern Methodist University, Cox School of Business
BS, Business Administration Marketing, University of Nebraska

She was invited to join the Tandy board because another male peer advocated for her who knew the CEO of Tandy. "Men generally have more access to board opportunities—because they hear about them in their networks and work," she says. She also relies upon her networks of women contacts.

"I don't think women on boards take less risk, but we take risk differently—with great thought and strategy, weighing the tradeoffs. A woman CFO learns to be collaborative as a problem-solver. Fact is, any CFO has to get the CEO of her own company to agree that she could take a board seat. For many women CFOs, getting their CEO's approval is the first challenge."

"I had to pitch hard to convince my boss to let me serve—that it would be good visibility for Match.com—because I would be on the board of a company listed on NASDAQ," she acknowledges. "It worked—he said okay."

McNabb received her bachelor's degree at University of Nebraska and her MBA from Southern Methodist University Cox School of Business. She was honored in 2011 as Distinguished Alumnae by SMU Cox School of Business and as one of the "Top 25 Women in Business," in Condé Nast's Dallas Business Journal.

She started out in sales and marketing, and then added finance and strategy—to qualify as CFO. She earned her MBA, then worked at a bank for two years—blending strategy and marketing.

Her advice is to build networks of both men and women, but make sure to find those who will act as a sponsor along the way. The man who introduced her to Nexstar was indeed someone she had known for years over her career, and he made sure she was considered for board opportunities.

GO IMMEDIATELY

TO

Chapter 6
Pathways through
Investment Banking,
Private Banking, and
Private Equity

PATHWAYS
6 Through Investment
Private Banking,

Banking, and Private Equity

INVESTMENT BANKING AS AN INDUSTRY HAS UNDERGONE RADICAL CHANGE OVER THE PAST TWENTY-FIVE YEARS AND IS now a productive pathway for women who want to become corporate directors. Women who have traveled in this career direction—whether their degrees are in business, finance, law, engineering, even Russian literature—have had significant success. Along with CFOs, they have often been the first women finance experts chosen for corporate boards.

The upside to this high-risk profession of investment banking can be lucrative and exciting; the downside can be devastating. Women are generally thought to be more risk-averse than men, so investment banking as a career pathway attracts women who are self-assured and extremely well prepared—important attributes for corporate directors as well.

There are many "firsts" in this chapter—women who have started in management consulting and advanced into banking and investment-advisory positions, constantly reinforcing and building their credentials for board service.

ALISON A. WINTER

Alison Winter is one of two co-founders of WomenCorporateDirectors (WCD). Her pathway to board service was not planned, yet critical decisions she made along the way led ultimately to her seat on the Nordstrom board—a dream directorship that combines many a career woman's favorite passions—shoes, clothing, and business.

ALISON A. WINTER
  Pasadena, California

Current Boards/Select Nonprofits:
  Nordstrom, Inc.
  WomenCorporateDirectors Ltd.
  University of Chicago Booth Graduate School
    of Business

Past Boards:
  Los Angeles Area Chamber of Commerce: Chair
  YMCA of Metropolitan Los Angeles
  YMCA of Greater New York

Career History:
  Braintree Holdings, LLC: CEO (current)
  Northern Trust Corporation: President, Personal Financial Services,
    Northeast Region; President, PFS Midwest; Co-President, PFS;
    CEO, Northern Trust of California; SVP and Head of Marketing and
    Sales for Personal Financial Services

Education:
  MBA, University of Chicago Booth School of Business
  BA, English, San Francisco College for Women

After graduating from a women's college in San Francisco, she joined the Northern Trust Company and began her career as an investment professional. She earned her MBA in Finance from the University of Chicago Booth School of Business, and subsequently the designation of Chartered Financial Analyst.

Her first executive position as president of Northern Trust of California, enabled her to serve on numerous charitable and civic boards. She was the first woman in its 110-year history to be selected as chair of the board of the Los Angeles Chamber of Commerce.

She was invited to interview for a board seat on one of two newly formed foundations created when Blue Cross of California changed from a mutual company to a public company, WellPoint. She was appointed to the California HealthCare Foundation (CHCF), which was funded primarily by WellPoint stock. The board's job was to monetize those shares to fund both of the new foundations, CHCF and the California Endowment. Winter's investment background and leadership skills made her a great match for this complex responsibility.

Winter collaborated with a fellow board member over their nine-year terms at CHCF, and they helped build a strong board, with a sustainable mission. After their terms ended, the same colleague recommended Winter for the Nordstrom board. By that time, she had returned to live in Chicago, and had just been named president of Northern Trust Midwest. Her leadership, financial and marketing strengths made her an attractive candidate, and Nordstrom was appealing to her because of its strong culture and focus on the customer. Winter was known to two other Nordstrom board members, who each supported her nomination.

Winter is an independent director on the Nordstrom board, sitting on the audit, governance, and nominating committees. She served as chair of the finance committee early on, and subsequently as chair of the compensation committee.

Her advice to women is to cultivate areas of expertise, such as finance or marketing, because "Boards tend not to look for generalists, unless they are sitting CEOs. They are usually looking for a specific skill set to fill a gap. More and more, boards are evaluating you as a candidate, based on the knowledge and expertise you bring that aligns with their strategy."

Winter is a fan of serving on nonprofits boards, having served on some twenty before she went on her first public board. "You gain a lot of governance experience and insight into how boards work, particularly by consensus," she explains. "Since financial literacy is a must for board service, you also learn a lot about finance on a nonprofit board. And, you meet influential people." In addition to her demanding career, board duties and nonprofit commitments, Winter has served two terms as chair of the Committee of 200, a preeminent organization of women executives.

Winter was the first woman elected to the Nordstrom board, but now there are two more. "I can truly say that our board is gender-neutral, and there is an open, respectful dynamic in all our discussions."

SUZANNE NORA JOHNSON

Suzanne Johnson sits on the public company boards of Intuit, Pfizer, Visa and American International Group (AIG). Now retired from her long career at Goldman Sachs, Johnson was among the first women to achieve a senior leadership position at GS. A graduate of Harvard Law School, she ultimately chose a career in investment banking, after practicing briefly with a New York law firm.

SUZANNE NORA JOHNSON
Los Angeles

Current Boards/Select Nonprofits:
Intuit Inc.
Pfizer Inc.
Visa Inc.
American International Group, Inc.
The Brookings Institution
Carnegie Institution for Science: Board of Trustees
University of Southern California: Board of Trustees

Career History:
Goldman Sachs: Vice Chairman (retired); Head, Global Investment
    Research Division; Head of Global Healthcare Business in the
    Investment Banking Division; Founder of Latin American business;
    Partner
Simpson Thacher & Bartlett: Associate
U.S. Court of Appeals: Law Clerk

Education:
JD, Harvard Law School
BA, Interdisciplinary Studies: Economics/Philosophy-Religion/Political
    Science, University of Southern California

As vice chair of Goldman Sachs and Chair of the Goldman Sachs Global Markets Institute, she engaged with a wide variety of stakeholders. She has spoken at the World Economic Forum in Davos, Switzerland, and other international gatherings of government officials and CEOs. She also served on the nonprofit boards of The Brookings Institution, The Carnegie Institution for Science, American Red Cross, RAND Health, and the Markle Foundation.

"I definitely did not view corporate board service as my ultimate goal, but given my financial expertise and global operating experience, I found there was a fair demand for business people with my background," she explains. "Fortune 500 boards are clearly looking for women who have had senior operating roles. Generally the highest value candidate is someone who has a broad base of operating experience and leadership success, so they can provide strong fiduciary oversight for shareholders and strategic guidance to management."

When she retired from Goldman Sachs, she received many calls about corporate boards from people she knew and from recruiting firms. "However, most of my board situations came from personal relationships who knew about my experience and reputation." Johnson advises women to develop strong working relationships with a wide variety of business and civic leaders so they feel confident passing along your name to search firms or nominating committees.

"I find many of the same names get recycled by the search community, so for many women it's very hard to get noticed for their first board. However, in the last several years, a number of search firms have worked hard to bring visibility to the wealth of qualified board candidates who are women."

GABRIELLE E. GREENE

A board member of Whole Foods, Gabrielle Greene earned two graduate degrees from Harvard, the first from Harvard Law School, and the second from Harvard Business School while she worked at Bain, the strategic management and consulting firm in Boston. Then she worked her way west at several investment banking firms.

"I chose a career in finance not as a strategy to get on boards, but because I had figured out that my strengths were more quantitative. I felt finance made me a more well-rounded professional. In retrospect, it was a wise choice."

Her first experience with boards, other than extensive nonprofit work, was with private boards of companies in which her company had invested. She was also invited by venture capitalists to serve on boards of pre-IPO companies they were funding. After each company went public, she would step down from its board. "When private companies are going public, one of the things on the checklist is to have at least one outside director. That's when I have been invited, at the pre-IPO stage. Those recommendations came about because I informed attorneys and investors that I was interested in board service." While she has served as an officer on the boards of several nonprofits—the Links, Boston Partnership and Boston Children's Museum—Greene believes her private board experience was more relevant to her current position on the Whole Foods board.

GABRIELLE E. GREENE
Pasadena, California

Current Boards:
Whole Foods
Stage Stores, Inc.
Johnson Products Company
SAFE Securities

Past Boards:
Bright Horizons Family Solutions
IndyMac Bancorp Inc.

Career History:
Rustic Canyon/Fontis Partners, LP: Principal (current)
Gluecode Software, Inc.: CFO
Villanueva Companies: CFO
Crown Services: CFO
BE/Greenwich Street Capital: Partner
HPB Associates: Principal
Commonwealth Enterprise Fund, Inc.: Principal
UNC Partners: Principal
Bain & Company: Associate Consultant

Education:
JD, Harvard Law School
MBA, Harvard Business School
BA, Urban Studies, Princeton

The chair of the nominating committee at Whole Foods, whose husband had been Greene's boss, recruited her to the board. The Whole Foods board wanted to find a director who was a financial expert, so her CFO experience was a key attraction. Greene says that the senior management of Whole Foods develops and promotes women. Two of the regional vice presidents are women, including the CFO, who has been there many years.

"I am also a fan of good food, and passionate about Whole Foods, so I have enjoyed my service on its board," she adds. "I really enjoy retail, and had always shopped Whole Foods!"

A woman who had previously served on the Whole Foods board became Greene's valuable mentor. "She watched out for me, gave me advice, gave me background about the board dynamics," she says. "I have tried to be that resource for other women as they joined the board."

When asked about how to find available board seats, Greene offers that there are many conferences in the venture capital and private equity worlds where companies in attendance would like to add gender diversity to their boards. Attending such conferences might be a good way to find a first board.

Greene foresees a growing demand for women board candidates with expertise in IT and in marketing. "Digital marketing is especially challenging, in the face of countless ways to reach the customer. In some enlightened consumer-oriented companies today, the marketing function is included in the C-suite." She sees a trend toward having more chief marketing officers or digital marketing experts on boards, both of which may become new pathways for women to the directors' table.

"There are much better business outcomes when you have a diversity of outlooks around the boardroom table," she says. "We have better conversations, and we get better results."

MARIA ELENA LAGOMASINO

Mel Lagomasino came to the U.S. from her native Cuba when she was eleven. She eventually attended Manhattanville College and earned her MBA at Fordham University and her MS at Columbia. She joined Chase Manhattan, where she became vice president for the bank's Latin American operations and ultimately the head of worldwide private banking.

When Chase merged with J.P. Morgan, Lagomasino was named CEO and chair of J.P. Morgan Private Bank. She later became CEO of GenSpring Family Offices, a $20 billion asset-management firm serving multi-generations of seven hundred families, and stepped down in 2012.

MARIA ELENA LAGOMASINO
New York City

Current Boards:
The Coca-Cola Company
Avon Products, Inc.

Past Boards:
Global Crossing Ltd.
Phillips Van Heusen Corp.

Career History:
GenSpring Family Offices: CEO (retired)
JP Morgan Private Bank: Chairman and CEO
Chase Manhattan: Head of Worldwide Private
    Banking Business
Chase Manhattan Private Bank: VP and Team
    Leader for Latin America

Education:
MBA, Fordham University
MS, Library Science, Columbia University
BA, French, Manhattanville College

Lagomasino served on the U.S. Secretary of State's Advisory Committee on Transformational Diplomacy and was appointed by President George W. Bush to find funding for disaster victims in Central America. President Bush also appointed her to the twenty-seven-member commission on White House Fellowships, which recommends exceptional men and women for selection as Fellows. She is a trustee of the Board of the National Geographic Society, and member of the Council on Foreign Relations and The Economic Club of New York.

Lagomasino was recruited for her first board—Phillips Van Heusen Corp. (PVH), well-known makers of shirts and apparel—by a banker who worked with nonprofit organizations. He knew Lagomasino from her nonprofit board service for Helen Keller International. Her nonprofit board connection was her link to serving on corporate boards, even though her global banking and investment credentials brought significant added value. She says her twelve-year service on the PVH board really taught her how to be a board member.

In 2000, Catalyst approached Lagomasino for the Avon Products board where there were other women directors. A year later, a friend recruited her to the Global Crossing board—a start-up technology company that placed fiber-optic cable across the floor of the Pacific Ocean to connect Asia to America. Her employer J.P. Morgan was also the banker for Global Crossing, so she stepped down from the Global Crossing board to avoid conflicts of interest.

An executive search firm recommended her to the board of Coca-Cola where she joined two other women at the time. Lagomasino, Alexis Herman, former U.S. Secretary of Labor, and Dr. Helene D. Gayle, CEO of CARE, now serve.

Lagomasino says that a finance background is the major qualifier for board candidates, whether men or women. She also thinks corporate boards need technology or media experience and those pathways should open up more opportunities for women.

She cautions, "Don't stay in a narrow field. Most large companies are looking for global experience today.

"In order to learn and grow toward serving on corporate boards, it's best to start small—at a nonprofit, or for-profit, where you feel strongly about its mission—so you will always make a difference and feel good about it.

"You'll never get recruited for a big company board unless you have previous board experience. Even early in your career, get started on a small company board or a private board. And grow from there."

SARA GROOTWASSINK LEWIS

Sara Lewis, the founder and CEO of Lewis Corporate Advisors, has more than twenty years of executive management, public company corporate governance, real estate and capital markets experience, including her work as a Wall Street research equity analyst covering publicly traded real estate companies. The equity analyst position led to her position as vice president of finance of Corporate Office Properties Trust, and then to become executive vice president and chief financial officer of Washington Real Estate Investment Trust (Washington REIT), both on the New York Stock Exchange.

Lewis spent many years reporting to a board in her career as chief financial officer, which gave her insights into the responsibilities of a director, allowing her to quickly become effective in that role.

SARA GROOTWASSINK LEWIS
Rancho Santa Fe, California

Current Boards:
CapitalSource
PS Business Parks, Inc.

Past Boards/Select Nonprofits:
San Diego Opera
Scripps Research Institute Advisory Council
Washington Hospital Center Strategic Planning Committee

Career History:
Lewis Corporate Advisors, LLC: CEO and Founder (current)
Washington Real Estate Investment Trust: EVP and CFO
Corporate Office Properties Trust, Inc.: VP, Finance and Investor
    Relations
Johnston, Lemon & Co. Inc.: Sell-Side REIT Equity Analyst
Riggs Bank (now PNC Bank): VP Commercial Real Estate
    Lending
Grand-Premier National Bank (now Fifth Third Bancorp):
    AVP Corporate Lending
U.S. Department of the Treasury, Office of the Comptroller of the
    Currency: Associate National Bank Examiner
First Midwest Bank: Commercial Real Estate Lending Officer

Education:
BS, Finance, University of Illinois, Urbana-Champaign
Chartered Financial Analyst
Certified Public Accountant, registered in the state of Illinois
National Association of Corporate Directors Board
    Leadership Fellow

Lewis was recommended to the board of CapitalSource, a commercial finance company with $8.6 billion in assets, by the external audit partner at Washington REIT. Her CEO at the time believed strongly that serving on outside boards was a great opportunity to broaden one's knowledge and to become a better executive. So he was supportive of her joining the CapitalSource board in 2004—her first. In effect, he was her sponsor. Lewis chairs the nominating and corporate governance committee, and serves on the audit and compensation committees.

Lewis is also a member of the board of PS Business Parks, where she is presiding director, chairman of the audit committee and also serves on the nominating and corporate governance committee. The company is a publicly traded real estate company that owns 27.2 million square feet of commercial office and industrial space, comprising 102 business parks throughout the country, where Public Storage facilities are located.

She observes that women seeking board positions are most likely to find their first boards in their own industries. Her advice to women is to be visible in your industry and do your job exceptionally well.

Lewis's best advice to aspiring board members is to sign up as an individual member of the National Association of Corporate Directors (NACD), where members may take advantage of its breadth of resources to build knowledge. Get daily emails from NACD and read these periodicals: *Corporate Board Member, Directorship* and *Agenda*, "which have a great deal of information that is helpful in understanding the role of board members."

SUSAN C. SCHNABEL

Susan Schnabel, a director of Neiman Marcus and Visant Holding Corporation, is managing director at Credit Suisse in the asset management division and co-head of DJL Merchant Banking Partners in Los Angeles. She came to investment banking through engineering—a career that ran in her family.

Schnabel grew up in the home of an independently minded mother, a role model *sine qua non*. Her mother was the first woman in East Germany to earn an advanced degree in mechanical engineering after World War II. She pursued her career fulltime when she came to the U.S., got married and had two daughters. Following in her mother's trail-blazing footsteps, Schnabel earned her degree in chemical engineering at Cornell and her MBA from Harvard.

Her own independent thinking showed up early in her career when Schnabel was exposed to corporate boards as a summer intern at First Boston, a leading investment bank. She was hired after being asked about her quantitative skills, and she gave a surprising answer to the question. "About the only quantitative skills necessary for that position were addition, subtraction, multiplication and division," she remembers. "So I offered to solve a thermodynamics equation instead, and my future bosses no longer questioned my quantitative skills." Because no one else on the team had chemical engineering experience, she was asked to present to the board of a client seeking to buy a chemicals company—an unusual opportunity for a summer intern.

SUSAN C. SCHNABEL
Los Angeles

Current Boards:
The Neiman Marcus Group
Specialized Technology Resources, Inc.
Visant Holding Corp. (formerly Jostens, Inc.)

Past Boards:
Rockwood Holdings, Inc.
Total Safety U.S., Inc.
Shoppers Drug Mart
Dick's Clothing & Sporting Goods, Inc.

Career History:
Credit Suisse Group: Managing Director, Asset
     Management Business and Co-Head of DLJ
     Merchant Banking Partners (current)
DLJ Merchant Banking Partners
PetSmart, Inc.: CFO
Donaldson, Lufkin & Jenrette: Managing Director
Drexel Burnham Lambert: Associate

Education:
MBA, Harvard Business School
BS, Chemical Engineering, Cornell University

Schnabel said her confidence was honed at Air Products & Chemicals, a large multinational Fortune 500 chemical company where she was one of the few women in an applied research and development department. "I easily stood out. I was the one wearing bright colors!"

After graduation from Harvard Business School, Schnabel knew she was not interested in a career in applied research and development. She pursued investment banking at Drexel Burnham Lambert in Beverly Hills, and then went to Donaldson, Lufkin & Jenrette (DLJ), another investment bank, when Drexel imploded.

While at Drexel and DLJ, she held positions in investment banking, specializing in public and private high yield debt and equity financing, and mergers and acquisitions advisory for the retail, telecommunications, technology and consumer products industries. After being promoted to managing director, one of the few women managing directors at DLJ, she decided to leave (much to the surprise of her peers) to take a corporate job as CFO of PetSmart.

In 1996, Schnabel returned to DLJ in the Los Angeles office as a senior member of DLJ Merchant Banking Partners, a middle-market private equity fund focused on investing growth capital and management buyouts in a variety of industries.

Schnabel attributes her success in investment banking and private equity, which are fields still mostly dominated by men, to her ability to "hold her own" among large groups of male colleagues. "Being 'noticed' has been an advantage to me in my career and on boards," she said.

She has been a director—many times the lead director—on more than twenty-five boards. Most were private, which she prefers "because decisions are made in a more timely manner. As shareholders themselves, everyone's interests are aligned—the investors only do very well if, and when, the company does well."

Before Schnabel is appointed to the board of a private company, she knows all the shareholders well. By virtue of doing the due diligence required before investing DLJ Merchant Banking Partners capital, she knows how the company operates, and then works in concert with other principals to select the board. She then serves on the private board to protect DLJ Merchant Banking Partners' investment and to help grow the new entity, often taking it public later.

In addition to Neiman Marcus and Visant Holding Corp. (including Jostens Scholastic), Schnabel is the lead director on the board of the NYSE public company STR Holdings Inc. Her private boards include Deffenbaugh Industries, Enduring Resources, Laramie Energy, Luxury Optical Holdings, and Summit Gas Resources.

ALISON DAVIS

Alison Davis has been a senior executive in the financial services business for many years, so it was a perfect fit when she was asked to join the Royal Bank of Scotland board where she is one of three women directors. With her BA and MA in economics from Cambridge, and her MBA from Stanford, she spent her early career at McKinsey & Co. as a management consultant, working with Citibank, American Express and other Fortune 500 companies.

Her first board was a technology start-up where she was recruited by a colleague at A.T. Kearney who became CEO. The company went from $0 to $285 million in six months and went public. It fell almost as precipitously. "You learn a lot on the board of a company like that," Davis recalls.

Several years later, when she was CFO of Barclays Global Investors with operations in the U.S., Europe, and around the globe, Catalyst recruited Davis for the board of First Data Corp., which also owned Western Union. They were particularly interested in her as a candidate because of her experience in strategy and payments. She made many important contacts on this board, among them Jim Robinson, former CEO of Amex. She helped recruit the former CEO of Bank of America, David Coulter, to the First Data board. "I really enjoyed the interaction with such smart people," Davis says of her board experiences.

She left Barclays to become managing partner of Belvedere Capital Partners— a private equity firm with a focus on buyouts. But in 2011 she decided to devote the rest of her career to board service, including public and nonprofit, the latter to give back to the community. She chairs the nonprofit board of Women's Initiative for Self-Employment (WI), which helps low-income women in the U.S. start their own businesses.

Unisys was one of the public boards Davis joined after leaving the financial services industry. She was recruited by a search firm, but also knew a board member. "If you do a good job on one corporate board, then you have great references for other board positions," she notes. "But to recommend you, people have to *like* you as well as respect your performance. For example, they want to see that you have a sense of humor and can remain steady in a crisis."

Davis doesn't believe it's necessary to have a finance background to be recruited for a board. "CEOs already have CFOs in their companies. They need board members with other experience who can strategize, bring perspectives from other industries, and be good advisors and mentors."

ALISON DAVIS
Tiburon, California

Current Boards:
Royal Bank of Scotland
Unisys Corporation
Diamond Foods
Xoom Corporation
GameFly, Inc.
SilkRoad Technology

Past Boards:
First Data Corporation
City National Bank
LECG Corporation
Dispatch Management Services Corporation
Presidio Bank
LesConcierges, Inc.
Broadlane Group
Professional Business Bank
Benefit Street
InterAct 911

Career History:
Fifth Era Financial: CEO (current)
Belvedere Capital: Managing Partner
Barclays Global Investors (now BlackRock), CFO
A.T. Kearney: Senior Partner and Financial Institutions Group Leader
McKinsey & Company: Strategy Consultant

Education:
MBA, Stanford University
MA, Economics, Cambridge University
BA, Economics, Cambridge University

When the topic turns to government-enforced quotas established in Europe to ensure that more women serve on corporate boards, Davis says, "I think quotas can be helpful, actually. Of course it would be better if it were voluntary—

for example in the UK some chairmen are competing to see who can get the best women on their boards! Once women get on boards, the men see what a great contribution women make and it becomes the new normal."

She, along with other directors in this book, says that boards today would benefit from having younger members who can bring fresh perspectives, especially when it comes to technology and social media. Quite a few boards she knows are looking for "Digital Directors." As noted before, this should open more board opportunities for women who qualify as digital directors.

"The key is to step into your power in your current role and enjoy it. Be as influential in your company and your industry as you can be. Women can be our own biggest enemies. We often find competition stressful and hesitate to use the word 'power'. Women often think that a promotion means more work, but really the more senior you are, the more you can hire people to help you." The mother of five children says, "With a high performing team on your side, it should be possible to have a life, too, and to sometimes get away at 3 pm to see your kids play soccer."

CONNIE K. DUCKWORTH

Connie K. Duckworth, retired partner and managing director at Goldman Sachs in Chicago, was the first woman sales and trading partner in the history of the company. To avoid conflicts of interest, executives of investment companies cannot serve on corporate boards until they retire. "Goldman always expected its partners to be involved with civic boards," she adds. So Duckworth developed her early board experience through large nonprofits—her in-depth financial expertise was a huge plus, and she made valuable connections along her pathway to future public boards.

In 1997, she was invited to join the board of NorthShore University HealthSystem, by its chair, Jerry K. Pearlman, retired CEO of Zenith Electronics. "They were looking specifically for a woman," she explains." I preferred to join a hospital nonprofit rather than an arts nonprofit because business is my lens." Duckworth eventually followed Pearlman as chair of NorthShore in 2006. "I didn't fully realize until I joined a public company board, how very much the NorthShore board operated like one. I also had the opportunity to serve with a group of CEOs who were among the leading business executives in Chicago."

CONNIE K. DUCKWORTH
Lake Forest, Illinois

Current Boards:
Steelcase, Inc.
Northwestern Mutual Life Insurance Company
Russell Investment Group

Past Boards:
DNP Select Income Fund
Nuveen Investments
Smurfit-Stone Container Corporation

Career History:
ARZU, Inc.: Founder and CEO (current)
Goldman Sachs: Partner and Managing Director

Education:
MBA, Wharton School, University of Pennsylvania
BA, Liberal Arts, Interdisciplinary Honors Program—Liberal Arts,
University of Texas

After retiring from her twenty-year career at Goldman Sachs, her first public company board was a closed-end mutual fund, the DNP Select Income Fund Inc., a several-billion dollar mutual fund, that was highly regulated. She had been referred by a friend in the Committee of 200, an organization of executive women.

Duckworth recalls that board as "very collegial," something she now looks for in any corporate board that may be recruiting her. "You want to work with people you like, learn something new, and have a good experience."

She planned a strategy to find three public corporate boards—hoping to add one each year, but consciously limited her choices to local companies or those that were in easy travel distance. She wanted time to devote to her own nonprofit called ARZU, meaning "Hope" in the Dari language, that models social entrepreneurship for women in Afghanistan. She serves pro bono as chair and CEO.

Her second corporate board was the Northwestern Mutual Life Insurance Company, which had been one of her clients at Goldman Sachs. She was invited to join the board because she knew the executives and the company well. "The board was quite diverse. I was the fourth woman, and three of the directors are African-American."

Jerry Pearlman recommended her for a third board—Smurfit-Stone Container Corp. Duckworth says her NorthShore relationship with Pearlman perfectly exemplifies the value of doing a good job on a nonprofit board where prominent business people can "see you in action." Smurfit was a major manufacturing company, which Duckworth says "was an opportunity to move out of financial services." But it ultimately went into Chapter 11, which she describes as "a challenging learning experience."

Next, Duckworth was asked to become an independent director of the Frank Russell Company, largely owned by Northwestern Mutual. She chairs the compensation committee. Her next board move came when a colleague from the board of Northwestern Mutual recommended her to Steelcase Inc., the global leader in the office furniture industry. "It was a good opportunity to learn about bricks and mortar."

Duckworth serves on the Board of Overseers for the Wharton School at the University of Pennsylvania, where she received her MBA. In 2011, Wharton awarded her its highest honor, The Dean's Medal.

LINDA FAYNE LEVINSON

Linda Fayne Levinson, who is currently on five public company boards, has served on more than fifteen other private and public boards. She is also on the U.S. advisory board of CVC Capital Partners, one of the world's leading private equity and investment advisory firms. From senior roles in venture capital, merchant banking, travel services, and technology, Levinson's career has been truly a succession of firsts. She was the first woman board member of several corporations—DemandTec, Genentech, Hertz, and NCR, among others.

Levinson is the consummate generalist. She understands the issues that apply to all businesses, and she does the homework required to gain expertise in specific industries. In 1979, Levinson became the first woman partner at McKinsey & Company, thereby establishing a precedent. She worked for several years as a partner at Global Retail Partners, LP, where she led investments in technology-driven, "consumer-facing" companies such as Overture (now owned by Yahoo!) and lastminute.com. She was senior vice president of Travel Related Services for American Express, where she ran the U.S. travel agencies and tour businesses, a partner at Wings Partners on the team that took Northwest Airlines private, and at CAA where she was involved in restructuring MGM Studios.

LINDA FAYNE LEVINSON
Santa Monica, California; New York City

Current Boards:
Hertz Global Holdings, Inc.
Ingram Micro, Inc.
Jacobs Engineering Group Inc.
NCR Corporation
The Western Union Company

Past Boards:
Bill Me Later, Inc.
CyberSource Corporation
DemandTec, Inc.
Egghead Software, Inc.
Genentech, Inc.
Homestead Technologies Inc.
Insperity, Inc.
lastminute.com plc
Mercata Inc.
Overture Services, Inc.
Wizards of the Coast

Career History:
Vendare Media (now Connexus Corporation): CEO (current)
GRP Partners: Partner
Creative Artists Agency LLC: Senior Executive
Wings Partners, Inc.: Partner
Fayne Levinson Associates: President
American Express Travel Related Services Company, Inc.: SVP
McKinsey & Company: Partner

Education:
MBA, New York University
MA, Russian Literature, Harvard
AB, Russian Studies, Barnard College

Levinson has an extensive network of contacts. A former McKinsey partner gave her name to the search firm retained by Genentech in the early 1990s. Subsequent board invitations came over the years through fellow directors and recruiters. "Being invited to join one's first board is the toughest because other members worry about how you will behave on a board, regardless of your previous success," she notes. "If you do well on that first board, others naturally follow—both by recommendation of your fellow directors and recruiters." Levinson says to fulfill your obligation as a board member, you have to "learn the business, do your homework, and be both courageous and respectful in asking the tough questions."

She is currently a director of Hertz, NCR, Ingram Micro, Jacobs Engineering Group, and Western Union. She is lead independent director at NCR and chairs the compensation committee at both NCR and Ingram Micro.

"If you want to be on a board, learn how to think like a CEO or a board member—not like an operating executive," Levinson advises. "Move from the purely operational to the longer term. Be able to exercise strategic judgment, recognize patterns and have the courage of your convictions."

GO IMMEDIATELY

TO

Chapter 7
Pathways through
Science/Engineering/
Technology/Math

PATHWAYS

7Through Science,

Engineering, Technology, and Math

PERHAPS ENERGIZED BY THE ODDS, THE WOMEN DIRECTORS IN THIS CHAPTER PAVED THEIR PATHWAYS TO CORPORATE boards by way of exceptional careers in what have historically been fields dominated by men: information technology, manufacturing, oil, utilities, telecommunications, pharmaceuticals and bioscience.

Many were the first women from engineering careers ever recruited to their corporate boards, many because they had significant management experience in operations, a preferred qualification for boards. Earning their engineering degrees in such male-dominated fields may have helped them develop the interpersonal skills, determination, and confidence to succeed in careers that led them to corporate boards.

Leadership in fields of science and engineering requires the same judgment and people skills as leadership in any other field. But it seems somehow more laudable and unusual when women make it to the top in fields of science, technology, engineering and math. Perhaps because men have naturally gravitated to these fields out of military background or by wanting to be astronauts or rocket scientists, there's a general assumption that women could not succeed, or would not be allowed, into those fields. Old stereotypes die hard.

Former U.S. Secretary of State Hillary Clinton often tells the story, "When I was about thirteen, I wrote to NASA and asked what I needed to do to try to be an astronaut," she explained. "And of course, there weren't any women astronauts, and NASA wrote back and said there would not be any women astronauts. And I was just crestfallen."

Fortunately, now women have role models in engineering and science. Many are featured in this chapter, and their pathways demonstrate the possibilities. In her 2012 research about how girls and women are depicted in television and movies, Academy Award-winning actor and advocate Geena Davis shows that only sixteen percent of women's roles are in executive or leadership positions. And only three percent have been shown in CEO roles. Davis is helping to change the depiction of women in entertainment. She says that when images of accomplished women appear on television and in movies, the audience embraces them and girls are inspired to believe in themselves.

DEBRA L. REED

Debbie Reed is one of the handful of women CEOs of Fortune 500 corporations in 2012. That year, Sempra Energy was ranked 266 on the Fortune 500, with ten billion dollars in revenues. Reed was promoted to CEO in June 2011 and then to CEO and Chairman in December 2012. She is featured in this chapter, rather than the CEO chapter, because she is a role model for success in engineering. She worked her way up to the pinnacle of the male-dominated utility industry from her first job as an intern at Southern California Gas Company while a civil engineering student at University of Southern California.

When she took those first steps through the door as a college intern, she probably never dreamed that someday she would be the chief executive officer of the whole corporation. Under the Sempra corporate umbrella there are two shareholder-owned utilities—SoCalGas and San Diego Gas & Electric. Reed served as CEO and president of both those utilities on her way to the top job at Sempra.

After college, she was hired as an entry-level energy systems engineer at SoCalGas. She gained a reputation as a productive team-member and creative problem-solver in operations, and moved up the ladder quickly. Over the years, she headed energy distribution services, finance, human resources and administration, learning all aspects of operating the business. Within ten years, she was named the first woman corporate officer at SoCalGas.

DEBRA L. REED
San Diego

Current Boards:
Halliburton
San Diego Regional Economic Development
Corporation

Past Boards:
Genentech, Inc.
Avery Dennison Corporation
Dominguez Services Corporation

Career History:
Sempra Energy: Chairman and CEO (current); Executive Vice President
San Diego Gas & Electric and Southern California Gas Co.: President
and CEO; President and COO; CFO

Education:
BS, Civil Engineering, University of Southern California

"I was viewed as someone who was always looking for opportunities and challenges," Reed explains. "That attitude was rewarded over time." Her CEO was her mentor, and sponsor, making sure she gained valuable experience that led to increased responsibility and promotions over the years. He recommended her for her first corporate board service—a public water company called Dominguez Services Corp.—so she could gain knowledge outside her own company to become an even better leader.

Throughout her career, Reed has been the champion for diversity at the Sempra companies. Under her leadership, Sempra has achieved higher diversity than other utilities in the nation when it comes to hiring, training, development and promotion of women and people of color, and also when it comes to opening contract opportunities for vendor companies that are owned by women and people of color.

"I found I brought back a lot of learning from my board work to my company—how to generate ideas and seeing how other companies handle similar issues. That's been my motivation for joining corporate boards." She joined the board of Halliburton in 2001, because she knew one of the other directors who recommended her.

Her third board was Genentech, but she did not know any directors serving on the board of the San Francisco-based biotech company. "Genentech was searching for a diversity candidate with financial expertise to chair their Audit Committee. I had been the CFO of my company, and I was recruited by their executive search firm." An extensive interview process was required since no one on the board knew her. But she had a deep interest in biotechnology and at one time had wanted to go to medical school. So she was keenly interested in the scientific work that Genentech does—developing medicines to combat the toughest human diseases.

"I'm sure they contacted directors on the Halliburton board as well as people in my company. I interviewed with the general counsel, the CEO and with two other board members. Then I interviewed with the CEO and the president of Roche—majority shareholders in Genentech. A few years later, Roche acquired all of Genentech, so the Genentech board ended."

Reed was next asked to serve on the board of Avery Dennison, the labels manufacturer based in Pasadena, California. But after she was promoted to CEO of Sempra, she realized there was not enough time to meet all of her commitments, so she stepped down.

"What I tell women who ask me how to get on corporate boards, is to get connected—do volunteer work, network in business, join community organizations—where others can see your skills being applied. Be a team player, demonstrate leadership, express your ideas constructively, and be solution-driven. All these attributes help in seeking your opportunity to serve on a board.

"Lastly, to the degree that you can broaden your work experience—either within your company or through your job progression in different companies—that's very helpful," Reed says. "Above all, get financial, operations and marketing experience to complete your portfolio of experience."

MARGARET S. DANO

Margaret Dano attended a Catholic high school for girls. Math and science came easily to her, so she wanted a career that would build on this as well as provide a great future. She was able to attend college at General Motors Institute where she earned her degree in mechanical engineering. Dano says "I didn't always want to be an engineer. I thought there would be nothing worse than sitting at a drafting table all day, but I found out that engineering is great training to learn how to think in a different way."

MARGARET S. DANO
Los Angeles

Current Boards:
Douglas Dynamics, Inc.
Superior Industries International, Inc.
Industrial Container Services, Inc.

Past Boards:
Anthony International
Fleetwood Enterprises, Inc.
Storm Industries, Inc.

Career History:
Honeywell: VP, Worldwide Operations, Garrett Engine
Boosting Systems (retired)
Avery Dennison Corporation: VP, Worldwide Operations
Black & Decker Corporation: VP, North American Operations
General Electric Company: Product Manager
General Electric Appliances: Plant Manager
White-Westinghouse: Plant Manager
Schick Razor: Process Engineer
General Motors: Manufacturing Engineer

Education:
BS, Mechanical Engineering, General Motors Institute of
Technology and Management

Engineering provides the ability to develop a process approach to problem-solving. That, in turn, led Dano to line jobs—the kind of operations experience boards are looking for—at Avery Dennison, GE and Honeywell, where she was vice president of worldwide operations for their $3 billion Turbo Technology unit with sixteen sites and 6,500 employees.

Her first board appointment came a few years after letting her friends at Catalyst know she would like to serve on boards. Dano was especially a "value-added" candidate because of her twenty-five years of operations experience in major public companies, GE and Honeywell, and because she had previously served on boards of private companies—from start ups, to small and large.

Dano recommends private boards as an ideal way to learn about board dynamics, procedures and responsibilities. Although she was active on nonprofit boards (she served ten years on the Los Angeles Alzheimer's Association board), she feels that private boards were, for her, ideal training for public boards, because the privates are directly related to the business world. Serving on private boards is more financially rewarding than nonprofits, of course. Typically, compensation is in equity, so if the company does well, so does the director. She is currently on the board of a portfolio company of Aurora Capital, a private equity company.

Fleetwood was Dano's first public company board, a Fortune 1000 company that made recreational vehicles. She currently sits on the board of Superior Industries—at $800 million, one of the largest producers of aluminum wheels. She has been a board member of six different companies during her career and after retiring from Honeywell.

SANDRA L. HELTON

Hired right out of college to work at a Corning plant in Kentucky, Sandy Helton, a mathematics graduate, was assigned to a new development venture for the company that required technical expertise and financial savvy. "Those econ courses at college really came in handy," she recalls. This was an important job for a young person right out of college (especially one whose only previous paying job was as a church organist), she acknowledges, "but if you think you can do it and you work hard, you can do it."

The project was successful, so she was promoted to headquarters in Corning, New York, where she was assigned another new project requiring skills in process engineering. This project, too, was a success—so much so that Corning paid for her to go back to business school full-time to earn her MBA degree, and paid her a partial salary while she pursued her studies.

SANDRA L. HELTON
Chicago; Tucson, Arizona

Current Boards/Select Nonprofits:
Covance Inc.
Lexmark International, Inc.
Principal Financial Services, Inc.
Northwestern Memorial HealthCare

Past Boards:
Telephone and Data Systems, Inc.
U.S. Cellular Corporation
Aerial Communications, Inc.
Lukens Steel Company

Career History:
Telephone and Data Systems, Inc.: EVP and CFO (retired)
Compaq: VP and controller
Corning Incorporated: SVP and treasurer; various positions
    in engineering, finance, and strategy

Education:
MS, Finance, Sloan School, Massachusetts Institute of Technology
BS, Mathematics, University of Kentucky

Helton stayed at Corning for twenty-six years, working her way up to treasurer of the company. As one of the top three people in the financial executive suite, she made many presentations to the board of directors. "I enjoyed learning about the board's perspective on our business." She also noted that early on Corning was a very progressive company with women at senior executive levels.

In 1995, she was recruited to her first board, Lukens Inc., an old-line steel company, and was recommended to the search firm by her boss at Corning, The board's practice was to rotate directors through all the committees during their three-year terms. Thus, Helton gained experience on audit, finance, and governance committees. Her board term ended when the steel company was acquired.

Helton left Corning for Compaq Computer Corporation and subsequently joined Telephone and Data Systems (TDS) in Chicago. Her mission was to partner with the CEO to change the company in key ways. As EVP and CFO, she sat on the boards of Telephone and Data Systems and its two publicly traded subsidiaries. "I thought I could make a difference," she reflects.

Her next independent board was Principal Financial Group, where Helton was one of four women on a board of thirteen. It was a very diverse board with African-American and Hispanic members. "The variety of voices lends credence to individual perspectives and contributes to richer discussion and better decisions," she notes.

Helton was recruited to the Covance board through the recommendation of an executive of Northwestern Memorial HealthCare Hospital in Chicago, where she served on the board. Headquartered in Princeton, New Jersey, Covance is one of the world's largest drug-development services companies with annual revenues greater than $2 billion, global operations in more than thirty countries, and more than 11,000 employees worldwide.

A fellow Principal board member gave her name to the search firm recruiting for Lexmark, a $4 billion company. Helton was chosen as the second woman on that board, though she is the lone woman on the Covance board at this writing.

Retired from her corporate career, Helton sits on three public corporate boards, which she enjoys because it keeps her involved in the business world, and she can continue to make a contribution.

SHARON D. GARRETT

Sharon Garrett is an information systems expert, with her BA in economics from UCLA and both her masters and Ph.D from the UCLA School of Public Health. She held the position of chief information officer at The Walt Disney Company from 1989 to 2000, after serving almost a decade in executive positions at UCLA Medical Center.

Being a CIO of a large and successful company led directly to her first public board position at Ross Stores, Inc., in 2000. As a senior Disney executive, she was known to search firms, and one of them recommended her to Ross. Garrett had been deeply involved in retail issues such as inventory and distribution, so she had the experience the Ross board of directors needed.

SHARON D. GARRETT
Pacific Palisades, California

Current Boards:
Ross Stores, Inc.

Past Boards:
Corio, Inc.
Catalytic Capital Investment Corporation, LLC

Career History:
American Medical Response, Inc.: EVP (current)
PacifiCare Health Systems: EVP, Enterprise Services
Zyan Communications: CEO
The Walt Disney Company: SVP and CIO
UCLA Medical Center: Deputy Director

Education:
Ph.D, Public Health, UCLA
MPH, Statistics and Planning, UCLA
BA, Economics, UCLA

"Many of the board members have been at Ross since its inception, so it's very collegial," Garrett says. She had more than enough professional credentials to qualify her as a board member, so the focus during her interviews was, in addition to specific expertise, whether or not she would be "a good fit."

Women senior executives with high profiles in large companies are the most obvious candidates to be targeted for boards by executive search firms. Garrett recommends that women who want to serve on public company boards should spend some of their professional careers in the executive ranks at one or more large, brand-name, publicly held companies. She also advises women to get international experience to learn to "fit in" and to navigate the subtleties of different country customs, language and "how business is done."

Some years after her Disney experience, Garrett returned to the health care industry as executive vice president, Enterprise Services for PacifiCare Health Systems. She is currently executive vice president at American Medical Response, the nation's largest ambulance company. In addition to her Ross Board membership, she serves on the board of a private-equity company.

Garrett's words of advice for women board candidates: Be knowledgeable, on top of your game and always prepared. And know all facets of your business, not just the piece of which you're in charge.

"When responding to questions (especially by company execs), sing shorter songs," Garrett says. "Give short, crisp, well-organized responses. Individuals who 'drone on' expose the fact that they aren't well organized and appear to be unconcerned about wasting other people's time. Regardless of how smart and knowledgeable a person is, if he or she cannot answer questions with short, crisp replies, it makes a very unflattering impression."

MARIE L. KNOWLES

Marie Knowles earned her bachelor's and master's degrees in chemical engineering, then went on to earn her MBA. These degrees led directly to her long and successful career at ARCO, a huge international oil company headquartered in Los Angeles, subsequently acquired by the multinational oil and gas company BP.

When Knowles began her career there, the women employees at ARCO were primarily in secretarial roles. Because of her education, Knowles was one of the few women professionals. "I had to establish my voice at ARCO." Knowles said. "If I hadn't had a voice, I wouldn't have had a career. So speaking up later in life as the only woman on a board was not really a problem for me."

Her bosses must have liked what they heard, because Knowles rose to SVP and president of a large subsidiary, ARCO Transportation Company and ultimately to EVP and CFO of the parent company. As SVP and president of ARCO Transportation, she reported regularly to the CEO and board of directors, who also reviewed top executives annually to evaluate them and develop their talent, "more in-depth and more regularly than other boards do," she says.

She was recruited for her first public company board by a search firm. Phelps Dodge, the international wire-and-cable manufacturing firm, was looking for a woman who had executive operating experience. Knowles was the first and only woman on that board from 1993 to 2007 when the company was acquired. As mentioned in the networking chapter, she was familiar with board dynamics, not only from her interactions with the ARCO board, but also through her work on nonprofits on behalf of ARCO.

MARIE L. KNOWLES
South Pasadena, California

Current Boards/Select Nonprofits:
McKesson Corporation.
Fidelity Fixed Income and Asset Allocation Funds
Santa Catalina Island Company

Past Boards:
America West Airlines (now US Airways)
Vastar Resources, Inc.
ARCO Chemical Company
URS Corporation

Career History:
Spirit Equestrian: Owner
Owen Washburn and the Five Ladies: Partner
Atlantic Richfield Company: EVP and CFO (retired)
ARCO: SVP/President, ARCO Transportation Company

Education:
MBA, University of Southern California
MS, Chemical Engineering, University of Southern California
BS, Chemical Engineering, University of Southern California

Knowles was on the advisory board of the engineering school at USC and served on the Smithsonian National Board. Because of this pro bono work, she was asked to join the board of URS, an engineering company, when ARCO was sold. The CEO of URS was also on the McKesson board, and he recommended her to the McKesson board, where two other directors are women. She is the chair of the audit committee.

Knowles was recommended to the board of America West (now USAir) by the CEO, who served on the Phelps Dodge board with her. An ex-ARCO executive recommended her to Fidelity, where she was invited to be a fund trustee. She served as audit chair for over ten years and is now vice chair of the independent trustees.

Although she's retired from her corporate career, Knowles is active in pro bono work as a board member of the Catalina Island Conservancy, and she owns and operates a training and boarding facility for horses. She still competes in hunter-jumper equestrian events..."just for fun."

CAROLYN CHIN

Carolyn Chin graduated from Rensselaer Polytechnic Institute (RPI) in the 1970s, when women were outnumbered by men fifty to one. As a result of her schooling, she was soon identified as a "technology expert," which she found amusing. "It only meant that I knew *just* a little more about technology than most people."

CAROLYN CHIN
Ft. Lauderdale

Current Boards:
The Bama Companies, Inc.
State Farm Bank
Woodard & Curran Engineering

Past Boards:
CH2M HILL
Holcim (US) Inc.
Zogby International
Commtouch
Allegiance Bank
Citi Retail Services

Career History:
Cebiz LLC: CEO (current)
Larasan Pharmaceutical: Chairman and CEO
SinglePoint: CEO, United States
Reuters America Inc.: EVP and Chief Marketing Officer
IBM: Corporate VP, General Manager e-Commerce Services
Citibank: VP and SVP
U.S. Department of Health, Education and Welfare: Executive Secretary
U.S. Department of Housing and Urban Development: Special Assistant to Executive Secretary

Education:
MBA, Harvard Business School
BS, Management Engineering, Rensselaer Polytechnic Institute

With an MBA from Harvard, she learned to develop increasingly sophisticated solutions to complex problems, often involving technology related to all aspects of a company, but especially to the customer experience. After she attended Harvard, a brief job as a sales clerk at Macy's led her to think strategically about customers. "To be good at retail, you have to make the customer happy—in ways neither I nor Macy's had even thought of. You have to be thinking ahead—seeing the possibilities."

That's just what Chin has done throughout her career in finance, technology, marketing and strategy. At Citibank in New York City, she was on the boards of Citi Retail Services and EJV Partners, created by Citibank and Salomon Brothers, "with men who made $20 million a year more than I did, but I had the same vote, representing one of the founders," she says with a smile.

Through her nonprofits, Chin has been rubbing shoulders with well-known CEOs and national leaders over the years. These include John Gardner, former Secretary of Health Education and Welfare and founder of Common Cause. He created the White House Fellows Program and chaired the commission when she was appointed a White House Fellow by President Jimmy Carter.

The White House Fellows Foundation Association is an exclusive alumni group from many different presidential administrations who keep in touch with one another. It is a powerful network, and Chin has often served as a board member. "It was the best personal and professional experience I ever had," Chin says of her year of meeting and talking with a wide range of historic figures such as Averill Harriman, Walter Cronkite, U.S. Cabinet Secretaries, and CEOs of Fortune 500 corporations.

Prior to being a White House Fellow, Chin was a founding board member of the Albert Einstein Peace Prize, where she worked with many of the top scientists in the country, some of whom were involved in the Manhattan Project. There, she also worked with Norman Cousins and Warren and Susie Buffett.

Chin says, "Throughout my career, people have told me that I speak like a man. Women often want to be certain of all the facts before they speak, and they anguish over what to say. Or even worse, say nothing. Men don't hold back, and I don't either."

Speaking up and knowing what she's talking about catapulted Chin to senior executive positions at IBM where she advocated programs to enhance professional development and opportunities for women and minorities. Her work on the IBM Women's Diversity Task Force ultimately led to IBM winning the Catalyst Award, the prestigious global award for companies that advance women.

Then as a board member of the engineering firm, CH2M Hill, she played a key role in establishing a diversity professional development program, patterned after IBM. CH2M Hill became the first company in the engineering industry to win the Catalyst Award.

She is one of two women directors on the board of State Farm Bank (a division of State Farm Insurance.) "We definitely have influence," she says. State Farm Bank is an incubator, looked to for creativity and innovation, like the division of Citibank where she worked years before. She was recruited for State Farm by a headhunter who knew her from the White House Fellows Program.

Another current board she serves is Woodard & Curran, a 650-person integrated engineering, environmental and operating company, where she is the only woman on the board and served with Angus King, until he was elected as U.S. Senator from Maine.

Chin's advice to women: "In your board interviews, anticipate what assumptions the interviewer may have about you and prepare to reinforce the positive or counteract the negative," she says. "The stereotype about Asians is that we don't communicate well, so I make sure I am very verbal and warm. Remember your interviews should highlight *all* your attributes because you are being evaluated on your personality, as well as your professional qualifications."

Chin sees her greatest strength as a strategist. She says she thinks the number one need for boards today is strategic planning, which she says is often not identified on the board's matrix of priorities. "The need for strategy experts may provide additional openings for women. Succession planning may be another avenue for women. It is not yet taken seriously enough at the board level." says Chin, speaking up, as usual.

JULIA R. BROWN

Julia Brown's passion is health. She studied microbiology and biochemistry at Louisiana Tech. She joined Eli Lilly and Company after college, and has devoted her career to pharmaceuticals, medical devices and diagnostics.

JULIA R. BROWN
San Diego

Current Boards/Select Nonprofits:
Targacept, Inc.
Biodel Inc.
UC San Diego Foundation Board of Trustees

Past Boards:
Labopharm, Inc.
Trius Therapeutics
Tanox, Inc.
MediQuest Therapeutics, Inc.
CovX Research, LLC

Career History:
Amylin Pharmaceuticals, LLC.: Advisor to the CEO (retired); EVP
Dura Pharmaceuticals, Inc.: EVP; VP
Eli Lilly & Company: VP, IVAC Corporation (division of Lilly);
    GM, Vital Signs Division

Education:
BS, Microbiology and Biochemistry, Louisiana Tech University

Although her career began in research at Eli Lilly, Brown moved into sales and marketing very early. "In those days, sales was a man's job," recalls Brown, who was one of the first six women in Lilly's sales organization. Julia spent many years in Lilly's international division and worked with subsidiaries all over the world. She became vice president of two Lilly subsidiaries—Hybritech, where she led worldwide marketing and IVAC where she was general manager of the Vital Signs Division. After retiring from Lilly, she became EVP of Dura Pharmaceuticals. Later with Amylin Pharmaceuticals, she served as executive vice president and advisor to the CEO.

Brown has served on seven corporate boards—four public, three private. All have been development-stage pharmaceutical or biopharmaceutical companies. "I am type-cast," she laughs. "My contribution is biotechnology industry experience, knowledge of drug development, partnering, and business development. My boards often include investors, but my added value is bringing a different viewpoint as one who works *inside* biotech companies."

A C-level executive, but never a CEO, Brown advises women who aspire to board service to "start early" and opt for line positions with profit-and-loss responsibility. "Women often gravitate to staff jobs. That is not the best career path to board service." While there is still a majority of male CEOs in biopharma, Julia says more women are starting life sciences firms and becoming CEOs. Women who are partners or managing directors in venture capital firms often become board members of companies where they invest.

Brown stays abreast of issues in corporate governance. She has taken board training courses at UCLA, Harvard and NACD and is a member of three organizations devoted to excellence in corporate governance. "You must take the job seriously," Brown says. "The field has been very dynamic. I never serve on more than three corporate boards at a time. In biotech, things happen that demand a lot of time. You have to give the company the time that's needed."

Brown is a trustee and chair emeritus of the UC San Diego Foundation. She also serves on the boards of two industry associations and Corporate Directors Forum.

"I think women tend to adopt different leadership styles than men," she says. "They bring complementary perspectives to decision making. Many studies have shown that diverse groups tend to make better decisions than homogeneous groups do. That applies to boards as much as to other business situations."

GERALDINE KNATZ

Geraldine Knatz is the executive director of the Port of Los Angeles, the largest port in the western hemisphere, and she is one of three women who run ports in the United States, all of them in California. Knatz began her maritime career as an environmental scientist at the Port of Los Angeles in 1977, and several years later was hired by its neighbor, the Port of Long Beach. Early on, she never dreamed she would someday be the most powerful woman in global shipping. Most people don't realize that together, the Ports of Los Angeles and Long Beach make up the seventh largest deep-water port complex in the world.

GERALDINE KNATZ
Long Beach, California

Current Boards/Select Nonprofits:
Bank of the West
International Association of Ports and Harbors

Career History:
Port of Los Angeles: Executive Director (current)
Port of Long Beach: Managing Director; Director
   of Planning; Manager of Environmental Planning
Port of Los Angeles: Environmental Scientist

Education:
Ph.D, Biological Science, University of Southern California
MS, Environmental Engineering, University of Southern California
BS, Zoology, Rutgers University

Knatz built her career by becoming active and visible in her industry. "Having hit the glass ceiling as managing director of the Port of Long Beach, I focused on building my reputation outside of my current job." She did that by getting involved in professional organizations—today she is the president of the International Association of Ports and Harbors. "When your bosses start hearing about you from others in the industry, they start to look at you in a new way. Sometimes you need to build your reputation outside your regular job with professional organizations to be noticed in your own organization."

But doing her "regular job" was already pretty impressive. As managing director for the Port of Long Beach, she was instrumental in creating and implementing an effective environmental improvement plan that enabled major new developments at the world's largest transportation and international trade hub.

"When you get into the pipeline of nonprofits and industry boards you become better known," Knatz observes. Her high profile led to a prestigious appointment to a special committee of the National Academy of Science in Washington, D.C. She was recruited by Lillian Borrone, then the maritime director of the Port of New York. That led to an invitation to join the influential Marine Board, a group she eventually chaired.

"By the time Los Angeles Mayor Antonio Villaraigosa interviewed me for the position of the Port of L.A. general manager, I was very well known in the port industry." She has since revolutionized the role of executive director of the Port of Los Angeles, and initiated controversial yet environmentally friendly programs. In addition to a steely focus on the port's core cargo handling business, she is building a visitor-friendly waterfront to turn the port into a destination for travelers and tourists, like San Francisco's Embarcadero.

A search firm recruited her for her first board at the Bank of the West, based in San Francisco. Owned by BNP Paribas, the Bank of the West was seeking a woman "with her finger on the pulse of L.A.," who had business and international experience.

"Doing business in the global marketplace requires that corporations have executives and directors who speak foreign languages in addition to English. Europe has always been way ahead of America on this score. Consider the acquisition of a second language part of your career path to corporate boards," Knatz says, noting that she regrets never having learned to speak other languages, especially French. "When I consider potential employees to work at the Port, bilingual skill is always an advantage."

Learning to navigate calm and rough seas has served Knatz well at the port, and as a director for current and future boards, she says.

MOLLY JOEL COYE, MD

Molly Joel Coye, MD, one of four women on the board of Aetna, said her network of professional women friends over the years has been key to securing her board positions. She initially caught the attention of Aetna's former CEO, Jack Rowe, who had led the turnaround of the company, at a working meeting in Washington with Tommy Thompson, former U.S. secretary of Health and Human Services. Eighteen months later, he invited her to have dinner, looking for a new board member with a combination of technology, government and health care experience.

MOLLY JOEL COYE, MD
Los Angeles

Current Boards/Select Nonprofits:
Aetna, Inc.
PATH
American Telemedicine Association
Prosetta Antiviral, Inc.

Past Boards:
Cholestech Inc.
American Hospital Association
American Public Health Association
The California Endowment
China Medical Board

Career History:
UCLA Health System: Chief Innovation Officer (current)
State of New Jersey: Commissioner of Health
California Department of Health Services: Director
Johns Hopkins Bloomberg School of Hygiene and Public Health:
    Head of Public Health Practice Division
Health Technology Center: CEO and Founder
CalRHIO, Chairman: CEO and Co-founder
Public Health Institute (Oakland, California): Senior Advisor

Education:
MD and MPH, Johns Hopkins University
Board Certified by the American College of Preventive Medicine
MA, Asian History, Stanford University
BS, Political Science, University of California, Berkeley

Her "old girls' network" had kicked in—when the CEO contacted a group of people he trusted to find out more about Coye, three of them happened to be women with whom she had worked closely or who knew her via executive networks. After meeting with Rowe, Coye was introduced to the other three women who were longtime members of the Aetna board, Barbara Franklin, Ellen Hancock and Betsy Cohen. Coye was elected to the board in 2005.

Recognized internationally for advancing innovative approaches to health-care delivery, Coye is now at UCLA Health System where she's the chief innovation officer, overseeing the Institute for Innovation in Health, and is responsible for the digital transformation of health care at UCLA—including redesigning the patient experience and incorporating telemedicine and remote monitoring systems.

She has extensive experience in universities, government and the private sector. Coye was commissioner of health for the State of New Jersey, director of the California Department of Health Services, and head of the division of public health practice at Johns Hopkins School of Hygiene and Public Health. After leaving public service, she led a large medical group in Santa Clara, directed product development at an early Internet disease management company, and advised venture capitalists about investing in health technology.

Coye received her MD and masters of public health degrees from Johns Hopkins University and is board certified by the American College of Preventive Medicine. She has a master's degree in Chinese history from Stanford, speaks fluent Mandarin, and is the author of two books on Chinese history. After living for several years in China early in her career, she decided to return to the U.S. and to work on health-care innovations that would help people around the world. Although she was later offered the opportunity to become a health anchor for a major TV-network affiliate, she chose to continue her work as a state health director in order to advance novel solutions for the AIDS epidemic, to extend prenatal care, and to increase insurance coverage for working families.

An entrepreneur, too, Coye founded and was CEO of the Health Technology Center (HealthTech), a nonprofit education and research organization that became the premier forecasting institution for emerging technologies in health care. She later founded and led CalRHIO, California's first statewide health information exchange organization.

Coye joined UCLA after working with the Public Health Institute in Oakland, California, where she chaired the advisory board for the Center for Technology and Aging and advised domestic and international programs regarding innovation and technology.

Aetna was not Coye's first for-profit board—that was Cholestech (one of the Fortune 200's Fastest Growing Companies), which was acquired by Inverness in 2007. "We went through the early days of working through the Sarbanes-Oxley regulations." she said. "As the only woman on the board, I had to learn quickly," This year she also joined the private board of Prosetta, Inc., a biotech company developing bioconformatics assays for a wide range of diseases.

JOAN E. HERMAN

Former president and CEO of the consumer business unit for WellPoint, Inc., the largest managed-care company by membership in the U.S., Joan Herman started on her pathway to public boards by serving on two corporate advisory boards—Bayer Medical Care and HealthData Insights.

Bayer's medical devices business unit was looking for an expert in managed care, and Herman was recommended by one of the founders of WomenCorporateDirectors. "Advisory boards are focused on strategy, not fiduciary responsibilities," explains Herman. "We helped management with succession planning and growth issues. As an advisory board member, you provide counsel to management based on your professional experience and business judgment. You build valuable relationships with top management and other advisory board members, and you add credentials to your future board resume, especially when it's a big-brand name like Bayer."

How do women make strategic connections to get on advisory boards? "Through networking," Herman emphasizes. "Find those consulting firms that help corporations build advisory boards, and let them know about your interest and about your professional skills and industry experience."

Her industry experience was sought by her next private advisory board, HealthData Insights, a recovery-audit contractor for Medicare that wanted to expand services to managed-care companies.

"Advisory board members are often paid per diem, far less compensation than public corporate boards pay, although the responsibilities are also fewer," Herman explains. "However, some private firms pay advisory board members with equity—which can be lucrative when the companies go public or are acquired."

JOAN E. HERMAN
Pacific Palisades, California

Current Corporate Boards/Select Nonprofits:
HealthSouth
Convergys Corp.
Qualicorp (based in Sao Paolo, Brazil)
DentalPlans.com
American Red Cross, Los Angeles region
Center Dance Arts (at the Los Angeles
   Music Center)

Past Boards:
Bayer Medical Care
HealthDataInsights
MRV Communications
American Academy of Actuaries
Jewish Venture Philanthropy Fund (Co-chair)

Career History:
Herman & Associates LLC: President and CEO (current)
WellPoint: President/CEO, Consumer Business Unit
Phoenix Life Insurance Company: SVP Strategic Development

Education:
MBA, Western New England College
MA, Mathematics, Yale University
BA, Mathematics, Barnard College, Columbia University

Strategic networking led Herman to an outside public board, MRV Communications, providers of optical equipment to telecommunications firms. While at WellPoint, she participated in CEO roundtables orchestrated by Jeff Weiss, founder of the Center for Corporate Innovation, which runs events primarily in the health care and technology industries.

Herman mentioned to Weiss that she would like to serve on boards, and he recommended her to the MRV CEO who wanted a director with large company policy-and-procedures experience, and who could help his entrepreneurial firm grow. The MRV general counsel also suggested her, having met Herman at a networking breakfast. That closed the deal.

"I learned a lot about technology from that board, even though it didn't relate to health insurance," explains Herman. "I saw many analogies in terms of how they dealt with customers, doing customization for large clients. That's what we had done at WellPoint, so I was able to help them delineate strategies for profitability as well as growth."

Building on what she learned from advisory boards and the MRV board, she now serves on the public boards of HealthSouth, Convergys, Qualicorp (based in Sao Paulo, Brazil) and privately held DentalPlans.com.

Herman heads her own consulting firm with a number of private-equity-firm clients. She was asked by one to review a potential investment in Qualicorp, one of Brazil's largest health care benefits administrators and brokers. Subsequently, she was asked to join the board, and remained when the company went public.

"At least two board meetings a year are held in Brazil," says Herman. "It's a long flight, but a very interesting experience. I fly to Dallas or Miami, then south to Brazil—about twelve hours—for a board meeting later that day. I don't speak Portuguese, but most of the meeting is conducted in English, and a simultaneous translator is always present."

Herman was recruited to her largest public board, HealthSouth, the biggest operator of inpatient-rehabilitation hospitals in the U.S., a firm with a market cap of over two billion dollars. She was recruited by two women partners at a global executive-search firm, one of whom she had met many years before when she worked at Phoenix Insurance in Hartford.

Herman brings her experience leading and profitably growing a diverse set of businesses in the highly regulated health care industry. She joined WellPoint Health Networks, Inc., in 1998 as president of specialty businesses. After taking on additional responsibilities for WellPoint's senior and state-sponsored businesses, she was named president and CEO of WellPoint's consumer business in 2007.

Throughout her career, Herman has served on nonprofit boards and been visible in the community. She serves with Jeff Weiss on the nonprofit South Central Scholars Foundation, which helps underprivileged Los Angeles youth succeed in college and in their careers.

Her other nonprofit boards include the Los Angeles Region of the American Red Cross, the Venice Family Clinic Foundation, Center Dance Arts at the Los Angeles Music Center, and Diavolo Dance Theater.

Herman grew up as a dancer and graduated from the renowned High School of Performing Arts in New York—where the movie *Fame* was set—but a back injury ended her dream of becoming a professional dancer. She comes from a long line of doctors and dentists, so she combined that family tradition with her mathematics degrees from Columbia and Yale, to create a successful career in health insurance—"it's probably more stable than dancing for a living," she smiles.

GO IMMEDIATELY

TO

Chapter 8
Pathways Through
Academia

PATHWAYS & Through

Academia

PRESIDENTS OF UNIVERSITIES AND COLLEGES, AS WELL AS DEANS AND FACULTY OF BUSINESS, MEDICAL AND LAW SCHOOLS have been sought by corporate boards for decades. Their business knowledge, management abilities, and knowledge of related fields of study all bring added value to companies. A corporation also gains a certain prestige when a respected educator sits on its board.

Leadership in higher education has been a primary avenue for women to gain the experience and gravitas needed for corporate boards in industries related to their fields of study. Women academic leaders profiled here bring added value due to their experience as entrepreneurs, executives and consultants.

Academic leaders with prior experience as entrepreneurs, or previous corporate experience, bring additional understanding of how business works in the real world outside the university, and are especially attractive to boards. Cynthia Telles served on several corporate boards leading up to General Motors. Maria Klawe learned business lessons from the failure of a small tech company she helped launch. Janet Kerr sees the importance of helping law students become business owners. The entrepreneurial center she established at a law school was the first in the country.

If you are below the level of president on a campus, but are a senior administrator with an MBA, and your field of expertise is organizational effectiveness, you might get noticed by a board recruiter, as happened to Judith Blumenthal. She had previously worked in human resources in a major public corporation, so her combination of academics, human resources, and business know-how was her ticket to the boardroom.

As reciprocal benefits to the academic institutions, the students and faculty may have access to these corporations for jobs, mentors, and real-world training, like this bonus to Harvey Mudd College from Maria Klawe's directorships: Microsoft hired ten of her 170 graduates in 2012, and she introduced one of her chip-design process professors to Broadcom, where he worked for the next few years. He then brought his knowledge and practical experience back to the students he teaches at Harvey Mudd.

MARIA M. KLAWE

Maria Klawe is president of Harvey Mudd College, the liberal arts college of science, engineering, and mathematics in Claremont, California. A career academic *and* an expert in mathematics and computer science, she was named president at Harvey Mudd in 2006 after serving as the dean of engineering and professor of computer science at Princeton University for three years. Before Princeton, she spent fourteen years in various faculty and administrative positions at the University of British Columbia. During her academic career, she was also involved in businesses—large and small. Klawe spent eight years with IBM Research, contributing her expertise in theoretical computer science and discrete mathematics.

Her first entrepreneurial venture was a start-up company called Silicon Chalk, a software product designed for colleges that provided all students with laptops—it compiled complete recordings of all class lectures and synchronized information. When this practice failed to grow in the early 2000s, the company failed. "We were ahead of our time," Klawe acknowledges. She also served on the board of another start-up technology company that was acquired by Dolby Laboratories in 2007.

Microsoft was her first public board. How did a college president find a pathway to her first corporate board—one of the largest companies in the world?

During fifteen years as a volunteer on the nonprofit board of the Anita Borg Institute for Women and Technology, which she chaired from 2003 to 2008, Klawe developed a friendship with her fellow nonprofit board member, Rick Rashid, who was the chief research officer for Microsoft.

MARIA M. KLAWE
Claremont, California

Current Boards/Select Nonprofits:
Microsoft
Broadcom Corporation
Math for America

Past Boards/Select Nonprofits:
Association of Computing Machinery
Anita Borg Institute for Women and Technology
Institute for Pure and Applied Mathematics

Career History:
Harvey Mudd College: President (current)
Princeton University: Dean of Engineering and Professor
    of Computer Science
University of British Columbia: Dean of Science
University of British Columbia: Vice President of Student
    and Academic Services
University of British Columbia: Head of the Department
    of Computer Science
IBM Research
University of Toronto

Education:
Ph.D, Mathematics, University of Alberta
BS, Mathematics, University of Alberta

"Microsoft wanted a real computer scientist to join its board, and they wanted an academic leader who was close to students. Rick told his board that the top of his list would be Maria Klawe," she recalls. "Bill Gates' sister had gone to Pomona College, and Steve Ballmer's son was coincidentally visiting Claremont McKenna at the time, so that helped to establish initial rapport during the interviews." Klawe is a member of the compensation committee and the regulatory and public policy committee at Microsoft. She notes that Dina Dublon is the other woman on the Microsoft board, and "I depended on her as my mentor for a year or so. She is great."

A few years after she joined Microsoft, Broadcom, headquartered in Orange County, California, was looking for a similar "unique combination" of technology and academia. Klawe was approached by a search firm consultant who was surprised to hear she actually had business experience. Klawe was able to assure the Broadcom recruiter that she was an entrepreneur at heart. Broadcom's CEO was really looking for a good fit culturally for the board. "Each board is different. Broadcom was much more focused on personal attributes," explains Klawe. "Microsoft is more complex and diversified. I think I am a better board member because of serving on both boards. I can see issues from different perspectives."

Klawe recommends all women candidates and directors take board-training courses. She attended Directors College at Stanford, and board-education courses through the National Association of Corporate Directors (NACD). Now, she is often invited to be a speaker on panels at both.

For visibility and to give back, Klawe built her industry contacts early, serving as a volunteer trustee of Mathematical Sciences Research Institute and president of the Association of Computing Machinery. She has been a board or council member of the American Mathematical Society, the Computing Research Association, and the Society for Industrial and Applied Mathematics. With her long list of accomplishments, it's no surprise that she is the recipient of several honorary doctorates.

MARY SUE COLEMAN

Mary Sue Coleman became the thirteenth president of the University of Michigan in 2002, following her seven-year tenure as president of the University of Iowa. Dynamic, engaging, and creative, she is also obviously indefatigable. *Time Magazine* named her one of America's Top Ten College Presidents.

Serving on the boards of Johnson & Johnson since 2003 and Meredith Corporation since 1997, she did not seek out board service. The boards came to her. Founded in New Jersey in 1886, Johnson & Johnson employs some 129,000 people worldwide and manufactures health-care products distributed around the world. Located in Des Moines, Iowa, Meredith operates well-known national publications and websites, including magazines *Better Homes & Gardens, Parents, Family Circle, Ladies' Home Journal, Fitness, More, American Baby, Every Day with Rachel Ray* and *FamilyFun* and online websites BHG, and Better Food Network.

MARY SUE COLEMAN
Ann Arbor, Michigan

Current Boards:
Johnson & Johnson
Meredith Corporation

Past Boards:
Gaylord Container Corp.

Career History:
University of Michigan: President (current)
University of Iowa: President
University of New Mexico: Provost and Vice President
   for Academic Affairs
University of North Carolina at Chapel Hill: Vice Chancellor
   for Graduate Studies and Research; Associate Provost
   and Dean of Research

Education:
Ph.D, Biochemistry, University of North Carolina
BS, Chemistry, Grinnell College

Coleman is known as an innovator—in campus life, in interdisciplinary studies, in collaborations with government, business, and universities in China, Ghana, South Africa and Brazil, opening up the world to her students. She has also opened the seven-million volume university library to Google to guarantee universal access and the preservation of recorded human knowledge.

One of six university presidents selected by President Obama to the Advanced Manufacturing Partnership, she helps bring together universities, industry, and the federal government to redirect and revitalize manufacturing in America. Coleman was also the 2010 co-chair of the National Advisory Council on Innovation and Entrepreneurship with U.S. Secretary of Commerce Gary Locke.

In addition to her many volunteer and civic responsibilities, Coleman runs the

University of Michigan with 59,000 students on three campuses. Her recent campaign called "The Michigan Difference," raised $3.2 billion—the most money ever raised for a public university.

Past chair of the Association of American Universities, representing sixty-one leading public and private research universities in the U.S. and Canada, she is also active in medicine and science. Coleman is a biochemist, who spent her career in research and teaching, and she is a Fellow of the American Association for the Advancement of Science. As a member of the Institute of Medicine, she co-chaired a major policy study, examining the consequences of "un-insurance," and has become a national expert on this pressing issue.

CYNTHIA A. TELLES

Cynthia Telles serves on the board of one of the largest corporations in the world, General Motors, proving an academic doesn't have to be a college president to be recruited for a corporate board. Telles has been a member of the faculty of the UCLA School of Medicine since 1968. Nonprofit board service, academic leadership, and public service led her to board positions at Sanwa Bank, Kaiser Permanente, and Burlington Northern Santa Fe, as well.

On the faculty of the department of psychiatry at UCLA since 1986, Telles has been extremely visible throughout her career on federal, state, and local commissions and through her leadership of nonprofit organizations. She also heads a UCLA psychiatric clinic for Spanish-speaking clients, where she is known to the huge Latino community in Southern California. Among its influential leaders, Vilma Martinez, now U.S. ambassador to Argentina, was a board member of Japanese-owned Sanwa Bank, a subsidiary of Sanwa Limited, which was the largest financial institution in the world. Martinez recommended Telles as one of four candidates for the Sanwa board. The president took each to dinner and chose Telles for the board because of her academic, government, and nonprofit experience, and also because of her visibility in the community.

"I cut my teeth on a financial institution board," says Telles. "It was enormously helpful to learn board responsibilities on a bank board." She learned about fiduciary duty, oversight, compliance, and governance of a complex, highly regulated business.

CYNTHIA A. TELLES
Los Angeles

Current Boards/Select Nonprofits:
General Motors
Kaiser Foundation Health Plan, Inc.
California Community Foundation
Pacific Council on International Policy

Past Boards:
Burlington Northern Santa Fe Corporation
The California Endowment
Sanwa Bank
Americas United Bank

Career History:
UCLA School of Medicine: Director of the Spanish-Speaking
    Psychosocial Clinic of the Neuropsychiatric Institute and Hospital;
    Associate Clinical Professor (current)
Los Angeles City Commissions: Status of Women (President); Ethics
    (Vice President); Library Commission (Vice President); Children,
    Youth & Families

Education:
Ph.D, Clinical Psychology, Boston University
BA, Psychology; minor, Latin American Studies, Smith College

Having served on one board, Telles was recommended for the Kaiser Permanente national board by a Kaiser board member, who had also served as a commissioner of the City of Los Angeles. When she was interviewed by Kaiser CEO George Halvorson, "There was a natural affinity, because of shared values about corporate social responsibility and public service," Telles recalls. "And because we both had a history with Hubert Humphrey." Halvorson is from Minnesota, and Telles had worked for Senator Humphrey in his Washington, D.C., office.

She contributed her time and talents over the years to large nonprofit organizations, including serving as board chair of both The California Endowment and the California Community Foundation. Her successful track record caught the eye of the federal government, and she was appointed to the National

Advisory Council for Substance Abuse and Mental Health Services during the Clinton Administration.

Former Los Angeles Mayors Tom Bradley, Richard Riordan, and James Hahn appointed her to influential commissions, She served as vice president of the Ethics Commission, president of the Commission on the Status of Women, and vice president of the Library Commission.

In 2010, when General Motors was emerging from bankruptcy, Telles was recruited by the chair of the new company, Ed Whitacre. She and Whitacre had served together on the board of Burlington Northern Santa Fe before it was sold to Berkshire Hathaway.

At the time of Telles's election to the board of General Motors, more than sixty percent of the company was owned by the government. The White House, pleased with her nomination, had recently vetted her for an appointment by President Barack Obama to the White House Commission on Presidential Scholars.

"Now is a good time for women to seek board service opportunities," Telles urges. "Because of economic uncertainties, many boards had extended the terms of their seasoned board members beyond the retirement age. Now that things are stabilizing, I think more seats will open up over the next few years."

JANET E. KERR

Janet Kerr, a professor of law at Pepperdine University School of Law, is recognized for championing the rights of women in law. She is the recipient of the Laure Sudreau-Rippe Endowed Chair, and she is the founder and executive director of the Geoffrey H. Palmer Center for Entrepreneurship and the Law. She sits on the boards of La-Z-Boy Inc., TCW Strategic Income Fund and TCW Funds, and Tilly's, Inc., a clothing retailer.

A nationally recognized author, lecturer and consultant in securities law compliance, banking law, corporate governance and general corporate law, Kerr has served as a consultant in several high-profile cases dealing with financial institution fraud. At Pepperdine School of Law, she teaches courses in corporations, securities regulations and entrepreneurship.

Her first corporate board was CKE (Carl Karcher Enterprises), a NYSE-traded company. Kerr says she always makes it a priority to get to know her students and meet with their parents. The father of one of her students was Andy Puzder, CEO of CKE restaurants. Two years after meeting Kerr at lunch, he nominated her to the CKE board, where she served for six years until the company went private in 2010. She was the only woman on the board; Betsy Sanders, also profiled in this book, had been the first woman director, but she had stepped down.

JANET E. KERR
Malibu, California

Current Boards:
TCW Strategic Income Fund, Inc., and TCW Funds
La-Z-Boy, Inc.
Tilly's, Inc.

Past Boards:
CKE Restaurants, Inc.

Career History:
Pepperdine University School of Law: Professor of Law (current)
The Geoffrey H. Palmer Center for Entrepreneurship and the Law:
    Founder and Executive Director (current)
Pepperdine University School of Law: Associate Dean
Hahn & Cazier: Attorney
Securities and Exchange Commission: Staff Attorney

Education:
LLM, Corporate Law, New York University School of Law
JD, Pepperdine University
BA, Political Science and Spanish, Pepperdine University

"I had never thought of serving on boards," says Kerr, but notes that after the Sarbanes-Oxley Act (SOX) became law in 2002, "My legal expertise in corporate law was in demand. Suddenly, companies had to have board members who knew something about SOX. So I sort of fell into board service."

Her next board was La-Z-Boy, which came as a result of a speaking engagement at a conference for general counsels, hosted by *The Economist*. "Speaking engagements, writing, and blogging about your expertise develop platforms," she advises. A board member of La-Z-Boy furniture came up to her after her speech and asked her to interview for its board. She joined in 2009 as the first woman, and, since then, another has joined. Kerr's story underscores how visibility as an expert in your field, confidence, and personality are helpful for anyone interested in corporate board service.

A directorship at Trust Company of the West Funds (TCW Funds) came through her friendship with the late California State Treasurer Matt Fong, who was on the board of regents at Pepperdine, where she teaches. He recommended her to Pat Haden, a TCW Funds board member. She is one of two women on the TCW Funds board. One of her former students became general counsel for Tilly's and recruited Kerr to that board prior to its IPO in 2012. She is the only woman on the Tilly's board.

At Pepperdine, Kerr started the first law school Entrepreneurial Center in the country, designed to train law students to start businesses. The Center has graduated three hundred lawyers in eleven years. Kerr recommends combining a law degree with business school, to earn a JD/MBA that can be an early step toward corporate boards. Another option might be law school with a vigorous program like Pepperdine's Entrepreneurial Center.

Kerr is also a successful entrepreneur herself, having founded several technology companies since 2000. X-Laboratories, a company she co-founded with HRL Laboratories, LLC, assists in the commercialization of technologies in research institutions. She also has consulted on entrepreneurial strategies for countries including the People's Republic of China, France, and Thailand.

Kerr says, "I see a great future for women on boards. We add great value. I look forward to the day when gender is not an issue."

JUDITH F. BLUMENTHAL

Judith Blumenthal, professor of clinical management and organizations at USC's Marshall School of Business, is a former associate dean of the Marshall School and chief alumni officer. She serves on the board of Guess?, a long-established fashion company in Los Angeles. She was recruited for Guess? by a major executive search firm. Guess? wanted another woman director, and Blumenthal believes her expertise in organizational effectiveness and strategy, along with her executive experience, and retail experience, were factors in her selection. Although it was rare at the time for women with human resources backgrounds to be considered for corporate boards, Blumenthal brought academic credentials that provided another added value. The Guess? board has two women on its seven member board.

JUDITH F. BLUMENTHAL
Los Angeles

Current Boards/Select Nonprofits:
Guess? Inc.
California Council on Economic Education
KUSC Radio Advisory Board

Past Boards:
Council for Advancement and Support of
Education, District VII
Natural History Museum of Los Angeles, Community
Advisory Council
USC Alumni Association Board of Governors

Career History:
University of Southern California Marshall School of Business:
Professor of Clinical Management and Organization (current)
University of Southern California: AVP, Alumni Relations and Executive
Director, USC Alumni Association; Associate Dean and Executive
Director for MBA.PM and Executive MBA programs

Education:
Ph.D, Business Administration, University of Southern California
MBA, Business Administration, University of Southern California
AB, English, Hunter College of the City University of New York

"Former USC President Steve Sample, used to say that students graduating from universities today will have five or more careers in their lifetimes," Blumenthal explains. "I have moved back and forth between business and academic careers, both of which helped prepare me for corporate board work."

On the business side, she worked in her twenties for Motorola in human resources for its semiconductor division as one of five top women among 30,000 employees. Three were engineers, two were in HR—Blumenthal and a colleague.

This was the 1970s when there were very few women in management positions. Blumenthal's female colleague was hired first, and when she was assigned to another position, she supported recruiting Blumenthal for her old job. Later, over a glass of wine, she confessed to Blumenthal that in supporting her, she also felt some uneasiness because she was afraid Blumenthal might outshine her.

"I remember that conversation vividly," says Blumenthal. "I admired her so much that, ironically, I felt intimidated trying to fill her shoes. But because she expressed her concerns, we both shared our misgivings, and suddenly a weight was lifted, and a wonderful communication and friendship ensued between us. The barriers came down, and we became an example for other women employees of how to work well together and support one another. I've been able to carry the lessons of that relationship to so many others throughout my career."

Blumenthal also sought professional development for her new job through the American Society for Training and Development and subsequently became an officer in that professional association so she could continue to learn and grow. She worked fifteen years in senior training, development, and organizational development positions.

Later in her career, Blumenthal went to graduate school at USC, and Warren Bennis, the renowned leadership expert at the USC Marshall School of Business, urged her to pursue a Ph.D rather than stop with an MBA. She was interested in broadening her knowledge of business strategy, but also in understanding businesses as complex social organizations. While a graduate student at USC, Blumenthal focused on blending theory and practice.

Following graduate school, Blumenthal taught at California State University, Northridge for more than eight years as a tenured professor. She was lured back to USC by an offer to be an associate dean in charge of MBA programs. Jane Pisano was USC's senior vice president for external relations at the time, and Pisano engaged Blumenthal as a consultant to develop a new strategic plan for the USC Alumni Association. A year later, Blumenthal became USC's chief alumni officer and executive director of the USC Alumni Association.

She recommends building networks of people you meet along the way, inside and outside your organizations. "My networks led to my board position, but you maintain contacts not just for what you can get out of them, but also what you can give." She values authentic relationships. "I never spend time with people who are just positioning themselves or posturing."

Being visible in a university career, plus business experience, and nonprofit board work can provide the pathway to boards. Capture and market the strengths that will be most useful to corporate boards. In Blumenthal's case, her expertise in organizational effectiveness was the added value she brought to Guess? Inc.

ANDREA L. RICH

During her thirty-four year career at UCLA, Dr. Andrea Rich worked her way up from assistant professor of communications studies to become the first woman executive vice chancellor and chief operations officer. In 1995, she was recruited away by the Los Angeles County Museum of Art to be its first president and CEO.

ANDREA L. RICH
Los Angeles

Corporate Boards/Select Nonprofits:
Mattel, Inc.
Douglas Emmett Real Estate Investment Trust
Save the Children (National Board)
Jules Stein Eye Institute
UCLA Brain Mapping Institute
ACLU Foundation of Southern California
The Private Bank of California
Pitzer College
Claremont McKenna College
La Plaza de Arte y Cultura

Career History:
Los Angeles County Museum of Art: President, CEO, and Director
University of California, Los Angeles: Executive Vice Chancellor
    and Chief Operating Officer; Vice Chancellor for Academic
    Administration; Assistant Professor, Communication Studies
Claremont Graduate University: Adjunct Professor

Education:
Ph.D, Speech, UCLA
MA, Speech, UCLA
BA, English/Speech, UCLA

Mattel, the largest toy company in the world and headquartered in Los Angeles, approached Rich for her first corporate board, during her early years at LACMA. Mattel saw value in her operations track record managing huge, complex organizations, her interest in children's education, and her visibility as a respected Los Angeles community leader with experience on major nonprofit boards.

When she was the second highest-ranking official at UCLA, Rich had overseen a vast academic enterprise that included the College of Letters and Science, eleven professional schools and the UCLA Medical Center. She led efforts to improve undergraduate education, renovate instructional facilities, and restructure the medical enterprise and academic arts programs. She orchestrated campus-wide interdisciplinary initiatives in public policy, environmental studies, and new media technologies. Six years after she departed, Rich was awarded the university's highest honor, the UCLA Medal for outstanding service.

Why did she leave UCLA? She had turned fifty, and had been one of the most senior administrators at UCLA for a long time, second only to then-Chancellor Charles E. Young. "It was a sense of timing—I knew if I didn't leave then, I probably never would," Rich recalled. "I thought I had one more big and challenging job in me. At the same time, my executive recruiter friend urged me to consider the Los Angeles County Museum of Art—something totally different."

At LACMA, Rich helped increase the endowment, expand educational programs, and enhance access and outreach to diverse populations. She completed a two-hundred-million-dollar capital campaign that doubled the museum's physical footprint, upgraded the collections, and converted the twenty-five-acre site into a welcoming and aesthetically beautiful green space in mid-city Los Angeles.

In her case, membership on the Mattel board came through an executive search firm—specifically, through a woman managing partner in that firm whom Rich had befriended years before through a women's network in Los Angeles. "I had not really set my sights on corporate board positions as my next goal, but I might have, had I known how to go about getting on boards."

Rich did her research. "I was impressed by Mattel's dedication to educating children through play, by its senior management who were expanding the company globally, and that Mattel had a woman CEO at the time, Jill Barad. So I said yes."

Rich joined two other women directors on the board—Barad, who was also chair of the board, and Pleasant Rowland, the founder of the American Girl Company, the doll maker which Mattel just had acquired. "The women were outspoken and the men were conservative," Rich said. "Most of the other directors were CEOs and/or financiers from the east coast. When Barad was terminated and Rowland left, I was the only woman. The new CEO was committed to recruiting more women board members, so now we have Cathy White and Fran Fergusson."

Rich acknowledged that at one time it took extra effort to find qualified women to serve on boards. "While serving on Mattel's nominating committee, I observed how committee members would typically recommend and recruit other businessmen they respected and with whom they had worked. The typical new recruit was someone who was friendly with, or connected to, existing members of the board and/or management. They usually turned out to be terrific board members. Finding and recruiting women candidates was a much more difficult challenge. There was no obvious reservoir of qualified women known to members of the committee, board, nor management. We had to proactively find women candidates."

Her nominating committee experience was eye-opening, Rich noted, especially when it came to trying to find potential directors among C-suite executives. "I found it's harder to recruit women to boards who held very high executive positions, since as female mentors, they are already called upon for duties beyond their positions," Rich explained. "Their time is in great demand. Often, their own companies don't want them to serve on outside boards for fear of diverting their attention from company business. The nominating committee also had an aversion to recruiting people who serve on too many boards and appear to be 'professional' board members—in other words, making a living on boards."

After Rich retired from LACMA, she was recruited to a new bank board. The founders were mostly lawyers, so the federal/state regulators told them they needed to have independent board members with considerable management and operational experience as well as roots and influence in the community to be served by the bank. The acting chairman of the new bank had been head of a foundation that funded many programs at LACMA. "He called out of the blue to ask if I would be interested," Rich recalled. "As it turned out, I was to be the only board member of the bank who had served on another public board. As a result, I helped the board members understand governance requirements—how to do compensation and performance reviews, and how board members should relate to management by focusing on policy and advice as opposed to micromanagement. Directors need to respect management's hierarchy of authority and follow appropriate communication channels when dealing with company personnel."

Rich added, "One of the things I believe is especially important for women— and men—is the reputation you have as a constructive member of a team. If you have a reputation for being difficult to get along with, prone to grandstanding or self-serving, or having your own agenda, it is unlikely you will be viewed as a desirable recruit for a board member position. Boards are not looking for superstars, but for experienced and accomplished professionals who play well within a team setting."

Author's Note:

Sadly, in the Summer of 2014, Andrea Rich passed away. In addition to being highly respected by her peers around the world, Andrea was a shining role model for women in business, education and art. Her impact will not be forgotten.

GO IMMEDIATELY

TO

Chapter 9
Pathways for CEOs
and Entrepreneurs

PATHWAYS
9 for CEOs

and Entrepreneurs

CHIEF EXECUTIVE OFFICERS ARE THE MOST SOUGHT-AFTER CANDIDATES FOR CORPORATE BOARDS. NOMINATING COMMITTEES TRADITIONALLY HAVE WANTED SEASONED CEOs who, because of their firsthand experience, know how to advise the CEO of a public corporation. Unfortunately, there are only twenty-one women CEOs of Fortune 500 companies, and most of them already serve on several boards in addition to those of their own companies. So boards that want to attract women will have to reach deeper into the C-suite for candidates, and expand the experience qualifications, because there are not enough women CEOs to go around.

Being a woman business owner historically has not been an ideal pathway to becoming a corporate director. Corporate boards are looking for candidates who have managed large complex organizations, multi-million-dollar P&Ls, and thousands of employees. Boards want directors who already understand what it means to be held accountable to shareholders. However, every large business started small. As the number of women business owners continues to increase, with more women-owned companies growing revenues and providing jobs, women entrepreneurs bring valuable experience to corporations. Especially when a corporation's prime customers are small-business owners, companies benefit from having the fresh and experienced-based perspectives of women business owners on their boards. The women entrepreneurs profiled in this chapter operated enterprises that started small and propelled them into circles of influence.

As of 2012, there were an estimated 8.3 million women-owned businesses in the United States, generating nearly $1.3 trillion in revenues and employing 7.7 million people, according to an American Express OPEN report on women-owned businesses. Entrepreneurs who show successful track records of growth and job creation are paving a new pathway toward future board membership.

From my own experience as a business owner, active in the National Association of Women Business Owners (NAWBO), I have watched women nurture and expand their companies from small private start-ups to very large companies. When a woman's own company expands, she has gained valuable experience that is necessary information for corporations—from building an enterprise, to expanding markets and engaging employees and vendors. And if the company goes public and the owner remains on the board of the newly public company, that board experience can lead to serving on even larger public boards, especially if the company is acquired by a large corporation.

The visibility and community presence that a small-business owner develops by growing her own company fulfills another significant requirement of the ideal board profile. Board experience gained from serving large nonprofit organizations, or private companies, is equally important. Often entrepreneurs are sought out by mayors, state legislators or members of Congress because of their leadership in the small business community for appointments to public advisory boards or commissions. Those credentials build visibility and networks of influential people for the business owner.

Linda Alvarado, owner of Alvarado Construction Company, based in Denver, is the first corporate board member I have known who was actually brought onto the board of a corporation precisely *because* she was an authentic small business owner. Pitney Bowes wanted to find a business owner for its board who would understand and reflect the target customer profile of Pitney Bowes. The corporation wanted the benefit of her insights as an entrepreneur and a business-builder.

More corporations are beginning to see the wisdom of having a business owner on board who understands small business customers, and the trend should escalate from here. Of course, Alvarado's construction company has grown very large—she builds major infrastructure and commercial buildings—throughout the U.S. and in other countries. Alvarado is an entrepreneur whose story may help diffuse this longstanding bias toward preferring only CEOs from large public companies on public boards.

Henrietta Holsman Fore and Linda Griego are successful women entrepreneurs who became highly visible through their government and civic involvements. Both were entrepreneurs first, but became well-known through their appointed roles or nonprofit boards before they were invited to corporate board membership.

In 2012, an American Express OPEN-commissioned study, "The State of Women-Owned Businesses Report," revealed that from 1997 to 2012, the number of women-owned business enterprises increased by 54%. This could mean that the women CEOs of the largest women-owned companies will be ready for corporate board service over these next few years, as current baby-boomer generation board members reach age seventy-two, which some boards have defined as the age for retirement.

- There are about ten million women-owned companies in the nation. California has 1.3 million women business owners—more than any other state.
- Metropolitan areas with the most women-owned businesses are Los Angeles, New York, Chicago, Miami, and Washington, D.C.
- 1.9 million firms in the U.S. are owned by women of color. (Source: Center for Women's Business Research.)

The American Express OPEN report says, "Women-owned companies are appearing in all industry sectors—with the highest concentration in health care and social assistance, educational services, and administrative and employment services." Not surprisingly, industries with the lowest concentration of women-owned firms are construction (just 8%) and finance/insurance. However, the report illustrates that women-owned firms are indeed staking a claim in all sectors of the U.S. economy.

According to this trend, there will be more women business owners whose companies have grown large, and perhaps been acquired, who will be poised for serving on corporate boards in years to come.

We start with a sister act—the first sister CEOs in American business history who concurrently run two major corporations: Denise Sullivan Morrison, CEO of

Campbell Soup Company, and Maggie Sullivan Wilderotter, CEO of Frontier Communications.

DENISE M. MORRISON

Denise Morrison has been the CEO of Campbell Soup Company since 2011. She knows the food industry inside-out, having spent her career at Procter & Gamble, PepsiCo, Nestle USA, Nabisco, Inc., Kraft Foods and now, she leads Campbell Soup.

DENISE M. MORRISON
Princeton, New Jersey

Current Boards/Select Nonprofits:
Campbell Soup Company
Grocery Manufacturers Association
Healthy Weight Commitment Foundation
Catalyst Inc.

Past Boards:
The Goodyear Tire & Rubber Company
Ballard Power Systems, Inc.

Career History:
Campbell Soup Company: President and CEO (current); EVP
    and COO; SVP and President-North America Soup, Sauces,
    and Beverages; President-Campbell USA; President-Global
    Sales and Chief Customer Officer
Kraft Foods: EVP and GM, Snacks and Confections
Nabisco Inc.: SVP and GM, Nabisco Down The Street Division
Nestlé USA: VP, Sales

Education:
BS, Economics and Psychology, Boston College

When she was general manager at Kraft Foods, Morrison wanted to find her first corporate board opportunity, and she felt she had developed the experience required. But according to Morrison, "I pounded the pavement visiting with recruiters in New York City trying to get on a board. I was told that I didn't fit the profile, and 'You can't be on a board unless you are a sitting CEO.' Since there were only four women CEOs at that time, I thought they would be pretty busy sitting on all those boards!"

Morrison is the first of the four "Sullivan Sisters," all business executives, who were featured in a *Wall Street Journal* story a few years ago called "Raising Women to be Leaders." Her other sisters Colleen Bastkowski and Andrea Doelling have held senior executive positions at Expedia Corporate Travel and AT&T Wireless. Maggie Wilderotter's story follows in this chapter.

Their father, Dennis Sullivan, was CFO of Cincinnati Bell and their mother, Connie, was in real estate. "The conversations around our dinner table were about profit margins and test marketing, not about school gossip," says Morrison. Connie modeled for her daughters that ambition was a part of femininity.

In true first-born sibling fashion, Morrison made a gutsy move in 1995. As vice president of marketing and sales for Nestle USA, she was asked to relocate from California to Cleveland due to a reorganization. Not wanting to move her daughter in her senior year of high school, she initiated an exploratory meeting with Doug Conant, then the president of Nabisco. They met for coffee in a Palm Springs diner amidst vacationers and retirees. "I recognized her immediately," Conant recalls. "She was the only person with a Day-Timer open on the table. It was a fateful meeting—the beginning of a fifteen-year business relationship."

Conant hired Morrison at Nabisco, where she was responsible for the innovative idea of packaging crackers and cookies together in a single serving. After he became CEO of Campbell Soup Company, he hired Morrison as president of global sales and chief customer officer in 2003. Eight years later, she succeeded him as CEO of Campbell Soup.

"I was very fortunate in having a sponsor—someone who has position and influence in the company, sees something in you, and opens doors," Morrison says. "But you can't force that. Those relationships grow over time from strategically putting yourself in a visible position." Echoing the importance of sponsorship, Catalyst President Ilene Lang, says she believes that advancing to the board level for women often requires having not just a mentor, but a sponsor in her own company. Lang mentions Conant specifically in this role.

Campbell Soup Company has five women on the board, including Morrison, reflecting the general population of its customers, eighty percent of whom are women. Four family members of the founder of the company are also directors. Morrison served on two outside corporate boards before being named CEO at Campbell Soup—the Goodyear Tire & Rubber Company and Ballard Power Systems, Inc. Recommendations to both boards came through her business contacts.

A founder of the Healthy Weight Commitment Foundation, Morrison is an industry leader in this initiative of manufacturers and retailers to combat obesity in the marketplace, the workplace, and schools through communication and education. She also chairs the Health & Wellness Committee of the Grocery Manufacturers Association.

In discussing leadership, Morrison says that Conant advised her at Nabisco to take time to build relationships and get to know people as people. "This was a moment of enlightenment—that leadership is about influencing and inspiring people," says Morrison. "Results may be the rite of passage in business, but building relationships gets you the rest of the way." Morrison is regularly listed among *Fortune* and *Forbes* Most Powerful Women.

MAGGIE WILDEROTTER

Maggie Wilderotter is chairman and CEO of Frontier Communications, a five billion dollar, Fortune 500 and S&P 500 company. She also sits on the boards of two other public companies: Xerox and Procter & Gamble. During her career, she has served on numerous corporate boards and was the first woman to sit on Yahoo!'s board of directors.

Wilderotter says her first "real" job was at CableData (now DST), a vendor to the cable television industry that merged communications, information technology, and media. By age twenty-eight, she was a vice president of this management, information systems, and billing company. Even then, she appreciated the value of networking and decided to join the governing body of the National Cable Television Association (NCTA). After being rebuffed the first time, Wilderotter was undeterred. She studied the organization's bylaws and discovered two seats were set aside for vendors. She called all two thousand vendors and asked them to vote their proxies for her. She made it. Being on that board was an ideal way to interact with customers and key CEOs in the cable industry, she explains.

MAGGIE WILDEROTTER
Nevada

Current Boards:
Frontier Communications
Xerox
Procter & Gamble Company

Past Boards:
Yahoo!
The McClatchy Company
Airborne, Inc.
Wink Communications, Inc.
Catalyst Inc.
Jacor Communications Company

Career History:
Frontier Communications (formerly Citizens Communications):
    Chair and CEO (current)
Microsoft: SVP, Worldwide Public Sector
Wink Communications (acquired by Liberty Media):
    President and CEO
Claircom (AT&T Aviation Communications Subsidiary): CEO
AT&T Wireless Services, Inc.: EVP of National Operations
McCaw Cellular (now AT&T Wireless): SVP
CableData (now DST): EVP and GM

Education:
BA, Economics, College of the Holy Cross

Wilderotter has since won NCTA's highest award—twice. Glenn Britt, now chairman and CEO of Time Warner Cable and a former director on the NCTA board with her, recommended Wilderotter to Anne Mulcahy, then chairman and CEO of Xerox, as a potential board member. Wilderotter has been on the Xerox board of directors since 2006.

Wilderotter was among the first women to be admitted to a previously all-male college. She entered Holy Cross in Worcester, Massachusetts, soon after the Jesuit school opened its doors to women. She says she was not at all intimidated. "I believed women could add value, and besides the male/female ratio was great for our social lives."

An avid sports fan, she became a sports announcer for the college radio station and toyed with the idea of radio as a career. Learning the work meant long hours for relatively little pay, she instead followed an entrepreneurial route. That brought her to CableData where, during her twelve-year tenure, she ran its U.S., Canadian, and European operations.

Her view of leadership was learned from her parents and buttressed by her Jesuit education. "You have to be value-centered," she explains. "You have to know that what you are doing is the right thing."

Wilderotter is one of the "Sullivan Sisters" (her sister Denise is profiled here as well) and was twice featured on the *Today* show. The four sisters were schooled in business at the dinner table by their father, an executive with AT&T, and their mother, a homemaker and top real estate salesperson in New Jersey.

Wilderotter worked at AT&T's Aviation Communications Division after it purchased McCaw Cellular Communications, where she had been a senior vice president. She later served as executive vice president of national operations for AT&T Wireless Services, Inc.

Her desire to run a company was strong, so Wilderotter left AT&T to become president and CEO of Wink Communications, Inc. After its purchase by Liberty Media, she went to Microsoft as senior vice president of worldwide public sectors and worldwide business strategy. Her job was strengthening customer and partner outreach in the government and education markets and working across business divisions to develop and coordinate forward-looking strategies. In 2004, she accepted the offer to lead Frontier Communications.

She confesses that professional success sometimes takes priority over family—"A lot of people don't want to say that, but it's true." The mother of two now-adult sons, she says she couldn't have done her job without her husband's unwavering support. Her husband Jay retired from the U.S. Air Force and took charge of the family front while running the family business, Wilderotter Vineyards.

In a *Wall Street Journal* article about female CEOs, Wilderotter had some advice for women in their jobs and in the boardroom: "Speak up—women have to take responsibility for the dynamics around them. You can't just say 'woe is me'."

About mentors, she says, "I picked the brains of a lot of senior executives. I had many mentors, but they didn't always know it!"

In October, 2012, Wilderotter was designated chair of the President's National Security Telecommunications Advisory Committee, following her service as vice chair since 2010. Why take this on, too? "Trying new things is in my DNA."

GERALDINE B. LAYBOURNE

Gerry Laybourne is "one of the foremost figures in cable-TV programming, as well as one of the most influential people in the television Industry," according to a profile in the magazine of the Museum of Broadcast Communications. Note that she is not referred to as one of the most influential *women* in the television industry. That's because she built Nickelodeon into a profitable and acclaimed source of children's programming that, when she left, had 56% of the kids-television viewing audience. She made a big business out of a category that others found unpromising.

GERALDINE B. LAYBOURNE
New York

Current Boards:
J.C. Penney Company, Inc.
Symantec

Past Boards:
Electronic Arts Inc.
Move, Inc.
Insight Communications Company, Inc.
KinderCare, Inc.

Career History:
Alloy Media + Marketing.: Chairwoman (current)
Oxygen Media: Chairman and CEO
Disney/ABC Cable Networks: President
Nickelodeon: President and Vice Chairman of MTV Networks

Education:
MS, Elementary Education, University of Pennsylvania
BA, Art History, Vassar College

Although she completed an art history major in college, followed by a graduate degree in education, Laybourne got excellent business training early in life. At age nine, she was accompanying her stockbroker father on business calls. He made her memorize all the symbols on the NYSE and know what companies they stood for. She managed his office when she was only sixteen.

Laybourne developed her keen instinct for a winner—the very instinct that told her she could turn the TV backwater of children's programming into a multimillion dollar success—when she was advising her father on those early business trips. Even though she was young, she had enough natural intuition about people that she could tell her father "Don't trust this guy" when she felt a person was not being truthful, or the business proposition didn't sound right. "He didn't always follow my advice—after all I was just a kid—but I turned out to be right more often than not," she says with a smile. "And that intuition has served me well throughout my career—in corporations as well as on corporate boards."

After college and graduate school, Laybourne taught school for a short time until she became an accidental entrepreneur in the television business. She and her husband started their own television production company, and she did research into what children really wanted to see on TV. The first client for their production company was Nickelodeon, a fledgling non-commercial children's programmer designed to improve the overall image of the cable television industry. Nickelodeon soon hired Laybourne full-time to work inside the young corporation. "In the early days, Nickelodeon was on no one's radar. No one in the industry wanted my job. We had no money, only ideas." So the girl with that instinct for a winner was in on the ground floor of the cable industry in 1980.

Nickelodeon was subsequently sold to Viacom, and Laybourne was named president while still in her forties. Viacom executive Frank Biondi suggested she go on the board of a bank, but Laybourne declined. She didn't see how her skills would translate to banking. She agreed that the next time a board opportunity came along, she would take it. This time it was KinderCare, a company owned by Viacom that involved children. The CEO of KinderCare invited her onto the board because he wanted to make big changes, and he knew of Laybourne's reputation for being outspoken.

"It was a great experience—even though the company endured sending its founder to prison, having multiple presidents, and going through bankruptcy," recalls Laybourne. "I met a lot of smart people on that board. Jack Greenberg, CEO of McDonald's, was a board member and a fabulous mentor to me."

In 1996, when she left Nickelodeon, she was recruited by Disney to be president of Disney/ABC Cable Networks. Since Disney does not allow its executives to sit on corporate boards, she resigned from the board of KinderCare. Laybourne left Disney in 1998 to form Oxygen, a multimedia content provider of programs for women, along with Oprah Winfrey and Marcy Carsey, the award-winning TV producer. She wanted to do something different, something with women for women, and she was surprised "how easy it was to raise money."

The founding of Oxygen was a result of "having a vision, and executing it," which is just what she did at Nickelodeon. She says that's her key to success. NBC Universal acquired Oxygen in 2007. During her tenure at Oxygen, she was recommended to the board of a company called Move Inc., as an independent director by the institutional investor pension fund CalSTRS, which had sued Move Inc. in a class action lawsuit. This might have been a difficult position for many board members to find themselves in, but for Laybourne, who loved real estate, it was a very good experience.

A fellow board member recommended Laybourne to John Tompkins, the CEO of Symantec in Northern California. The company was interested in marketing technology to women and was looking for a woman board candidate who knew marketing and had an interest in the technology industry. At Symantec, Laybourne is the only woman on the board. The board has brought on only one new member since Laybourne was appointed—a CEO, who, in fact, later replaced the sitting CEO. She also sits on the board of J.C. Penney Company, where she is one of three women.

Laybourne doesn't get deterred by the fact that there are so few women CEOs in Fortune 500 to fill the seats on America's boards—indeed, she doesn't believe it's necessarily true that CEOs make the best board members. "Lots of CEOs are not financial wizards—look at me!" she says. "What CEOs have to offer is success in building a company. But there are other skills that boards need as well, including human resources. 'Compensation' has become the new 'Audit'—in terms of committee challenges and requirements.

"Companies understand that they must have diversity, especially young people who understand modern forms of communication and technology. A career in digital technology is a good pathway for women today to get on the track to become CEOs and board members. Look at Marissa Mayer, now CEO of Yahoo!."

Laybourne says she believes that there was a period of time, before the collapse of Enron, when women, who were the right age with the required executive experience, were eager to serve on corporate boards. But when the Enron scandal happened, she said, that "chilled the momentum."

Currently she chairs Off The Sidelines, the branding initiative of New York Senator Kirsten Gillibrand. This effort encourages women to go into politics, into government, into sports and onto corporate boards. Its slogan is "When more women stand up to play, America wins." That was proved by the many gold medals won by U.S. women athletes in the 2012 Summer Olympics that propelled the U.S. to the top of the medal count. And it was further proved by the record number of women elected to Congress in 2012, increasing female representation in the Senate and House of Representatives tenfold since 1992. One day soon, when the number of women increases similarly in the nation's business leadership, America will truly be at the top of its game..

Laybourne's advice to women before interviews with search firms or board recruiters, "Put out a positive message about yourself." Laybourne urges women who are seeking directorships to create one page of talking points about their strengths as a potential board member. "That's what I did, and it worked," she explains. "Don't be shy. Speak out about your successes. Research shows that women do as well as men on just about everything *except* putting ourselves forward." She says that women are the fastest growing category of new board members. "But women have to be in charge of recruiting if we want to have lots more women on boards."

A great champion of women, Laybourne asserts: "Every move I make is to advance women."

LINDA G. ALVARADO

Linda Alvarado, CEO and owner of Alvarado Construction Inc. headquartered in Denver, sits on the boards of 3M and Pitney Bowes, and previously served on six others: Pepsi-Cola Bottling Group, Lennox, Qwest Communications, Engelhard Corp., Cyprus Amax Minerals Co., and United Banks of Colorado, later acquired by Norwest (now Wells Fargo).

LINDA G. ALVARADO
Denver, Colorado

Current Boards:
3M Corporation
Pitney Bowes

Past Boards/Select Nonprofits:
Pepsi Bottling Group
Lennox International
Qwest Communications
Engelhard Corp.
Cyprus Amax Minerals Co.
United Banks of Colorado
United Banks of Denver
United Bank of Littleton, Colorado

Career History:
Alvarado Construction, Inc.: President and CEO (current)
Colorado Rockies (Major League Baseball): Co-owner
Martinez Alvarado Construction Management Corp.: Founder and CEO

Education:
Pomona College, Economics

Truly a woman of many "firsts," she was the first woman and the first Latino owner (male or female) in Major League Baseball history who actually cofounded a franchise, along with seven men co-owner/investors, and she remains the only woman owner of a Major League Baseball team today. She didn't inherit nor marry into team ownership—she put her own savings and her own reputation on the line to start the Colorado Rockies in Denver in 1992.

A native of Albuquerque, New Mexico, Alvarado has been an entrepreneur throughout her career. She started her company in 1976, and today Alvarado Construction is a multimillion dollar commercial general contractor, construction management and development company with offices in several states. Her company builds commercial, retail, office, government, industrial, institutional, heavy engineering, technology, medical health facilities, and sports venues throughout the U.S. and internationally. In fact, Alvarado's company built the NFL Denver Broncos' Mile-High Stadium, next door to the old stadium, which remained in operation until the new one opened. Then she demolished the old one.

"It helps to have grown up as the only girl in a family with five brothers—I was surrounded by lots of sports, academics, and church," she posits. "Culturally, Latinas did not play sports, so I'm not sure how I went down this career path, because my parents were not entrepreneurs." Cultural stereotypes didn't get in Alvarado's way, however. "Obviously I am quite comfortable in male-dominated environments," she laughs. "You don't have to be a man to get along well with men, but having sports knowledge does come in handy. Men are impressed by a woman who reads the *Wall Street Journal*, but they are *really* impressed when they meet a woman who reads the sports page. When you talk about sports, you talk about strategies for winning, using terms that men understand. Getting into the big leagues of serving on boards, we women have to be over-prepared, add value to the discussions, bring aptitude and attitude, *and* speak their language."

Alvarado got into construction during summers when she was at Pomona College in Claremont, California, by working as a sub-contracts administrator on construction sites. "Quite frankly, that was the determining factor to my becoming a contractor—it was exciting, but also radical and naive on my part—because women were simply not on construction sites in those days," she recalls.

"But I learned early that construction is not just about brawn; it's really about brains. Early in my career as a woman in this non-traditional role, people would question my capability, credibility, character and cash flow." She started her construction company in California, then got married, moved to Colorado, and restarted there.

Alvarado proved her credibility initially by getting involved on nonprofit boards, in industry and construction trade associations, and in her community. She was the only woman founding member of the Denver Hispanic Chamber. She also served on the Downtown Denver Partnership, the Tennyson Center for Abused Children, and the Colorado Women's Forum, a group of women from corporations, nonprofits and entrepreneurs that advocates for advancing women in business, and of course, onto boards of directors.

"The turning point was serving on the Boy Scouts of Denver board, where most of the other board members were men who were CEOs of the state's largest companies," Alvarado explains. "Conversation was always about business, state of the economy, banking, and of course, sports." She was introduced to her first board by a fellow Boy Scouts board member—it was a small publicly owned bank—United Bank of Littleton, Colorado. That small bank was under the holding company of United Banks of Colorado, and Alvarado graduated to that larger board. "I advise women to get started on boards of smaller public companies that have a chance to be acquired by bigger companies, so you can move up as opportunities arise," she offers.

Alvarado joined her next public board after being noticed as a speaker at a construction industry conference. "The stereotype of a woman contractor was 'big and brawny,'" she recalls. "But I started when I was only twenty-seven years old, and looked more like a secretary than a construction company owner. No one had ever seen a young woman in construction. There were no affirmative action programs then. So I did speaking engagements to prove my credibility."

At the conference, she met the chair of the board of Lennox International Inc., a leading manufacturer of heating, venting, and air conditioning equipment. Just two weeks later, he asked her to serve on the board, which was still family-held and controlled, but in growth mode. He was the first non-family chair of that board, and wanted another external perspective. Lennox had never had a contractor on its board, someone who knew about working with unions, pricing of products, service expertise, and more. She stayed on the board from 1989 to 2010, a period which included taking the company public in 2000. She stepped down after more than two decades to move onto other boards. The company honored her for years of service by endowing an engineering scholarship for college women in her name.

Speaking at a Catalyst event in New York, Alvarado met George Harvey, then chairman of Pitney Bowes. He called her a few weeks later. Although she thought he was trying to sell her postage meters, instead, he invited her onto his board. Pitney Bowes was ahead of its time with two women directors already seated. The board was looking for a business-owner, a successful entrepreneur, who would bring the perspective of business owners who buy their services. Pitney Bowes wanted to expand its brand and distribution into mail-processing services for corporations and for the U.S. Postal Service. The board needed someone with business acumen to look at the business models differently. Alvarado brought a fresh perspective to the board as the only director from west of the Hudson River.

What's the story behind starting the baseball team? Alvarado received a call from Colorado Governor Roy Romer, who wanted to put together a group of investors to acquire a baseball franchise for Denver. Alvarado was the only woman. "There was no requirement to have a woman investor—they wanted a credible business person with an entrepreneurial spirit and track record who was willing to take a calculated risk," she explains. She had met all of the other investors previously through business and civic involvement—including Peter Coors, whom she knew because he hired her company for construction services at Coors Brewery. Together, competing against five other cities, they launched their bid to Major League Baseball for an expansion team.

"This was indeed high risk—to convince MLB that we could produce enough profits for revenue-sharing with the other teams," she reflects. "I had to write a huge deposit check, knowing it could be totally gone if we lost the bid. But we won. And the redevelopment of abandoned areas in downtown Denver has been a major benefit of our bringing the team here. Not only am I proud of what we've done for Denver, I'm also an example that women are—and should be—team players involved at the highest levels, who can make a difference like this."

LARRAINE SEGIL

Larraine Segil was born in South Africa and came to the U.S. in 1974, qualifying as a lawyer, but soon went into business, building several companies. She co-founded a thrift-and-loan company, and a series of freestanding medical clinics. Following those endeavors, a business school friend approached her with the opportunity to turnaround a distributor providing products and services to aerospace and electronics companies.

LARRAINE SEGIL
Los Angeles

Current Boards:
Frontier Communications

Past Boards/Select Nonprofits:
World Health Organization, Tropical Diseases
Strategic Alliances Board, Geneva
Vantage Partners, LLC
Association of Strategic Alliance Professionals, Inc.
LARTA Institute (Technology Commercialization and
Entrepreneurship)

Career History:
Little Farm Company: CEO (current)
Rockin' Grandma Music: Founder (current)
Committee of 200: Chair of Foundation and Vice Chair
of Governing Board (current)
Larraine Segil Inc.: CEO (current)
Vantage Partners LLC: Partner
The Lared Group: Partner

Education:
JD, Southwestern University
MBA, Pepperdine University
BA, Latin Classics and English, University of the
Witwatersrand (South Africa)

As a supplier to the aerospace industry, Segil was asked to join the board of SoCalTEN, an organization of CEOs, very few of whom were women. SoCalTEN was formed as a network of chief executives to exchange information and resources across tech industries. Segil also joined the private board of one of the electronic companies in the network, having previously served on the board of the financial services company she co-founded.

When she sold the aerospace distribution company, Segil cofounded The Lared Group, a consulting company focused on advising companies in multiple industries on their critical business relationships and strategic alliances. This company was later purchased by Vantage Partners, LLC. As a partner and board member of Vantage, Segil consulted with the Global 100 and Fortune 500 companies. She did not serve on another board for twenty-five years, because of potential conflicts of interest with her consulting clients.

Segil joined the Committee of 200, an executive women's network, where she met Maggie Wilderotter, then the most senior woman executive at Microsoft, who engaged Segil and her consulting firm to provide services. Within a year after Wilderotter became CEO of Citizens Communications, Segil joined her board of directors. Over the next eight years, led by Wilderotter, the board was transformed to become one of the most diverse public company boards first on NYSE and then on NASDAQ.

Citizens Communications changed its name to Frontier Communications and bought Verizon's rural assets to become a $5 billion company. Segil serves on the Compensation and Nominating/Governance Committees.

Segil is an author of seven books and a keynote speaker on the benefits of establishing strategic alliances in business. For twenty-four years, she taught an executive education course on strategic alliances at Caltech in Pasadena, California, and is recognized widely as a global-thought leader.

"Board nominations are all about whom you know and who knows you, unless you are an operating CEO in a public company," she opines. "Someone on the board has to be willing to nominate you and lobby other board members on your behalf." She advises women to get P&L experience in either a private or public company, and network strategically "to meet people who can recommend you."

JULIE A. HILL

Julie Hill is a CEO and entrepreneur who has held leadership positions in the real estate development and housing construction industries in the U.S., Australia, and the U.K. Proving her high school counselors wrong, she found her career pathway in these male-dominated fields.

JULIE A. HILL
Newport Beach, California

Current Boards:
WellPoint, Inc.
The Lord Abbett Family of Mutual Funds

Past Boards:
Lend Lease Corporation Ltd.
Holcim (US) Inc.
Resource Connection, Inc.
Costain Homes Inc.

Career History:
The Hill Company: Owner (current)
Hiram-Hill Development Company: Founder, CEO and Owner
Costain Homes Inc.: Chairman, President, and CEO
Mobil Land Development Corp.: VP and General Manager

Education:
MA, Marketing and Management, University of Georgia
BA, English, UCLA

Hill's first public board was WellPoint/Blue Cross of California where she was the first woman. She continued on that board when WellPoint merged with Anthem in 2004 to become the nation's leading health benefits company. She also serves on the board of the New York-based Lord Abbett Family of Funds (the oldest mutual fund group in U.S. with $100 billion under management), and she recently stepped down from the Lend Lease board in Australia.

All this, despite advice from a high school counselor, who told her, "Pretty little girls shouldn't go into business." Hill says, "That was the conventional wisdom in 1964—but it took me a while to figure out it was wrong." The classic example of brains and beauty, this high school valedictorian was elected Mardi Gras queen in her junior year and homecoming queen during her senior year at UCLA.

After graduation from UCLA, she dutifully became an English teacher for two years, an "appropriate career for a woman." Hill says she admires teachers and the hard work they do, but she wanted to pursue a career in business instead. So, to earn her master's degree in marketing and management, she enrolled at the University of Georgia in 1975, and found her calling through her first entrepreneurial effort in Atlanta.

The housing market there was on a downhill slide, but Hill saw a marketing opportunity. Banks were trying to unload houses but had no marketing plans, while developers were building three-story townhouses for empty-nesters, who preferred single-level homes. So Hill launched a real estate research and marketing firm to help banks reach target buyers. She says this was not rocket science, but market segmentation was new to the housing industry.

She moved back to California to raise her son near her family, and was hired by one of the home builders with the Irvine Company, which was master-planning a development of 100,000 acres. Her marketing savvy was sought by developers who faced new guidelines and challenges working within the limitations of a master plan.

Hill was lured back to Atlanta by Mobil Oil's Land Development Division that focused on planned communities. Throughout her career in home building, she has been active in her industry trade associations—which she advises all women to do for visibility. She was named "National Marketing Professional of the Year" by the National Association of Home Builders. Her high profile as a woman executive in the industry attracted the attention of the global CEO of Costain, a London-based international company, one of the builders of the England-to-France Channel Tunnel ("The Chunnel") and the Hong Kong Airport.

He recruited her to be one of four senior vice presidents of the U.S. division—the only women above the level of bookkeeper in the entire international company. Not much time passed before he promoted her to CEO of the U.S. division. "It was the first time ever for Costain to have a woman CEO—very rare for the Brits," she notes.

In 1998, she was urged to start her own business—The Hill Company—by an entrepreneurial benefactor, who offered to invest a million dollars, with no strings attached. "I paid him back within two years," she says. "I was able to get started thanks to his generosity and confidence in me."

Hill has served as chair of several private, public, academic, and nonprofit boards, including the CEO Roundtable of UC Irvine. Her networks and visibility helped establish her reputation as an effective leader.

"I have a bias toward action," Hill admits. "If you are going to be the boss, you have to be ready to shoot from the hip when necessary, to make decisions even if you don't have perfect information. You can't always second-guess yourself and wait for the perfect data set. You have to be able to rely on your instincts when pressed. I think sometimes women have a problem with this. I knew nothing about health insurance when I joined Blue Cross, but the CEO wanted my operations experience. I wanted to learn about the health-care industry, and he wanted to add a woman to his board. I met Leonard Schaeffer over a lunch that turned into a several-hour conversation."

That WellPoint introduction came through her executive women's networks. She was approached by Jane Hurd, then a partner at Korn/Ferry executive search. Both belonged to the International Women's Forum, a global membership group of accomplished women. Known for her sense of humor, Hill came across a magazine ad where she had years before posed as a secretary seated at a desk, holding a Blue Cross insurance card. She put the ad in a picture frame with the caption, "Yes, and someday I will be on the board of this company. Leonard displayed it on the WellPoint boardroom for years."

"Being the first woman on the WellPoint board created a significant difference in the topics the board talked about," Hill recalls. "There was a discussion early on about whether women's mammograms should be covered—for me as a woman director, that was a no-brainer."

Hill has become an agent for change, even on boards where she has been the only woman. As chair of the WellPoint Nominating Committee, three years after joining the board, Hill recruited Betsy Sanders (also interviewed for this book). Five years later, they brought on a third woman. "Women should be well-represented on boards of all companies—especially in the health care industry," she says.

Hill was recommended to the board of the Lord Abbett Family of Funds by William Bush, who was then a fellow WellPoint board member. Given her advocacy for women, Hill was amused by the irony of playing golf with other Lord Abbett directors at the storied Augusta National Golf Club when that all-male bastion in Georgia did not allow women. In 2012, they invited two women to become members—former U.S. Secretary of State Condoleezza Rice and businesswoman Darla Moore from South Carolina, who had been the first woman on the cover of *Fortune*.

Hill became the lone woman director on the Lend Lease board in Australia, introduced by a global executive search firm, Egon Zehnder, because of her industry experience. She was motivated and wanted to join the Lend Lease board because it was a large, diversified, and international firm in her industry, "despite its being a serious old boys' network," she said. Hill says she stays in close touch with her contacts developed over the years at executive search firms, and recommends that women seeking board positions do the same.

"Lend Lease had thirty senior managers, only one of whom was a woman— and she was paid substantially less money than her male counterparts," Hill says. "Needless to say, I objected to unequal pay for women and insisted on parity for her and future women employees. As a result, the chairman of the board was not happy with me, but it had to be done. And it took a woman director to be outraged enough to bring up the issue."

Hill explains, "I have always worked as hard as I possibly could—I was always over-prepared. My advice to other women is, always say "yes" at the door of an opportunity, despite any doubts and against all odds. Take a chance and seize the moment."

JAYNIE MILLER STUDENMUND

Jaynie Studenmund, on the boards of Western Asset Management, Orbitz, Pinnacle Entertainment, CoreLogic and Forest Lawn, began her career in financial services and then became a pioneer in the Internet.

"Having financial skills is important for board members, all of whom need to understand financial statements," she says. "But operations experience, with a successful P&L record, is invaluable."

JAYNIE MILLER STUDENMUND
Pasadena, California

Current Boards/Select Nonprofits:
Pinnacle Entertainment
CoreLogic
Orbitz Worldwide, Inc.
Western Asset Management
Forest Lawn Memorial Parks
Huntington Hospital
Flintridge Preparatory School

Past Boards:
MarketTools
eHarmony
aQuantive
Countrywide Bank

Career History:
Overture Services, Inc.: COO (retired)
PayMyBills.com: President and COO
Home Savings of America (now JPMorgan Chase): EVP, Head of Retail Banking
Great Western (now JP Morgan/Chase): EVP, Head of Retail Banking
First Interstate Bank of California (now Wells Fargo): EVP, Head of Retail Banking
Booz Allen Hamilton: Management Consultant

Education:
MBA, Harvard Business School
BA, Economics, Wellesley College

Studenmund is an example of the added value that high-tech experience can bring to today's corporate boards. After fifteen years in financial services, she shifted into the emerging Internet world in 2000, as president and COO of PayMyBills, an online bill-management company.

Next came Overture, the California-based company that pioneered paid search results, a concept which resulted in an industry that now generates more than $15 billion in revenue. As the chief operating officer, Studenmund helped grow Overture from a $100 million to a $1.2 billion company in three years—a successful growth record, to say the least. The company was acquired by Yahoo! in 2003 for $1.63 billion.

"I was very fortunate to have C-level jobs, including key line positions, at several corporations at a young age, and I was even luckier to be in the forefront of the Internet," acknowledges Studenmund, who is the daughter of former U.S. Senator Jack Miller of Iowa. She grew up in Iowa and Washington, D.C..

Her first board was a bank holding company started by her former boss at First Interstate Bank where she had been chief marketing officer and EVP of retail banking. He also knew her through her nonprofit work in the community. Another early board was for a number of funds managed by Western Asset, which she learned about from another former boss at First Interstate. "In both cases, I had stayed in touch with these incredible men," Studenmund explains. "I had shared with both my interest in someday serving on corporate boards. So when opportunities arose relevant to my experience, both remembered me as a potential candidate."

Studenmund served on the bank holding company board for five years and is still on the Western Asset board. The next opportunity came when Overture was sold to Yahoo!, and she was asked to sit on the board of one of Overture's major business partners, aQuantive, which was purchased by Microsoft in 2007.

She confirms that digital careers are a good pathway to boards. Having been an operations executive in both financial services and Internet companies, she says such a background translates well to board service, even for companies that are not currently involved in e-commerce but need to understand online risks.

In 2012, Jaynie joined the boards of CoreLogic and Pinnacle Entertainment. At Pinnacle, it turns out, she was the second board member to graduate from Wellesley College and Harvard Business School. Although the two women had not met before, "It was an unusual and happy coincidence," Studenmund commented.

When Yahoo! purchased Overture, Studenmund decided that she would put seventy-hour-plus work weeks behind her. She wanted to spend more time with her husband and teenage children. Rather than finding another executive position, she devoted herself to serving her corporate and nonprofit boards.

"Board service allows me to stay very engaged in the corporate world, work on critical issues, and partner with talented people," she says. "I love what I do."

STEPHANIE A. STREETER

Stephanie Streeter is the current CEO of Libbey Inc., the largest glass tableware manufacturer in the western hemisphere, and former board member of the Green Bay Packers and the U.S. Olympic Committee. Her passion for sports has been a key to her visibility and board connections. She serves on two Fortune 500 boards, Kohl's and Goodyear.

STEPHANIE A. STREETER
Toledo, Ohio

Current Boards/Select Nonprofits:
Libbey Corporation
Goodyear Tire and Rubber Company
Kohl's Corporation
Catalyst Inc.

Past Boards:
United States Olympic Committee
Green Bay Packers, Inc.
Banta Corporation
Parker Hannifin Corporation

Career History:
Libbey Corporation: CEO (current)
United States Olympic Committee: Interim CEO
Banta Corporation, Chairman: President and CEO
Idealab: COO
Avery Dennison Corporation: Group VP, Worldwide Office
    Products; VP and GM, Label Division

Education:
BA, Political Science, Stanford University

Serendipity placed her on the cover of *Forbes Magazine* as the woman executive in a business suit dribbling a basketball. Streeter came by both her cover status and basketball by hard work and her love of sports. She was an executive at Avery Dennison Corporation at the young age of forty, and had been a four-year starter on the Stanford varsity women's basketball team. When the *Forbes* photographer was in her office, he saw the basketball on the shelf and suggested a picture of the rising-star woman executive with a basketball would be an eye-catcher. It was a game-changer for Streeter's career.

The *Forbes* cover photo, plus Streeter's operations performance running the largest division of Avery Dennison's Office Products Group, caught the attention of Pat Parker, then-CEO of Parker Hannifin Corporation, a Fortune 500 company in Cleveland, who asked her to join his board in 1996. In 2012, Parker Hannifin is a $13 billion manufacturer of motion-and-control technologies and systems for mobile, industrial, and aerospace markets. The company today employs approximately sixty thousand people in forty-eight countries around the world.

"I ran about an $800 million dollar business at Avery Dennison at the time of the article in *Forbes*," recalls Streeter. "I'll never forget what Pat Parker said to me when I asked him why he would consider me. I said, 'I thought only CEOs were invited to join boards of directors, especially a Fortune 500 company.' He said in good humor, 'The board told me I had to get a girl, and you were the best one I could find.' That was 1996."

After fourteen years at Avery Dennison, where she developed general management and operations expertise, Streeter left to become the COO of Idealab, an Internet incubator "where I thought I would find an idea to start my own company, but it didn't work out that way." She departed the Parker Hannifin board because she didn't think she would have enough time to devote to both. "Frankly, it was a mistake to leave the board, but I didn't think so at the time," she recalls. "I believed I would be so consumed by the work at Idealab that I wouldn't have time to do the kind of job that I wanted to on the Parker Hannifin board. They were sorry to see me go and tried to talk me out of leaving, but I was stubborn and foolish."

Streeter was recruited away from Idealab to become president, COO and ultimately CEO and chairman of the board of Banta Corporation, a $1.5 billion NYSE-listed company. Banta was a major printing, imaging, and supply-chain management company based in Menasha, Wisconsin. Founded in 1901, it was acquired by Chicago-based RR Donnelley in late 2006.

The Green Bay Packers board opportunity came about because one of the directors of Banta was on the executive committee of the Packers. "As we got to know each other at Banta, he asked if I would be interested in the Packers board, the answer was obviously yes!" she explains. "He worked behind the scenes to help make it happen."

Her introduction to the U.S. Olympic Committee came through a partner of a search firm she had met years before at Idealab who served on the U.S. Ski Team Foundation and Los Angeles Sports Council. Four industry-associated people were required for the new board construct as part of the reformation, when they drastically pared down the size of the board. She served on the USOC board from 2004 to 2009, and then became CEO, responsible for leading day-to-day operations. The USOC is recognized by the U.S. Congress and the International Olympic Committee as the sole entity in America with authority and oversight for Olympic and Paralympic athletes and sport organizations.

After Parker Hannifin, her next public board was Kohl's Department Stores, which came through her networks—a friend of a friend—in Wisconsin. When Banta was sold, Streeter contacted people in her strategic networks to look for her next career move. A well-connected Wisconsin friend introduced her to an attorney who served on the Kohl's board.

"Only about two weeks after he and I had lunch, he gave me a call and said 'I have these guys I'd like you to meet,'" she remembers. "They were Kevin Mansell and Larry Montgomery from Kohl's Corporation. Larry was at the time chairman and CEO, and Kevin was president and successor to Larry. We met and really hit it off. One thing led to another, and I joined the Kohl's board in August 2007."

As of 2012, Kohl's operated 1,146 stores in forty-nine states. The company also provides online shopping through its website kohls.com. Streeter was about to become the mother of twins, so she brought both the perspectives of a businesswoman as well as a mother to the department store board.

Streeter was recommended to Goodyear by a former Avery Dennison executive who had become Goodyear's chairman and CEO and had asked her several times over the years to join the board. So busy leading Banta, she declined. But after Banta was sold, she accepted the invitation to the Goodyear board in 2008. "Board service is very different from being a leader in your own organization," Streeter adds. "I actually like it because you get to play Monday morning quarterback somewhat. You see how others approach business issues. You learn how boards think. It's quite different. It's not your day job, so you don't have the level of detail that you would have running your own organization—what's really important is that the board focuses on strategy and overview. Board service really helped me be a better CEO."

When she moved from Wisconsin to Ohio in 2011 to become the CEO and board member of Libbey Inc., Streeter had to resign her seat on the Green Bay Packers board, since the bylaws say that Green Bay board members must live in Wisconsin. But she remains an avid Packers fan and admits that knowing sports has helped her in her career. "It's all about teamwork," she adds.

"Having been a team sports player helped me because you recognize how to get along with people almost instinctively," Streeter says. "The unspoken requirement is that directors have to have something in common to talk about, whether it is sports or golf or other avocations. I think it is no different than any other social situation. I just advise women to be up-to-date on what is going on in the world and be able to have conversations about it."

SUSAN E. ENGEL

Susan Engel is the CEO of Portero, Inc., and she is an experienced CEO in retail and customer service. She has served as chief executive of Department 56, a giftware and collectibles company; Champion, which included brands such as Hanes, L'eggs, Bali, and Coach; and The Lenox Group, makers of fine china and glassware.

Her degree in labor relations from Cornell University and a Harvard MBA landed her a job at JCPenney, where she worked in HR and marketing. She later joined Booz Allen Hamilton for fourteen years as a consultant with a focus on retail and consumer goods. Among her clients were Sara Lee, Grand Union and Coach. Their executives were helpful in recommending her for public corporate boards. Her first board was K2 Skates, an inline skating and ski company in Los Angeles, and her second was Piper Jaffray, the investment bank and asset management firm, that was sold to U.S. Bank. No longer on her first two boards, she is now on the board of Supervalu, Inc., and a director of Wells Fargo, where she is on the credit, finance, and human resources committees.

SUSAN E. ENGEL
New York City

Current Boards:
Wells Fargo
Supervalu, Inc.
Coolibar, Inc.

Past Boards:
Lenox Group, Inc.
K2 Skates
Piper-Jaffray

Career History:
Portero, Inc.: CEO (current)
Department 56, Inc. (now Lenox Group, Inc.): Chair
    and CEO; President and COO
Sara Lee Corporation: President and CEO,
    Champion Products Division
Booz Allen Hamilton: VP

Education:
MBA, Harvard Business School
BS, Industrial and Business Relations, Cornell University

Supervalu, Inc., is a large national grocery, pharmacy and supply chain company with 2,700 Independent locations including Albertsons and Jewell. She says she is happy to report that there are two women on that board and three on the board of Wells Fargo.

"Boards are looking for diversity, and women on boards are the biggest proponents of other women joining them," Engel notes. "You have to have a senior—big picture—perspective and be able to think strategically. You don't have to know how to create a derivative or trade, but you do have to have some understanding of how the company makes money. Some fundamental finance background is essential for every board member."

Engel recommends the boards of nonprofits and private companies for making contacts and as stepping stones to public board service. "The fun part of being at mid-cap or smaller companies is helping them grow," Engel says.

"People in private equity are eager to have capable women on their boards who are still building their board experience. Also, the smaller companies may be acquired or acquire other companies, and you could be in the right place at the right time."

She is also a fan of being active in your industry trade association, and maintaining relationships with auditors, accountants and lawyers. They are often asked for recommendations. "Think 360 degrees—all the places where your life intersects with people who serve on boards. Let them know of your interest."

Engel does not believe there should be quotas placed on the number of women who should sit on boards. "Why thirty percent? Why not fifty percent? If you get on a board as part of a quota, you'll always think you were brought on as a 'token woman.'"

GO IMMEDIATELY

TO

Chapter 10
Rewards and Risks

DIRECTORSHIP—
10 Many Rewards

and a Few Risks

THE GAME OF RISK HAS REWARDS. THERE MAY BE RISKS TO SERVING ON CORPORATE BOARDS, BUT THE REWARDS OUTWEIGH THE POTENTIAL RISKS.

Corporate directors of large public companies sit atop the global business pyramid, which is why it's such a long climb to get there—especially in high heels. Chief executive officers of public companies and their boards of directors are the elite of business leadership, and to be among them is the ultimate validation of one's career and professional reputation. It's also a big responsibility. Entrusted as the fiduciaries representing the shareholders, board members influence the global environment, the economy and society, in addition to the company.

Several years ago, former U.S. Secretary of Labor and one of this country's most venerable corporate directors, Ann Korologos, wrote an article for *Directors & Boards* to answer women who ask her how to get on a corporate board: "Why on earth would you want to—in today's anti-business, regulation-infested, overtaxed, anti-globalization, protectionist-minded, constantly investigated, negative headline-filled governance environment?"

Because serving on boards has many rewards—career enhancement, high-level business contacts, advanced learning, lasting friendships, annual compensation, and the satisfaction of making a difference. But as any board member will caution, there are indeed risks—potential crises, lawsuits, whistleblowers, disappointments, and perhaps personality conflicts with the CEO or other board members. Calendar restrictions are challenging: board schedules, travel days, preparation time, and keeping up on industry issues and trends can become time-consuming—novice board candidates are not always prepared for the work outside of the boardroom that adds to the time involved in a director's commitment.

Yet women and men are still clamoring to get on corporate boards. Korologos urges potential board member candidates to avoid these decidedly false expectations:

- The "prestige" factor: "Board service is a lot of hard work. It is not a social club. There are significant fiduciary responsibilities and liabilities. Prestige can turn into a nightmare when you hit bumps—or a crater—over regulatory challenges, a soured acquisition, or inappropriate or illegal executive behavior."
- The "get-rich quick" factor. "Don't join a board for the money. Clearly if a company does well and there are stock awards and ownership for directors, then wealth creation for all shareholders is being achieved. But it is not a sure thing. In fact, an extraordinary amount of time spent over a challenging CEO succession or an acquisition gone awry may make your board fees lower than the hourly minimum wage."
- The "I was an important member of Congress or government or a former CEO, and I deserve it" factor: "Don't join a board in the belief that you can run the show; the CEO runs the show—not you—so understand there is a lot you don't know."

The Rewards

The women interviewed in this book agree that the rewards for serving on corporate boards are numerous and outweigh the risks. Even for executives who have had corporate careers involving frequent interaction with directors, the real training and learning begins when one steps into the corporate boardroom for the first time as a new director.

ANN D. MCLAUGHLIN KOROLOGOS
Washington, D.C.; Basalt, Colorado

Current Boards/Select Nonprofits:
AMR Corporation (American Airlines)
Kellogg Company
Host Hotels & Resorts Inc.
Harman International Industries, Inc.
Vulcan Materials Company
The Aspen Institute
RAND Corporation
Anderson Ranch Arts Center (Chairman)
Cristo Rey Network

Past Boards:
Microsoft Corporation
Nordstrom
Fannie Mae
General Motors
Union Camp Corporation
Unocal Corporation
Donna Karan

Career History:
Ann Korologos Gallery: Owner (current)
Benedetto, Gartland & Company, Inc.: Senior Advisor
McLaughlin & Company: President
Braun & Company: Manager, Washington, D.C.
Union Carbide Corporation: Assistant Director of State and Local
    Government Relations
U.S. Department of Labor: Secretary of Labor
U.S. Department of the Interior: Under Secretary
U.S. Department of Treasury: Assistant Secretary
President's Commission on Aviation Security and Terrorism
    (Pan Am 103): Chairman

Education:
Executive MBA, Wharton School, University of Pennsylvania
English Literature, University of London
BA, English, Marymount College

Nordstrom board member Alison Winter says, "Our board is very collegial, but not complacent. The relationships are intensified by a united focus—shareholder value—in a pressure-cooker environment, where our decisions have wide-ranging impact."

Board membership has historically been an exclusive club, verified by how difficult it's been for anyone other than Anglo males to get in. But the changes in the makeup of corporate boards today are welcomed by many men as well as women.

Precisely because being selected for a corporate board is a rare achievement, members who are brought onto boards are automatically viewed as experts in their fields. After serving on the first board, a director is considered "pre-approved" and among the inner circle. Other corporate directors nominate experienced board members they know from one board to the next.

Board membership burnishes careers and creates a formidable network of contacts. It provides opportunities to learn best practices from other companies—those of the company where you are a director, and the companies of other board members, who bring their experience, expertise and ideas to board discussions.

"You have the opportunity to look at a company—from the top down—at the 50,000-foot level. I don't think you can get such overall perspective any other way," says Andrea Van de Kamp, a former director of The Walt Disney Company, City National Bank and Jenny Craig.

The board member's role is to advise the CEO and senior officers, but *not* to get involved in the day-to-day management of the corporation. Such advice-and-consent perspective enhances a director's view on the problems their own companies may face, and can positively influence the director's input as a leader. Different technology systems, management practices and corporate structures offer valuable parallels and potential applications to their own companies.

Sitting on an outside board helps the director better appreciate what his or her own company's board of directors goes through. When you understand the perspective and valuable input that outside directors can bring, you will benefit from closer working relationships with your own company's board members.

ANDREA VAN DE KAMP
Pasadena, California

Past Boards/Select Nonprofits:
The Walt Disney Company
Sotheby's North America
City National Bank, City National Corp.
Jenny Craig, Inc.
MPG Office Trust, Inc.
Carter Hawley Hale Stores, Inc.
Maguire Properties, Inc.
The Music Center, Los Angeles (Emeritus,
    Founding Member)

Career History:
Van De Kamp Consulting: Owner (current)
Sotheby's North America: SVP and Managing Director
    of West Coast Operations
Independent Colleges of Southern California: President and CEO
Carter Hawley Hale Stores, Inc,: Director for Public Affairs
Dartmouth College: Associate Director of Admissions
Occidental College: Associate Dean of Admissions

Education:
MA, Teacher's College, Columbia University
BA, Psychology and Counseling, Michigan State University

Judy Olian, dean of the Anderson School at UCLA, says many women MBA graduates seek "self-actualization" in their careers and lives, over power and wealth. "I believe that making a contribution is a primary component in how women view their success in life." UCLA Anderson offers a Director Education and Certification Program designed to help officers and directors of private firms prepare for the higher level of scrutiny in advance of taking their companies public.

Traditionally, generations of women have made a difference through service to nonprofit organizations. While their husbands worked downtown, women of previous generations managed charities and helped heal society's ills. Today, women are making a difference in business, too. Perhaps the concept of "self-actualization" for women will evolve to embrace their full potential in lives that include business as well as family and nonprofit service.

Margaret Dano, former board member of Fleetwood, and current member of Superior Industries, says, "Before I join a board, I ask myself, 'Will the shareholder be better served because I am on board?'"

That simple statement reflects deep commitment to purpose. Women directors often talk about their responsibility to shareholders as people rather than as numbers, and they express personal satisfaction in being able to perform their duties for the benefit of shareholders and employees, not just to increase the company stock value.

Having women on corporate boards is an obvious benefit to the corporation in terms of marketing and customer service. When Van de Kamp, served on the board of City National Bank, she advocated for financial services that were better suited to the specialized needs of women. "That subsequently helped the bank expand and develop a completely new market. There are also intangible ways that women add value to boards—through their intuition, their greater sensitivity to the dynamics of relationships, and their collaborative working style," Van de Kamp says.

"I have been told by several board members that the questions I ask are very different from those men typically ask in the boardroom, and the men tell me they appreciate those questions," says Julie Hill, on the board of WellPoint. "The presence of women in the boardroom does truly give permission to bring up the more intuitive side of topics and issues for discussion."

Adds Hill: "I think women board members are better at managing relationships and communication with executives. When one of my boards was about to quite abruptly fire a senior executive, I could see the ramifications of what could happen. I was able to suggest a much more graceful solution that allowed the individual and the company to maintain credibility."

Women tend to ask the tough questions at board meetings. Betsy Sanders, who stepped down from her last corporate board in 2005 after twenty-three years of service in boardrooms of some of the country's best-known companies, told me she was often better able than men to ask the tough questions because she was not concerned with "losing face" if she were asking for more information. "In the minority as a woman," she says, "there have been times when I was less hesitant to speak up than some of the men were, especially when my question could be about a controversial factor in decision-making.

BETSY SANDERS
Sutter Creek, California

Past Boards:
Wal-Mart Stores, Inc.
Wolverine Worldwide, Inc.
Washington Mutual Savings Bank
Wellpoint Health Networks, Inc./Anthem
H.F. Ahmanson & Company
Denny's
National Bank of Southern California
Carl Karcher Enterprises
The Vons Companies
Sport Chalet, Inc.
St. Joseph Health System
Bimbo Bakeries, USA
Dacor

Career History:
The Sanders Partnership: Founder and Principal (current)
Nordstrom, Inc.: Corporate VP and GM Southern California

Education:
M.Ed, Secondary Education, Boston University
BA, German Language & Linguistics, Wayne State University

"From my experience, for the board to have real impact on how a company actually performs requires the goodwill of the CEO and senior management team and an absolute desire to work with the board. The CEO has to believe that the board has value as trusted advisors."

Sanders shared an example of how a woman's perspective can bring value in logical ways that may be unexpected:

"I was the only woman on the board of a well-known supermarket chain, and I was the only board member who *ever* actually had gone into a grocery store to buy food for my family!"

Visibility through board service and among networks of board colleagues often leads women to rewarding opportunities as speakers, conference panelists, authors, college professors, or professional advisors to boards of directors.

"Board service is a phenomenal 'second' career," says Susan Engel, a director of Wells Fargo. "So many women have so much to contribute. Board service is a great way to take advantage of all their experience in business, and the women keep learning while giving back."

Another reward of being on boards is the opportunity to bring more women into the boardroom. Every woman corporate director is in a position to recommend and recruit additional women when board openings occur, and when planning ahead for succession. Women directors have long known where and how to find other board-ready women—the challenge has been to convince nominating committees and chairmen. Now those nominating chairs have many more resources to access prospective women candidates directly.

WomenCorporateDirectors keeps updated profiles of its 1,800 members on its membership roster. WCD member profiles include current and previous board experience and career qualifications. The Women's Forum of New York offers a database of "CEO-sponsored" women candidates for companies and search firms to access—at no charge. CalPERS and CalSTRS launched the 3D database, also free to use. And Catalyst provides to its corporate a database of CEO-sponsored women's profiles.

Jan Babiak, a member of the board of Walgreens and WCD co-chair in Nashville, keeps a database of upwards of 150 qualified women and men candidates. When search firms or friends call her about serving on boards that are not well-suited to her background, she checks her files against the qualifications and recommends prospective candidates—men as well as women. "So far, most of those considered have been women because the men were already on the lists," she says. "Out of some seventy prospects I have recommended, seven women have been selected."

Chairing the nominating committee is one way to proactively pursue this goal. The responsibility of the chair is, of course, to find the best-qualified candidates for open seats—so she should insist that women be sought out and included as candidates for consideration.

Sanders says, "When we draw board members from a too-narrow candidate pool of marquee names and CEOs, we overlook both men and women of talent and expertise who can bring important and diverse thinking to our boards. As boards are often considered to be old boys' clubs, healthy boards are always challenging themselves to raise the standards and ensure vitality and relevance."

Even if not on the nominating committee, any director can still advocate for more gender equity on the board. The first priority for women directors is to do a stellar job on the boards they serve. This helps dilute lingering reluctance other members may have about inviting more women to join. Whatever your position, women must recommend and sponsor other women candidates for the board, to proactively increase the overall percentage.

Serving on the board allows women directors to help women in senior management advance in the company—which Catalyst has shown is a benefit to women working their way up. Lulu Wang, board member of MetLife, one of the Fortune 500 companies with thirty percent women directors, recommended that the CEO allow women executives to make presentations to the board, so they can interact with and learn about boards of directors. She said one of the best perquisites about sitting on the board is the opportunity to meet the women who work inside the company and help develop opportunities for their growth and advancement.

When Julie Hill served on the board of Australia's Lend Lease Group, she also led a successful charge to expand opportunities for women within the company. She chaired board committees on diversity, gender equity and sustainability— committees that did not exist before her arrival. And she made a lasting difference. The women of the company hosted a farewell salute to her when she retired from the board.

Sanders served on the board of a major retailer and observed that key management meetings were regularly held at seven o'clock in the morning, which meant that working mothers who needed to drop their children at daycare could not attend. She observed that the women were missing key management opportunities to learn and advance. Women board members asked senior management to schedule essential meetings later in the day so more women employees could participate. And it worked.

"When being considered for board service, and in evaluating my contributions over the years, my gut-level dedication to the customer and to organically growing revenues has been considered a great asset," asserts Sanders. "My twenty years spent learning and living 'servant leadership' at Nordstrom, captured in my book *Fabled Service*, provided an invaluable and unusual bedrock for passionately committed board service, too."

Another reward of serving on a board, is a sense of pride that comes from knowing that women directors positively affect the bottom line of companies.

The 2012 research from Credit Suisse firmly established that companies whose boards include women perform better, have less debt and are slightly more risk averse. Having women on boards may not directly *cause* better company performance—although it often does. But there is an obvious cause and effect of having enlightened management that welcomes a diversity of voices, including women, who bring their varied experience and perspectives to participate in decision-making.

Compensation, including cash and equity, is the most tangible reward for corporate board service. Most corporations pay their directors in cash as well as stock ownership earned over a period of years. Directors who own stock better represent the shareholders, because when the share value increases, all investors benefit. An expert in compensation for boards and CEOs, Robin Ferracone, owner and CEO of Farient Advisors in New York and Los Angeles says, "Compensation should not be the main reason people seek to join boards. Boards want directors who don't need to earn a living at this, but who want to make a difference and have the objectivity to best represent shareholders."

According to Ferracone, compensation for directors has been increasing over the years, but tends to stagnate during recessions. As reported by the National Association of Corporate Directors (NACD), annual compensation for serving on advisory or private boards usually averages from $10,000 to $50,000 per year, and for public company boards from $85,000 to $250,000 per year. This includes annual cash payment, equity, and fees for committee service. Compensation is measured more by the overall time commitment required throughout the year, rather than by attendance at meetings. Additional compensation is earned for leadership roles, such as chair of the board, serving as lead director, or chair of compensation or audit committees.

"Today, most equity for boards has relatively short vesting periods (one to three years) and is delivered in full-value shares, rather than stock options," Ferracone adds. Full-value shares align the directors with the shareholders they are representing, while also compensating them for how well they are doing the job. Directors are expected to hold their shares throughout their board service.

Ferracone recommends that women considering a board seat learn about all aspects of compensation—in advance. What is the form of compensation—cash and stock. How much stock is a director required to hold? When can directors liquidate the stock? What is the board culture about these matters? It is also good to know what happens to stock ownership when a director leaves the board. What happens to directors' shares if the company is acquired? On entering the board, a new director should know what the "exit" protections are.

While compensation is most tangible, the other rewards of board membership are equally appealing to women. Women directors reported how much they learned and grew as a result of the interaction with highly intelligent people they respected. In every case, they said the environment and the company forced them to "up their game" in all aspects of corporate governance. They grew from the experience—from recruiting more women, to taking on more responsibility, to seeing the company through difficult times.

Women board members *do* make a difference—inside and outside the companies they serve. Their ultimate reward, is to use their expertise, experience, and leadership to positively influence business decisions, large and small, that affect the daily lives of countless people and communities. All the women interviewed for this book expressed their satisfaction in contributing their time and talents to making a significant difference in this all-important sector of business and in the world economy. The benefits, they agree, far outweigh the risks.

The Risks

The good news is you have been invited to sit on a board. But is it the right board for you? Have you considered what you need in terms of your own goals? Have you done your due diligence?

Many women directors caution eager board candidates not to jump at the first opportunity without doing lots of research. They advise that finding the right board should be as strategic as shaping a career. Selecting a board means learning everything possible about the company, the executives and the board members—before saying yes.

Every finalist for a board position meets the CEO and other board members. But every finalist should also assertively ask to meet all the C-suite executives in order to assess their strengths and weaknesses. This is a must, an essential part of due diligence—the only way to get those trustworthy gut feelings—and spot any red flags that may become apparent when interviewing the people who run the company.

More ways to discover any potential risks attached to a board seat: Review the company's finances with an outside CPA and meet the firm's general counsel to discuss pending litigations and determine how litigious the company is. Inquire of the CEO, CFO and the general counsel about intangibles. Lulu Wang says to ask important questions such as: Are the board dealings transparent? Is transparency a key value in the company? Is there good communication between management and staff? Is management enthusiastic about suggestions made by the board? She advises that learning the answers at the outset can reduce risk and avert disappointment later.

Many directors also recommend meeting with sitting board members one-on-one to gain their personal perspectives on the executive team, other board members, and board dynamics. The collegiality factor is important to decision-making as well as to your personal comfort. You are going to be spending a lot of time with these fellow directors over the years ahead, so make sure they are people you like and admire.

Board members earn their fees by dedicating a great deal of time and effort attending and preparing for meetings. Required advance reading includes documents that can be hundreds of pages long. Boards meet for one to three days, plus travel. If the meetings are held in distant cities, directors can spend days traveling. Time spent doing advance preparation and study is especially critical, due to heightened scrutiny and additional regulations governing board actions and decisions.

The time adds up quickly, says Linda Griego, a CBS board member: "It takes time to prepare and read board materials—you have to get on it right away, as soon as you receive the packet in the mail. Don't put it at the bottom of your pile of things to do!"

Some women directors said they felt compelled to turn down opportunities for board recruitment because of the time commitment—their jobs were too demanding; or they were already on two other boards and didn't believe they could adequately serve on a third, or the board calendar conflicted with their other board meetings. Since attending board meetings is mandatory, a director's calendar must allow adequate time for board days, committee days, and travel days. Many directors decide to only accept seats on boards that are local or in the same time zone, to provide sufficient time in their already busy schedules. However, focusing on only local boards may limit the number or scope of boards one would be asked to consider.

In order to have greater control over their calendars and schedules, many women executives who serve on three or more public boards decided to retire from their high-pressure corporate jobs and started their own consulting companies. Board service keeps them current with technology developments, the regulatory environment, and expanding markets, and they all enjoy staying actively involved in business.

Today, additional financial responsibility—that is, *risk*—exists because of business disasters such as Enron and Lehman Brothers. The increased regulations that resulted, including Sarbanes-Oxley and Dodd-Frank legislation, complicated governance issues. Some directors say Sarbanes-Oxley emphasizes the board's responsibility to ask important questions and follow through, and penalizes them for not asking the essential questions—thus making boards more accountable. Board members not only should be current and knowledgeable about pertinent issues facing the corporation, they should also be fully cognizant of their duties and responsibilities so as to prevent the board and the corporation from running afoul of regulations.

Reputation is an important risk factor to consider. According to a survey by Eisner Amper, a national consulting and accounting firm, among the five things that board members worry about most, three involve the company's reputation: crises related to product quality; personal and professional integrity, and public perception.

Public trust is the only viable currency between a public company and its many audiences. Once trust is shattered, it's extremely difficult to get it back. Tainted medicines, scalding coffee, sexual harassment and indiscretion, international bribes, and criminal behavior are among the many difficult crises that have faced boards in recent years. And the fallout of tainted reputations can land on directors. Media coverage can drag on far too long, squandering the company's hard-earned goodwill.

Such crises can damage personal as well as professional reputations, resulting in pressure to step down, not just from that board, but also from others. Further, your name may be included in lawsuits, and you may risk not being considered for public board searches in the future.

Davia Temin, president and CEO of Temin and Company in New York, a consultancy to boards on reputation, crisis management, and marketing strategy, also writes a column, "Reputation Matters" for *Forbes.com.* She is amazed at the public's level of anger at the business community, which she sees in many of the corporate crises she is called in to address. "It's very hard to imagine what the reaction is going to be to any given controversy," she notes. That's why she advocates for a diversity of perspectives on corporate boards. A person capable of seeing things differently can help the board understand all sides of a crisis.

Temin explains, "A crisis-ready board underscores the need for diversity of all kinds because there is a better chance that someone will recognize a potential crisis. Differing points of view lead to deeper discussions and better decisions, and a wider variety of people increases the chances that someone is more likely to have had personal experience with the issue." She encourages prospective board members to ask about reputation risk. The fact that something new exists called "reputational insurance" indicates there are increasingly serious risks due to insistent worldwide media that can spread a rumor in minutes or start a revolution almost as quickly. When there is a crisis, board members may share in bad publicity about management wrongdoers, because the company's failings are ultimately the responsibility of its directors.

Some boards keep track of potential problems by creating a phone line that any employee can call with anonymous tips, a kind of hotline for whistleblowers. These calls should not be screened or edited—they are a means of risk avoidance. A corporate executive monitors the hotline and reports to the board. Temin says, "Whistleblowers should be able to share their concerns directly with board members. Since boards are seen as the conscience of the company, it is a critical responsibility for directors to know what's happening inside the corporation. Directors should welcome hearing concerns directly from employees, and make time to discuss them at board meetings." In these days of heightened skepticism about institutions, and social media access that can propel an incident to international awareness, corporate boards must be alert to issues that can potentially impact product quality, integrity or public perception.

Possible harm to a director's personal and professional reputation is an inherent risk of board membership. However, if there is a crisis and the situation is handled well, dealing with a difficult challenge can strengthen reputations. One woman director told me that she decided to step down from a board after she helped the company survive a crisis, because she no longer felt she shared the values of the CEO. Ironically, because she handled the crisis well, other board members later asked her to join other boards. She urges all board members to have their own personal crisis plans in place.

Another board member says her reputation was actually enhanced when she sat on the board of a company that declared bankruptcy. She was the lead director, managed the crisis quickly, and satisfied all parties—no easy feat! Several other boards subsequently sought her out precisely for the leadership she had shown and the expertise she acquired through the crisis.

Almost as soon as Donna James joined the board of a subsidiary company, the CEO of the parent corporation (who had suggested her for this board) decided to buy back the subsidiary at below-market price. She was appointed to lead the lawsuit on behalf of the subsidiary's shareholders, to negotiate a fair price for their stock. "It was a difficult position to be in, but my responsibility was clear, and I felt good that I was able to protect the shareholders," James said. "If you keep governance issues and shareholder value at the center of your thinking, you are a much more effective board member."

A few years later, the CEO, who had been so impressed by the way she negotiated on the shareholders' behalf, invited James to join the board of the holding company. She became known as an expert on mergers, spin-offs, and acquisitions—her unique value-added for future board consideration. James is on the board of Time Warner Cable and Marathon Petroleum (where twenty-five percent of board members are women).

Besides having their reputations at risk, board members are often automatically named in lawsuits against the corporation. From employee discrimination suits to alleged improper actions of the CEO—lawsuits can be unexpected and time-consuming. In the extreme event of a criminal investigation, email records and computers of board members can be subpoenaed.

Directors and officers (D&O) insurance is provided by the corporation to cover all directors and corporate officers against lawsuits and personal liability. New regulations require boards to have directors who are finance experts as chairs of audit committees, responsible for analyzing and monitoring the balance sheet and detecting small problems before they become crises. This new regulation reduces the risk of incompetence or fraud. Board members must sign off on the company's annual audit statements and financial documents, which can put directors in the spotlight for potential lawsuits.

Many women directors say the risk of being personally sued is extremely low. If the board members can demonstrate that the board used sound business judgment according to the established processes and procedures for analyzing risk, D&O insurance kicks in, and they cannot be held personally liable for corporate losses.

However, to avoid such potential lawsuit exposure of serving on public boards, one cautious investment banker says she prefers to sit on private boards, rather than public. She says the private companies are often more tightly controlled by shareholders, and can move more quickly to resolve crises. She feels public company board service is overrated, and potentially risky, primarily because of the personal liability.

Many companies have formal ways to evaluate the risk involved in each major project, so it's important to know if a board has a system for its own enterprise risk analysis. Which C-suite executives report to the board to explain the risk involved in certain decisions? Does the board dedicate a committee to analyze risk? Does the responsibility rest with a risk officer, or is it the entire board's responsibility to discuss and identify risks? Global supply chain issues topped the list of enterprise risks—in 2012, Wal-Mart was charged with paying bribes to local officials and suppliers in Mexico. Directors of companies are expected to know how their companies do business and make money—globally. The U.S. government requires that all companies doing business in foreign countries have to abide by the Foreign Corrupt Practices Act of 1977 (FCPA).

The FCPA prohibits U.S. firms doing business in foreign markets from making payments to corrupt foreign officials for the purpose of obtaining or keeping business. In addition, other statutes such as mail and wire fraud laws, which provide for federal prosecution of violations of state commercial bribery statutes, may also pertain. The U.S. Department of Justice is the chief enforcement agency, also the Securities and Exchange Commission (SEC) and the Department of Commerce.

Finally, before you accept any directorship, be sure you like and respect the CEO. Veteran board member Van de Kamp, who has now retired from all her public corporate boards, believes the most critical factor for success is to try to be sure there's no personality conflict between you and the CEO. Sometimes this is hard to assess before joining the board, when you are still a candidate. Van de Kamp's term was not renewed on the Walt Disney Company board of directors after a public disagreement with the CEO.

"Actually, I always believed I was acting on behalf of the shareholders, " explains Van de Kamp. "I didn't dislike the then-CEO, I just disagreed with him.

Directors are all on the same side—everyone wants to see the company be successful. But as a director you have a fiduciary responsibility above all."

Van de Kamp also cautions, "Being the lone woman on a board, especially the first woman on a board, has many challenges—overt and subtle. Before you accept, if your due diligence turns up the fact that three women have left the board in recent years, you would be wise to have a candid conversation with at least one of them. You don't want to be the fourth one to leave unexpectedly. Women need to remember that eagerness could lead to choosing the wrong board."

Every candidate for a board seat should evaluate these risk factors, as well as the more subjective factors such as personality, compatibility, and shared values, before making the decision to become a candidate for a corporate board. Weigh the potential risks and the rewards—as the women in this book have done. All women who have devoted years of their lives and careers to board service, they have proved that by carefully evaluating the directorships you accept, the rewards trump the risks. That's how you win The Board Game.

GO IMMEDIATELY
TO
Chapter 11
Your Turn—
Focus on YOU

11 YOUR TURN—
Focus on

YOU

YOU take it from here—whether your career is in the DEVELOPING, ESTABLISHED, OR ADVANCED STAGE. Here are the specific action steps you can take today and tomorrow, this year and next, to strategically move closer to your first corporate board—by no means a trivial pursuit.

The clear message of this book is that serving on a corporate board is not something you casually think about doing someday when you retire. Your efforts throughout your career should be intentional and strategic. Think of your goal to serve on a public corporate board as "a purpose-driven pursuit," says Doug Conant, former CEO of Campbell Soup.

At What Career Stage Are YOU?

- *Developing*—there's plenty of time to build networks, learn board dynamics and make strategic, purpose-driven career choices regarding jobs, companies and industries—maybe even public service.
- *Established*—there's still time to evaluate your own career achievements, and make course changes—add to your nonprofit board experience, expand your skill set, and focus on gaining more visibility for your accomplishments at your job and in the business community.

- *Advanced*—at the height of your productive career, you must now activate your contacts, clearly define your achievements, and inform people in your networks that you want to sit on a corporate board. Even if you have not paved your way by strategic steps toward a Fortune 500 corporation, there are many private companies and smaller public companies that can benefit from your business knowledge and experience.

Developing Stage of Your Career

You are starting out. By reading this book, you have just learned that someday being on a corporate board of a public company could be your ultimate career goal. You may still be searching for your ideal career grounding. So here are the steps for your first phase to start the long process early. Enjoy the confidence that no matter what career pathway you choose, you will perform your best, look for opportunities to learn, and be a team player. You might even pick up a team sport at your gym along the way. For women who didn't learn team sports at school, it's not too late.

- Become visible throughout your company. Be recognized as a person who not only does her job expertly, but also volunteers for tough assignments, seeks additional responsibility, and performs well on a team.
- Speak up when you've achieved a milestone, met the goal, built an effective team. Use your company newsletter or intranet to share your team's success. Don't brag, and never take all the credit. Success is all about relationships and teamwork.
- Ask your supervisors for feedback so you can course-correct, as needed— don't wait for your annual performance review. Spend time on your own self-evaluation, separate from performance reviews. Denise Morrison, CEO of Campbell Soup, says women spend hours on proposals and presentations, but tend to give short shrift to their own self-evaluations.
- State your achievements in terms of results. Don't just describe what you've done. State what you achieved, preferably including numbers, demonstrating management of people and budgets. A sample resume is in this chapter.
- Find mentors or sponsors during the course of doing good work. Informally, stay alert for more senior people in your work environment you admire who might coach and direct you. If formal mentorships are encouraged at your

company, find a senior person to sponsor you—someone who can help make sure you are considered for promotions and opportunities for learning and growth. Develop working relationships with people you admire and respect. Capture "mentor moments" where you pick up tidbits about best ways to do things successfully.

- Learn about networking, Don't spend countless hours chained to your desk to prove you work hard. Do a good job, but also carve out time to build beneficial working relationships with others—inside *and* outside your company. Seek out business and industry associations where you can meet business contacts.

- Join 2020 Women on Boards, 85Broads, and other women's organizations that are advocating for more women on boards.

- Expand your professional circles outside your own company. Stay in touch with classmates from college and graduate school. Join the women's branch of your professional association or become a member of an organization whose mission is to advance women in the workplace. It's never too early to start building your professional networks.

- To get involved in well-connected nonprofit organizations, ask your senior management which affiliations your company has with community services and volunteer agencies. Let the senior executives know you are seeking leadership development on nonprofit boards where you can learn. Ask executives for advice about the organizations. Look for nonprofit organizations where you can spend early years in the trenches as a volunteer—at a medical center, a prominent national service organization, a high-profile cultural institution.

- Guard your image now that you are a serious, dedicated professional. Be judicious and tempered on social networks—Facebook, Tumblr, Twitter, etc. Pictures or comments can come back to haunt you. And they *will* come back to haunt you, at just the *wrong* time.

- Buy stock—even just a few shares. Get to know and understand the stock market. As a shareholder you receive quarterly reports and should gain a full perspective about all companies you invest in. Read the financial news and annual reports. Financial literacy is a must for board appointments. Start now.

- Decide what you love to do, and then orient your career toward developing expertise in that discipline, whether in operations, marketing, finance, information systems, technology, or human resources. Learn everything you can about the function, and use that information, and your performance, to demonstrate your competence and expertise.

- Avoid getting stuck in a professional silo. Be willing to step out of your comfort zone to accept assignments across disciplines. If you believe you can do it, you *can* do it.
- Take classes. Attend seminars that give you information to expand your understanding of business functions outside your own expertise. If you're a marketer, take classes in finance, etc. Consider educational seminars and university courses about corporate board service. Attend leadership seminars. Keep learning.

Established Stage of Your Career

You have moved up, and proved your ability to manage people and budgets. Take your management skills to the board of your favorite nonprofit. Seek membership on a corporate advisory boards where you can meet and be seen by senior executives. Remember: You have to be *known* before you can be recruited.

- If you don't already have a corporate sponsor who is dedicated to your success at the company, do your best to find one. Share your interest in leadership development and career advancement with the most senior person you have come to know well at your company, or outside your company. Ask for her or his counsel, without imposing on this busy executive's time. Relationships are two-way streets—try to help that person achieve what he or she needs to accomplish, and a senior executive who is fair will return the favor. It may take time to see this pay off, but it should.
- The majority of women corporate directors were recommended for their first corporate board by colleagues they knew on their large nonprofit boards. Based on your previous volunteer work, offer to serve on the board, and take on challenging projects as a board member—like chairing a capital campaign or orchestrating a partnership that will increase the reach and resources of the organization. This is a key strategy for gaining the respect of your fellow board members, a prerequisite for corporate board consideration.

- Board recommendations also come from your colleagues in the women's organizations you have already joined. There are undoubtedly several business women's groups in your area, either in your profession or in various areas of advocacy for women in the workplace. Research and join groups that sound like a good fit for you. Also contribute to Catalyst, an international research nonprofit focused on women in the workplace, or 2020Women on Boards, or the Thirty Percent Coalition. (See the Resource Guide.)

- Now that you're a supervisor or vice president, if you don't have your MBA degree, consider going back to business school for an MBA in a program for the full-time employed. Or take opportunities to broaden and deepen your learning through business classes offered at most colleges and universities, board training programs at most business schools, and board "boot camps." (See the Resource Guide.)

- Look for opportunities to get operations experience. Responsibility for P&L is a major calling card for board recruitment. If you're already a financial wizard, take on a marketing position or a role in HR to broaden your experience portfolio. Donna James, chair of President Obama's National Women's Business Council, spent her career in finance at Nationwide Insurance, but she says she reluctantly took on the HR responsibility to handle a merger, at the request of her CEO, and said, "It made me a much better executive."

- If you are not visible inside your company, seek the counsel of your corporate communications staff. Ask for help to package a possible story about the company for the general media that will highlight your team's successes. The public relations team often welcomes leads about potential stories.

- Use your position to advance the careers of deserving women in the company. Mentor them. See that they are considered for promotions and opportunities for professional growth.

- Pursue leadership roles in your industry or trade associations. At first, volunteer to manage events, find speakers for conferences, write white papers for the industry, and help find articles for the industry trade publication. Geraldine Knatz, general manager of the Port of Los Angeles became well known in her industry association as a diligent volunteer board member—and that increased her visibility for higher-level positions.

- Make your interest in serving on corporate boards known to all your associates and ask for help through all of your networks, including your attorney, accountant, family, and friends.

- Check out advisory boards in your industry or among your clients/customers. While advisory boards don't have fiduciary responsibility, you will be introduced to the issues that company faces, and you will make contacts among board members and senior executives of other companies.

- To find your first board position, try private and venture capital-backed boards. Research private company boards that may be family-held, or new companies being formed by venture capitalists. Many women interviewed in this book said their first company boards were private.

- Get involved in your community. Research how to get appointed to a government or community commission. Take opportunities to contribute to civic initiatives. If your company is a partner in public/private partnerships, volunteer to participate. Get to know major players in the community and business leadership. Represent your company on the Chamber of Commerce or in Rotary—all good visibility and opportunities to hone your leadership experience.

- Become more active in executive women's business organizations. There is a wealth of information, knowledge, and contacts to be made. Women's networks were valuable leads and support for women in this book on their pathways to boards.

- Serving on the board of your industry/trade association provides invaluable contacts. Maggie Wilderotter, CEO of Frontier Communications, waged a one-woman proxy fight to be elected to a seat on the all-male board of the National Cable Television Association. Only a few years later, she was given the association's highest award for excellence—and a fellow board member recommended her for her first corporate board.

- Craft your own reputation as an influential expert in your field by writing articles, appearing on panels, being active and visible in business and community outreach programs. You don't have to be a lobbyist to represent your industry and your profession to government entities—local, state, federal—through your associations.

- By now you are a shareholder in publicly traded companies, and you are always informed and current with the financial markets. As a shareholder, use your proxy to urge the board to include on its agenda the issue of more women directors. Demand that women be included on the slate of nominees for the corporate boards of companies in which you own stock.

New legislation and regulations have empowered shareholders (large and small) to become activists by giving them a more formal voice in the process. Even small shareholders are bringing forward their concerns and opinions at annual meetings, challenging excessive pay packages for executives and raising questions about governance issues that concern financial risk, diversity, questionable ethics, and performance of board members. There were more proxy fights in the first half of 2012 than in the entire year of 2011, according to Institutional Shareholder Services (ISS) in Washington, D.C., which provides proxy voting services and corporate governance research, and monitors more than 35,000 shareholder meetings annually around the world.

- Nominate yourself for the 3D Database and other databases of potential women board candidates. Demonstrate your commitment to pursuing corporate boards and your profile will be open to nominating committees and search firms that use databases among their many resources.
- Get to know current women board members, who have similar professional backgrounds to yours. If you can arrange it, take these women to lunch and ask their advice. Just like you network with people who have the corporate jobs you aspire to, introduce yourself and get to know other women who serve on corporate boards. Get to know the women who serve on the board of your company, or other board members who know you from business or nonprofit connections.

Advanced Stage of Your Career

You are at the top of your career. You are an officer in your local business group, a member of ION and probably have attended several leadership training programs, maybe even OnBoard Bootcamp. You have distinguished yourself on the board of at least one major community service organization and, perhaps, have been a director at a private company.

Since you now are poised to sit on a public board, plan to secure the seat(s) long before you retire from your executive role. Corporations want directors who have current business relationships and knowledge. Boards generally have a retirement age of seventy-two or seventy-five, so they don't want new candidates who are near retirement age. They want the added value of a new board member's counsel for years to come. Boards are also eager to learn what active and current business contacts new directors can bring with them .

Define the added value you immediately bring to a board based on your experience and your network. Scrutinize every important aspect of your resume. Evaluate your experience, both in your work world and your previous board work. And take a look at your network to see whom you know that can help you now to achieve the goal you've been working toward. This is the time to use all your strategic skills:

- Call upon mentors and sponsors who have supported your career. Ask them for introductions that could lead to board placements. If your sponsor is a CEO, ask him or her to endorse you to be included in the database of the Women's Forum of New York (see Chapter One).

- Leverage your board experience—corporate, private or large nonprofit—current and previous. Determine who you know who can make a direct contact for you. If you don't have a direct contact, it's very possible that you are just two degrees of separation from the board you want to join. Since the majority of women corporate directors were introduced to boards by fellow board members of large nonprofits, analyze your boards—whom do you know from your nonprofit, advisory, or private board who will recommend you? Contact those people now and ask if they will recommend you to a specific board.

- Add a brief written statement to your resume about your financial expertise that prepares you to serve on an audit committee, i.e., have you managed a P&L, are you experienced in complex, global financial issues? Check out Sarbanes-Oxley requirements for "finance expert." Craft a succinct statement that captures the pertinent experience you bring, and share with your contacts, so they are updated on your specific experience that would bring value to a corporate board.

- If you are a current CEO or senior C-suite executive of a large publicly held company, or a division president, you have the ticket to get on boards. Emphasize your credentials.

At the Advanced stage of your career, you have already gained the experience in many areas—whether it's international management, ownership of your own company, technology fields, HR—so you need to capture the best value you bring to the board in a powerful punch-list of accomplishments. Geraldine Laybourne did just that. She developed a one-page "marketing brief" of her expertise and added value. Laybourne points out that even people who may know you well, may not know your outstanding accomplishments, the specifics of your areas of expertise, and their direct benefits to the board.

Your Board-Ready Resume

As co-owner of an executive search firm Berkhemer Clayton since 1994, I have counseled hundreds of executives over the years and seen thousands of executive resumes—and no resume is ever perfect. In fact, I'm convinced there isn't a "perfect" one. But with some careful attention, you can be sure your resume is Board-Ready. If it is, it will clearly show the nominating committee precisely what the directors are looking for—at a glance. Your resume paints the picture of your leadership, strategic thinking and the results you have achieved everywhere you've worked, and on each board where you've served—nonprofit organizations, private or public company boards. So you'll want your resume to be as effective as it can be.

Corporate boards look for director candidates who have the wisdom and leadership experience to help guide their companies—candidates who understand the company's business, are able to strategize within the global framework, and who have a solid track record and stellar reputation. So your resume must demonstrate that your leadership, people management, financial management and social understanding have served the test of time. Its reader should immediately see an executive who is well-rounded, and mission-driven, and that you bring good judgment and imagination to the decision-making process. Corporate CEOs have to trust their boards to be reliable counselors. Company shareholders must be able to rely on independent directors to represent their interests.

I have counseled hundreds of executives over the years and seen thousands of executive resumes—most have been far from perfect, despite strong careers filled with excellent experience and great success. But in most cases, the nominating committee of a board has to dig deep to discover the salient information about the candidate. So your job is to make it easy for them.

If you have not updated and revised your resume in a while, you may never have constructed one that showcases the added value you bring to board service. Your value-added achievements should be shown with measurable results—such as the percentage increases in business growth and revenues—to document the difference you have made to your company, the nonprofits you are involved with, your industry, and your community. Through what you have already accomplished, you can demonstrate how your leadership will specifically benefit the company. Your accomplishments show the entire picture of an executive who has a track record of expertise in given areas—finance, operations, technology, management, marketing, human resources. Focusing on your achievements, not skills, shows you are strategic, well-rounded, and will bring experience, judgment, and imagination to the decision-making process. Showing results in measurable numbers (percentage increases or dollars) highlights what a difference you have made to your company, your nonprofits, your industry, and the community.

The Board-Ready Resume format that follows will be helpful at all stages of your career—from the first years out of graduate school, to mid-career, to later when you are poised to serve on a corporate board. Even if you are early in your career and you have not yet been in a position to have made key achievements, the sample resume should help you develop your resume and fine-tune it over time, citing your achievements as your career progresses. Your resume should always be a "work in progress." Your career takes years to build, so your resume should grow accordingly.

Your resume is your personal marketing document. It doesn't just say what you've done. It shows how you think, how you approach problems, and the results of your efforts. The sample resume I've created will help you craft your own, a document that paints a clear picture of your leadership, your strategic thinking, and the results you have achieved at every company where you've worked, and on each board on which you've served—nonprofit, private, or public.

Here are some important details to remember:

- **Carefully proofread your resume and cover letter**—It sounds so basic, doesn't it? You'd be amazed how many people don't take the extra time it takes to proof the most important document in their business life. Your resume shows your level of attention to detail, so be sure to proof it with an attention to detail—one stray comma might just irritate a would-be colleague on a board. If you are a good proofreader, use your skill; if not, ask a friend to read it thoroughly. A second pair of eyes is always helpful.
- **Use your name and date as the document title**—When sending your resume as an attachment to an email, be sure the title of the attached document is your name and the current date. For example, you should entitle the document "Mary Smith Resume June 2013." Do not simply attach a document named "Resume" from your computer desktop. This may be basic Resume-101 courtesy, but you should see how many attachments I receive that are simply titled "Resume."
- **Customize the email cover letter**—Another basic courtesy that many people forget—in the salutation of your letter, address a person at the executive search firm or an executive at the company you are approaching. If you are sending to a search firm, send your resume and cover letter intentionally to the head of the board-search practice.

What Does a Board-Ready Resume Look Like?

Every resume is different, because every story is unique. Here's an easy-to-follow template designed to help you create your own Board-Ready Resume, a resume that will succinctly state your overall achievements and the value you bring to the boardroom. (In the sample below, any resemblance to an actual individual or real companies is unintended and purely coincidental.) Following the sample resume is an example of a cover letter in bullet format, since every Board-Ready Resume must be accompanied by a cover letter that gets right to the point.

Sample Board-Ready Resume

MARY E. SMITH

123 Elm Street

City, USA, or Country

Contact info: email or other online access

Phones: Office, home, cell

OBJECTIVE

Seeking a board of directors seat on large publicly held corporate board where my finance and operations experience in manufacturing durable goods, and my business contacts in industry and government will bring added value. My budget oversight experience ranges from $50 million to $600 million; I have been an effective board member of a privately held corporation and large nonprofit organizations, and successfully helped raise major contributions and investments.

CORPORATE BOARD SERVICE — *List current and past*

SYNTHETIC GLASS PRODUCTS   (elected to board May 2010)

(NYSE: SGP) $1 billion revenues, 60,000 employees with operations in 5 countries

Chairs Finance Committee; and serves on Compensation Committee.

www.syntheticglass.com

If you have no public or private corporate boards, then list largest nonprofit board first

WXYZ CORPORATION (privately held)   (elected to board June 2005)
Headquartered in Tucson, Arizona; with 40,000 employees; operations and facilities in 13 states, and distribution network to 30 countries.
www.wxyzcorp.com

KANSAS TRANSPORTATION COMMISSION
                (Governor appointment, June 2004. Six-year term ended Dec 2010)
$3 billion budget, 18,000 employees, managing infrastructure for Kansas state highways, toll-roads, rural routes for vehicles, multi-axles trucks, trailers, and emergency communications; meets quarterly in Topeka. Chaired Budget Committee; and served on Audit Committee.
www.kansas.gov/services/transportation

NONPROFIT BOARD SERVICE

KANSAS LEUKEMIA FOUNDATION—Kansas statewide board (May 1999 to present)
Nonprofit 501(c)3 organization which raises $3 million annually for research related to new treatments. Chair of the Board (2005 to 2009) and Finance Committee (2001 to 2003)
www.klf-kansas.org

List current and past

UNIVERSITY OF TOPEKA MEDICAL CENTER (June 1994 to June 2004—ten years)

Board of Trustees responsible for governance of $30 million university medical center, with 3,000 students in medical and dental schools; 6,000 employees, managing three hospitals, 750 beds, with 3,500 patients annually. Committees: Finance and Human Resources.

www.kansasuniversitymedicalcenter.org.

EDUCATION

List all degrees with most recent at top

University of Kansas, MBA, emphasis in Economics, June 1987

If no degree, say "attended"

Yale University, BS, Mathematics, June, 1985

Certifications: CPA, 1998

UCLA Anderson School of Management: Corporate Directors Training, May 2010.

Languages: Fluent in Spanish; conversational French.

CAREER HISTORY

MIDWESTERN STEEL & BRASS PRODUCTS, INC. (NYSE: MSBP)   May 2006 to present

Wichita, Kansas

www.midwesternsteel.com

Largest steel manufacturing company in Kansas, tenth largest in U.S., $1 billion revenues, 35,000 employees, operations in four countries; primary business is infrastructure repair and rebuild.

Chief Financial Officer   Sept 2007 to Current

- Reporting directly to CEO since Sept 2007.
- Managing staff of 30, including finance professionals and investor relations communications team. (staff budget of $250,000)
- Managed growth from $650 million to $1 billion over eight-year period.
- Implemented new corporate governance and operating model for business development and innovation through venture capital, existing assets, and commercialization of new business concepts.
- Orchestrated 25% increase in shareholder communications through investor relations staff, also increased numbers of analysts following our company from 7 to 15.

Vice President, Finance and Treasury   May 2006 to Sept 2007

- Completed strategic rationalization of four different businesses to determine the best growth and value options for the future. As a result, over $300 million in additional invested capital was redeployed to better investment alternatives; and completed exit strategies for two business units in two years.
- Secured $500 million in acquisition capital for new business ventures.
- Recognized by CFO Magazine on list of "Most Influential" CFOs in U.S. in 2012.

ABCD LIFE INSURANCE, INC. (Member-owned) Sept 1996 to May 2006

Headquartered in Chicago, Illinois, owned by 500,000 members, third-largest life insurance company in the U.S, provides life and retirement savings products to individuals and institutions, including 401K plans, 457 plans, life insurance annuities, and investment advisory-related products. More than 4,000 employees and 10,000 independent broker dealers.

VP Finance Jan 2000 to May 2006

Director Strategic Planning Sept 1996 to Jan 2000

LARGE CPA FIRM, Tax and Audit Services Jan 1988 to Sept 1996

Kansas City, Kansas. Staff auditor and audit supervisor for large and small business clients in the public and private sectors in the insurance, retail, manufacturing industries.

ORGANIZATIONS, ASSOCIATIONS

This section paints the picture of your strategic networks—Industry associations, professional organizations, chamber of commerce—include purpose of the organization, how large, annual revenues, and volunteer positions held. Also include your service on fund-raising or finance committees.

AWARDS, HONORS, LECTURES, ARTICLES

> *This is the visibility section—list awards won, recognition of achievements, speaking engagements, and articles you have written related to business, governance and corporate citizenship—not personal travel articles for example.*

PERSONAL

Golf, tennis, recreational chess. Writing once-a-year travel column for Condé Nast magazines.

Married, three children (two college graduates, one teenager still at home)

ONLINE PROFILE is located at (online address).

> *Your online profile must include your professional headshot photo and the text must match your resume, presenting the same work history. Be sure to update online profile to be accurate and current.*

Sample Cover Letter or Introductory Email letter

Dear [CEO, Corporate Secretary Nominating Chair or Executive Search firm]:

(Your letter should be addressed by name to the gatekeeper for board searches.)

I am writing to introduce myself as a potential candidate for your company's board of directors. I have worked for two decades to develop the credentials, leadership strengths, and business networks that I believe would bring value to the *(company name)* board of directors. My business acumen has been honed in the trenches at *(name your publicly held companies where you currently or previously worked)*. I understand the requirements and dynamics of board governance through making presentations to corporate boards and by serving on significant nonprofit boards. For your consideration, I respectfully submit these achievements to reinforce my candidacy:

- Serve for five years on board of WXYZ nonprofit organization, with annual revenues of $10 million, and 200 employees. Its mission is to provide health and human services to underserved populations in the state. I led the fund-raising team, which generated an incremental increase of $500,000 for the general operating fund.

- Oversee finances of a publicly held company with $1.2 billion annual revenues; handled mergers and acquisitions that doubled the size of the corporation and increased the number of employees by 18% to a record 10,000. I understand the issues and interests of shareholders.

- Provide strategic counsel to the CEO, including overall risk assessment, global supply-chain management, and message development as needed for challenging situations, internal and external.

- Make quarterly presentations to my company's board of directors which has sharpened my knowledge about governance, and how to best provide essential information to help board members make strategic decisions.

While I have not yet served on a public board, I have worked toward board service as my ultimate goal for the culmination of my career. Thanks to my history working for three large publicly held corporations, I know the fiduciary duties of board service, and I would like to take on such a leadership role at your company. I would like to request an exploratory meeting in hopes my credentials might fulfill current or future needs on your board. When opportunities for openings arise in the future, thank you for keeping my expertise in mind. My CEO has approved my dedicating the time required to become an excellent outside director for you and *(company name)*.

Best regards,

Mary Smith
(address)
(cell phone, home phone, office phone)
(email address)

How Will Serving on Corporate Boards Benefit You?

So, where is the win/win for women? Here are just some answers that perhaps you haven't thought about. By winning The Board Game—and getting your first seat on a public corporate board, you will be able to:

- Bring your perspective as a woman to the decision-making process at the highest levels—changing the communication dynamics in the boardroom and the decisions that can affect millions of people.
- Represent the interests of shareholders and benefit the environment, the employees, and the social and governance aspects of companies where you serve—companies you believe in.
- Gain knowledge and training to become a CEO yourself someday, if you are not already there.
- Earn additional income in director's fees and stock in companies where you serve.
- Provide added value from your years of business experience to benefit corporate boards, and learn best practices you take back with you to the company where you are employed, or that you own.
- Enjoy a sense of gratification when you help mid-cap and smaller companies grow into something bigger, something special. You will have the satisfaction and pride of knowing you made a difference.
- Generate top-level business contacts who will be beneficial connections throughout your career.
- Help senior women executives at the company move up in their careers, and sponsor women you respect and admire so they may someday serve on corporate boards.
- Enjoy a productive, active second career—during and after your primary career—as board member and role model.

As YOU Move into the Winner's Circle

This book explains the rules of The Board Game. Now it's up to you to play to win your first seat. I have introduced you to outstanding women who have played The Board Game and won. They've shared their moves, their strategies, their alliances, and the often-lucky cards they drew or obstacles they overcame along the way. They've talked about risks and rewards to help you devise strategies toward directorship. And finally, I hope my personal career advice is helpful to you. This last chapter has focused on *you*—your pathway, your visibility, your resume, and your strategic networks.

Women bring win/win collaboration, consensus building, and communication. Women leaders may not be motivated so much by the desire for personal power and wealth as they are by a desire to make a difference—to ensure that business survives and thrives not only for the financial benefits to shareholders, but also for the benefit of the employees, the environment, the consumer and the community. They also use power as directors to bring other women into the boardroom and to assist high potential women to advance through the ranks of the corporations they direct.

Yes—*win/win*.

Remember to ask every CEO YOU know:
- Are there upcoming retirements on your board, and are women being considered in your board's succession plan? Tell the CEOs about the Credit Suisse research that demonstrates companies with women on their boards perform better than those without women.
- Do you have more women on your board than your competitors? If not, challenge every CEO to do so. When CEOs start competing for more gender-balanced boards, everyone will surely benefit.

Enjoy the journey ahead. Please let me know when you pass Go, and join your first corporate board. Your goal for a few years from now: to have followed the rules, successfully played the game by creating your own strategies, building your networks, and serving the community through nonprofits. By gaining the experience and credentials needed by specific companies, you will have earned your ticket to be considered for your first corporate board. Congratulations.

But remember, this is just the beginning.

GUIDE TO
RESOURCES AND REFERENCES

Women seeking their first corporate board seats will find many pathways to the goal, as described in *The Board Game*. The following resources and references are meant to help you learn along the way. Many of the research studies, articles, and books are referred to in the chapters of this book. But others are included as additional reading, to help you forge your own pathway and become more informed about corporations and their boards of directors.

Research References

Research studies referenced in *The Board Game* spell out the current statistics for women on corporate boards. These provide context and definitive conclusions showing that greater gender balance is good for business.

The Alliance for Board Diversity

Missing Pieces: Women and Minorities on Fortune 500 Boards—2010 Alliance for Board Diversity Census. Published online on July 21, 2011 by the Alliance for Board Diversity (www.theabd.org), a collaboration of four leading organizations—Catalyst, the Executive Leadership Council (ELC) the Hispanic Association on Corporate Responsibility (HACR), Leadership Education for Asian Pacifics, Inc. (LEAP).

Catalyst

2012 Catalyst Census: Fortune 500 Women Board Directors; appendix to *2012 Catalyst Census: Fortune 500 Research Project* (www.catalyst.org/knowledge/2012-catalyst-census-fortune-500).

Credit Suisse

Gender Diversity and Corporate Performance, Credit Suisse AG Research Institute; authors Mary Curtis, Christine Schmid, Marion Struber. Zurich, Switzerland, August 2012 (www.infocus.credit-suisse.com). See pages 17-19, "Rationalizing the link between performance and gender diversity."

The Glass Hammer

How Do Women Improve Board Performance? Let Us Count the Ways by Melissa J. Anderson (January 31, 2013; www.theglasshammer.com/ news/2013/01). The Glass Hammer is an online community designed for women executives in financial services, law, and business.

ION—the InterOrganization Network

Follow the Leaders: It Can *Happen Here—The Ninth Annual Status Report of Women Directors and Executive Officers of Public Companies in 16 Regions of the United States*; principal author Toni G. Wolfman; Susan M. Adams oversaw data collection and presentation (December 2012; www.ionwomen.org/ion-reports).

McKinsey & Company

Unlocking the Full Potential of Women in the U.S. Economy, by Joanna Barsh and Lareina Yee, (December 2012; www.mckinsey.com/client_service/ organization/latest_thinking/unlocking_the_full_potential).

Spencer Stuart Executive Search

Spencer Stuart U.S. Board Index 2012 (November 2012; www.spencerstuart.com/research/articles/1621). The Spencer Stuart Board Index is an annual study that examines the state of corporate governance among S&P 500 companies.

WomenCorporateDirectors and Heidrick & Struggles

2012 Board of Directors Survey; conducted by Dr. Boris Groysberg, Professor of Business Administration, Harvard Business School and Deborah Bell, researcher; facilitated by Heidrick & Struggles and WomenCorporateDirectors (September 2012; www.heidrick.com/PublicationsReports/ Documents/WCD_2012BoardSurvey.pdf). See sections "Board Diversity" and "Board Governance and Effectiveness" on pages 3 and 4.

Additional Research and Suggested Reading

For more information about women in the world, women in business, and women on boards, here are articles and books that inspired *The Board Game* and provide additional information.

Articles and Books

Bart, Chris, and Gregory McQueen. "Why Women Make Better Directors." *International Journal of Business Governance and Ethics* 8, no. 1 (2013).

Davidson, Amy. "Elect Women to Positions of Power, Get Positive Change." *More Magazine*, December 2012.

DeDominic, Patty, and Maureen Ford. *Life Moments for Women: 100+ Extraordinary California Women Share a Turning Point in Their Lives*. Santa Barbara, California: Blue Point Books, 2012.

Donaldson, Mimi. *Necessary Roughness: New Rules for the Contact Sport of Life*. Marina Del Rey, California: Mimispeaks, 2010.

Doyle, Anne. *Powering Up! How America's Women Achievers Become Leaders*. Bloomington, Indiana: Xlibris, 2011.

Ellig, Janice Reals, and Kathryn S. Wylde. "Boardroom Parity in the U.S. by 2022: For Gender Diversity, That Is. And Yes, It Can Happen—without Quotas. Here's How." *Directors & Boards*, June 7, 2012.

Entrenched Board. Key Metrics Series. www3.gmiratings.com/home/2012/10/key-metrics-series-entrenched-board/

Frankel, Lois P. *See Jane Lead: 99 Ways for Women to Take Charge at Work*. New York: Warner Business Books, 2007.

Friedan, Betty. *The Feminine Mystique*. New York: W.W. Norton, 1963.

Ghaffari, Elizabeth. *Outstanding in Their Field: How Women Corporate Directors Succeed*. Santa Barbara, California: Praeger/ABC-CLIO, 2009.
—. *Women Leaders at Work*. Berkeley, California: Apress, 2011.

Goman, Carol Kinsey. *The Silent Language of Leaders: How Body Language Can Help—or Hurt—How You Lead.* San Francisco: Jossey-Bass, 2011.

Green, Jeff. "The Boardroom Is Still the Boys' Room." *Bloomberg Businessweek*. October 25, 2012. www.businessweek.com/articles/2012-10-25/the-boardroom-is-still-the-boys-room

Grossman, Leslie. *Link Out: How to Turn Your Network into a Chain of Lasting Connections*. Hoboken, New Jersey: Wiley, 2013.

Kanter, Rosabeth M. *Men and Women of the Corporation.* New York: Basic Books, 1977.

Kaye, Beverly L., and Julie Winkle Giulioni. *Help Them Grow or Watch Them Go: Career Conversations Employees Want*. San Francisco: Berrett-Koehler Publishers, 2012.

Kaye, Beverly L., and Sharon Jordan-Evans. *Love 'em or Lose 'em: Getting Good People to Stay*. San Francisco, California: Berrett-Koehler Publishers, 1999.
—. *Love It, Don't Leave It: 26 Ways to Get What You Want at Work*. San Francisco: Berrett-Koehler, 2003.

Korologos, Ann McLaughlin. "Abandon Certain Misconceptions." *Directors and Boards*, 2005, Third Quarter ed.

Kramer, Vicki W., Alison M. Konrad, and Sumru Erkut. "Critical Mass on Corporate Boards: Why Three or More Women Enhance Governance." Wellesley Centers for Women. 2006.

Kristof, Nicholas D., and Sheryl WuDunn. *Half the Sky: Turning Oppression into Opportunity for Women Worldwide*. New York: Alfred A. Knopf, 2009.

Liswood, Laura A. *Women World Leaders: Fifteen Great Politicians Tell Their Stories*. London: Pandora, 1995.

Orr, Sarah Smith. "Women Directors in the Boardroom: Adding Value, Making a Difference." In *Boardroom Realities: Building Leaders Across Your Board*, by Jay Alden Conger. San Francisco, California: Jossey-Bass, 2009.

Pelosi, Nancy, and Amy Hill Hearth. *Know Your Power: A Message to America's Daughters*. New York: Doubleday, 2008.

Pointer, Dennis Dale., and James E. Orlikoff. *Board Work: Governing Health Care Organizations*. San Francisco: Jossey-Bass, 1999.

Forum of Executive Women. 2011. www.forumofexecutivewomen.com *"The Power of Three."*

Roberts, Cokie. *Founding Mothers: The Women Who Raised Our Nation*. New York: William Morrow, 2004.
—. *Ladies of Liberty: The Women Who Shaped Our Nation*. New York: William Morrow, 2008.

Rosener, Judy B. *America's Competitive Secret: Women Managers*. New York: Oxford University Press, 1997.

—. "Ways Women Lead." *Harvard Business Review*, November 1990.

—. "Women on Corporate Boards Makes Good Business Sense." Directorship, May 2003.

Ross, Emily, and Angus Holland. *100 Great Businesses and the Minds Behind Them*. Naperville, Illinois: Sourcebooks, 2006.

Shellenbarger, Sue. "The XX Factor: What's Holding Women Back?" Wall Street Journal. May 7, 2012.
online.wsj.com/article/SB10001424052702304746604577381953238775784.html

Shipman, Claire, and Katty Kay. *Womenomics*. New York: Collins Business, 2009.

Shultz, Susan. "Diversity." In *The Board Book: Making Your Corporate Board a Strategic Force in Your Company's Success*. New York: Amacom, American Management Association, 2001.

Stautberg, Susan, and Theresa Behrendt. *Selected Quotations That Inspire Us to Think Bigger, Live Better and Laugh Harder.* Quotation Media, 2012.

Steinem, Gloria. *Revolution from Within: A Book of Self-Esteem*. Boston: Little, Brown and, 1992.

Thomson, Peninah, Jacey Graham, and Tom Lloyd. *A Woman's Place Is in the Boardroom: The Roadmap*. Basingstoke, England: Palgrave Macmillan, 2008.

Van Der Zon, Kim. "Bring The NFL 'Rooney Rule' Into Corporate Boardrooms." *Forbes*. May 09, 2012.

Wittenberg-Cox, Avivah, and Alison Maitland. *Why Women Mean Business*. Hoboken, New Jersey: Wiley, 2009.

Publications About Boards
- *Agenda* (www.agendaweek.com) Weekly newsletter for corporate board members about relevant issues in the boardroom, Financial Times, London, UK
- *Directors & Boards* (www.directorsandboards.com)
- *Directorship* (NACD) (www.directorship.com/magazine)
- *Harvard Business Review* (www.hbr.org)

Organizations and Informational Websites

- BoardSource (www.boardsource.org) / BoardSource is a nonprofit, dedicated to advancing the public good by building exceptional nonprofit boards and inspiring board service.
- Broads Circle (www.broadscircle.com)
- Catalyst (www.catalyst.org) / Catalyst is the leading nonprofit membership organization with a mission to expand opportunities for women in business.
- The Conference Board (www.conference-board.org)
- 85Broads (www.85broads.com)
- InterOrganization Network (ION) (www.ionwomen.org)
- National Association of Corporate Directors (NACD) (www.nacdonline.org)
- National Association of Women Business Owners (NAWBO) (www.nawbo.org; California chapter www.nawbo-ca.org)
- 100 Women in Hedge Funds (www.100womeninhedgefunds.org)
- The Thirty Percent Coalition (www.30percentcoalition.org)
- Toastmasters International (www.toastmasters.org)
- 2020 Women on Boards (www.2020wob.com)
- Women Lawyers (American Bar Association) (www.directwomen.org) / DirectWomen for women attorneys
- WomenCorporateDirectors (www.womencorporatedirectors.com)
- WCD Global Nominating Committee Launches Campaign to Raise Number of Women on Board Worldwide, WomenCorporateDirectors, New York NY December 2012, www.womencorporatedirectors.com

Registries for Board-Ready Candidates

We are accustomed to finding information about ourselves in databases, but don't usually have a specific intention—or even ability—to *create* a record. But if you are ready for board service, you want to make yourself visible to boards seeking qualified candidates. Here are five registries to consider:

- Catalyst (www.catalyst.org/catalyst-corporate-board-resource): The Catalyst Corporate Board Resource allows member company CEOs to sponsor top women executives for board positions, premised on a recent Catalyst report that demonstrated how sponsorship can offer high performers greater access to advancement and the opportunity to excel.
- DirectWomen (www.directwomen.org): For women attorneys, this

organization identifies, develops, and supports attorneys who are qualified directors for board service, while promoting the independence and diversity required for good corporate governance.

- Diverse Director DataSource (www.gmi3d.com): Launched by CalSTRS and CalPERS and managed by GMI Ratings (www.gmiratings.com), board-ready women and people of color may register their profiles on the Diverse Director DataSource (also known as the "3D Database"). It is provided as a resource to executive search firms and corporations.
- WomenCorporateDirectors (www.womencorporatedirectors.com): Available to corporations and executive search firms seeking directors and advisory board candidates.
- Women's Forum of New York Database (www.womensforumny.org/index.cfm/layouts/ceo-sponsorship-portal): A national database of CEO-sponsored, board-ready women candidates.

Corporate Governance Education

A selection of corporate director training courses for women and men who want to improve their governance knowledge and keep current on updated regulations, best practices, and resources.

Non-University Training Programs

- OnBoard Bootcamp Training (www.onboardbootcamps.com) was launched by Susan Stautberg (co-founder of WomenCorporateDirectors) and multi-board director Carolyn Chin. OBB is designed for women who are interested in serving on boards and want to hone their preparation in a one-day seminar.
- DirectWomen Board Institute (www.directwomen.org/institute/) is an annual two-day program providing an orientation for exceptional women attorneys and updates on key issues facing current and future directors. Its goal is to position an elite group of exceptional senior women attorneys for service as corporate directors.
- BoardRoom Bound (www.boardroom-bound.com) offers a Chicago-based program "Boardology" to help train future board members.
- Women in the Boardroom (www.womenintheboardroom.com) produces programs to educate women for board preparation.

Professional Associations and Industry Training Programs
- Deloitte Center for Corporate Governance (www.corpgov.deloitte.com)
- The Directors' Consortium (www.directorsconsortium.org)
- The Directors' Network, Inc. (www.directorsnetwork.com)
- Energy Industry Directors Conference (business.rice.edu/energyboardconference) is designed for board members of energy companies at Rice University, Jones School of Business.
- Forum for Corporate Directors (www.fcdoc.org)
- KPMG Institutes (www.kpmginstitutes.com)
- National Association of Corporate Directors Board Leadership Conference (www.nacdonline.org)
- The FT (*Financial Times*) Outstanding Directors Exchange (www.ftconferences.com/ODX2012)
- Society of Corporate Secretaries (www.governanceprofessionals.org)

University Business Schools
- Columbia Business School, Columbia University, New York (www.gsb.columbia.edu)
- Dartmouth College, Tuck School of Business, Lindenauer Center for Corporate Governance, Hanover, New Hampshire (www.dartmouth.edu)
- Duke University, The Fuqua School of Business, Durham, North Carolina (www.fuqua.duke.edu)
- Emory University, Goizueta Business School, Atlanta, Georgia (www.goizueta.emory.edu)
- Harvard Business School, Cambridge, Massachusetts (www.hbs.edu)
- Indiana University Kelley School of Business, Institute for Corporate Governance (www.kelley.iu.edu/icg)
- New York University, Stern School of Business (www.stern.nyu.edu)
- Northwestern Kellogg School of Management, Evanston, Illinois, Executive Education—Women's Director Development Program (www.kellogg.northwestern.edu/execed/Programs/women.aspx)
- Oklahoma City University, Meinders School of Business (msb.okcu.edu)
- San Diego State University College of Business Administration, Corporate Governance Institute, San Diego (cbaweb.sdsu.edu/cgi)
- Stanford Graduate School of Business, Palo Alto, California (www.stanford.edu)

- University of California, Berkeley, Haas School of Business (www.haas.berkeley.edu)
- University of California, Irvine, The Paul Merage School of Business (merage.uci.edu)
- UCLA Anderson School of Management, Director Education & Certification Program (www.anderson.ucla.edu/executive-education/individual-executives/management/corporate-governance)
- University of Chicago, Booth School of Business (www.chicagobooth.edu)
- University of Denver, Daniels College of Business (www.daniels.du.edu)
- University of Georgia, Terry College of Business (www.terry.uga.edu)
- University of Maryland, University College: National Leadership Institute (www.umuc.edu/nli)
- University of Michigan, Ross School of Business (www.bus.umich.edu)
- University of Pennsylvania, The Wharton School, Philadelphia (www.wharton.upenn.edu)
- University of Southern California, Center for Effective Organizations, Marshall School of Business, Los Angeles (ceo.usc.edu)
- University of Tampa, Directors Institute (www.ut.edu/floridadirectorsinstitute)
- University of Texas at Austin, McCombs School of Business (www.mccombs.utexas.edu)
- University of Texas at Dallas, Naveen Jindal School of Management, Institute for Excellence in Corporate Governance (jindal.utdallas.edu/centers-of-excellence/institute-for-excellence-in-corporate-governance)
- Washington University in St. Louis, Olin Business School (www.olin.wustl.edu/pages/default.aspx)
- University of Wisconsin–Madison, Wisconsin School of Business (www.bus.wisc.edu)

ACKNOWLEDGMENTS

MY GRATITUDE GOES OUT TO EVERYONE WHO ENCOURAGED ME ALL THE WAY TO THE FINISH LINE, INCLUDING:

The many women corporate directors and experts featured in *The Board Game*, including three Fortune 500 CEOs—Debra Reed, Denise Morrison, and Maggie Wilderotter. For their tireless efforts on behalf of women on boards, Susan Stautberg, Alison Winter, and Henrietta Holsman Fore, co-chairs of WomenCorporateDirectors; and Ilene Lang, CEO of Catalyst. Male CEO advocates who are in *The Board Game*: Peter Ueberroth on the board of Coca-Cola; Mark Bertolini, CEO of Aetna; George Halvorson, CEO of Kaiser Permanente; Doug Conant, former CEO of Campbell Soup; and Joe Keefe of Pax World.

My collaborator Keven Bellows, longtime friend and author, for her ideas, her help with writing and editing—I could not have done this without her. And Betsy Nolan, my literary agent in New York and San Francisco.

My publishers/editors Paddy Calistro and Scott McAuley, owners of Angel City Press in Santa Monica, California, who made the dream come true—when I thought it couldn't be done. Jeff Burbank, who re-introduced me to Paddy— I first knew her before she co-founded her publishing company twenty years ago, when she was a well-known columnist at the *Los Angeles Times*. And to Hilary Lentini, designer of this book and owner of Lentini Design in Los Angeles—we met as co-speakers on a panel of women business owners years ago, and coincidentally met again through Angel City Press.

Fred Clayton, my hard-working and dedicated business partner, co-founder of Berkhemer Clayton in 1994, headquartered in Los Angeles, with an office in Hong Kong. Thanks to our client corporations, universities, and large nonprofit organizations who retain our firm to find senior executives for corporate communications, finance, investor relations, and boards of directors. Our staff at Berkhemer Clayton—Krista Haley, Ben Lambert, Elaina Schmitz, Anne Weber, Alicia LaFarga, Wanda Kilbourne, and Mike Bindman in California—and Sai Pradhan in Hong Kong. Special thanks to Alicia, for her help with countless book-related details. You all make it fun to go to work every day.

My friend for twenty-five years and radio co-host Renee Fraser, owner of Fraser Communications, a marketing, advertising, and digital agency, one of the largest woman-owned companies in the West. In 2009, she and I created "Unfinished Business" a weekly hour-long radio talk show to encourage entrepreneurs, on KFWB News Talk 980 in Southern California. Special thanks to our close friend Tammy Tucker, vice president of Anthem Blue Cross, who was our first advertising sponsor; to our producer Carolyn Branson, and to our champion, Rosemary Hernandez, at CBS Radio.

My author friends/scholars and speakers: Anne Doyle from Detroit, Martha (Marti) Hammer, Linda Sivertsen, Elizabeth Ghaffari, Kate Kelly, Mimi Donaldson, Dr. Tessa Albert Warshaw, and Sarah Smith Orr, executive director of the Kravis Leadership Institute at Claremont McKenna College, who interviewed me for the book *Boardroom Realities* and invited me to speak to the women students at the Claremont Colleges. And to ION board member Toni G. Wolfman at Bentley University Center for Women and Business.

At my alma mater UCLA: Chancellor Gene Block, Dean Judy Olian of the UCLA Anderson School of Management; Dr. Al Osborne, leader of its Corporate Director Training and Certification Program; and Associate Vice Chancellor Carol Stogsdill.

Dean Jim Ellis of University of Southern California Marshall School of Business; Martha Harris, retired EVP of University Relations at USC and her husband Morgan Lyons, now residents of New Orleans; and to Mount St. Mary's College, for producing its annual Report on the Status of Women and Girls in California.

I salute my revered National Association of Women Business Owners, where I serve on the NAWBO-California statewide board, am past statewide president and past president of the Los Angeles chapter, and was honored to receive the NAWBO-Los Angeles Lifetime Achievement Award in 2004.

I thank my women business-owner friends: Jane Skeeter of UltraGlas; Beverly Kaye of Career Systems International; Cristina Rose and Maureen Kindel, former owners of Rose & Kindel Public Affairs; Karen Hill Scott and Alice Walker Duff, founders of Crystal Stairs; Patty DeDominic, leadership coach, former owner of PDQ Careers, and International Women's Festivals founder; Billie Greer, former public affairs agency owner; Madelyn Alfano of Maria's Italian Kitchen Restaurants; Chris Hershey of Hershey|Cause; and renowned architect Brenda Levin.

Leslie Grossman in New York, author of *Link Out*, and Andrea March, both founders of Women's Leadership Exchange; Janice Bryant Howroyd of Act One Group; Gayla Kraetsch-Hartsough of KH Consulting; Frieda Caplan, founder of Frieda's Produce, and her daughter CEO Karen Caplan; and Hiroko Tatebe, founder of the Global Organization for Leadership and Diversity (GOLD) conference that builds relationships among women leaders in Japan and the U.S.

Joan Payden of Payden & Rygel global investment management firm in Los Angeles; Sandy Gooch, founder of Mrs. Gooch's Natural Foods Markets; and Debbi Fields, former client and founder of Mrs. Fields Cookies.

To the late Adrienne Hall, the first woman co-owner of a national advertising agency, Hall & Levine. A champion for women leaders around the world, Adrienne founded The Trusteeship, the Los Angeles affiliate of the International Women's Forum (IWF).

Judy Miller, vice president and director of the Hilton Humanitarian Prize at the Conrad N. Hilton Foundation; Michelle Jordan, Jordan LLC, strategic communications for leaders; Jane Hurd, executive coach, board search consultant.

Corporate directors Monica Lozano, CEO of ImpreMedia, board member of Bank of America and Walt Disney Company; Bernee Strom, founder and CEO of Gemstar/TV Guide International and Priceline.com; and former director Vilma Martinez, now U.S. Ambassador to Argentina. And to Janice Reals Ellig, past president of the New York Women's Forum.

Geena Davis—founder of the Geena Davis Institute on Gender in Media, dedicated to changing portrayals and gender stereotypes of women and girls in movies and TV.

Lise Luttgens and Carol Dedrich of the Girl Scouts of Greater Los Angeles; Faye Washington, CEO of YWCA of Greater Los Angeles; and Ann Reiss Lane, founder of Women Against Gun Violence.

My role models: Hillary Clinton, Gloria Steinem, Dianne Feinstein, Madeleine Albright, Betty Friedan, Peg Yorkin; U.S. Representatives Lucille Royball-Allard, Karen Bass, Jackie Speier, Judy Chu, and Janice Hahn; California Secretary of State Debra Bowen; former California State Controller Kathleen Connell; California legislators Holly Mitchell, Hannah-Beth Jackson, Bonnie Lowenthal, Carol Liu, Mimi Walters, and Cheryl Brown. Los Angeles Deputy Mayor Aileen Adams and former City Controller Laura Chick.

Wendy Greuel, the first woman to run for mayor of the city of Los Angeles.

Friends Anne Shen Smith, president of Southern California Gas Company, and Kimberly Freeman, director of community relations; JoAnn Bourne of Union Bank; Gail and Brett Guge; Sally's Dinner Group—Sally Jameson, Jackie Doud, Barbara Goen, Sue Whitfield, and Linda Deacon. Darya Allen-Attar, founder of

Broads Circle, and to all members of the Organization of Women Executives (O.W.E.) in Los Angeles. To Andrea Schaffer and Marguerite Rangel of Pacific Advisors; and my Spanish teacher, Elizabeth Vanegas.

My sisters, Dorothy Perry, Bonnie Vincent, Rosemary Joyce, Suzanne Furlong, brother Dick Brooks, and his wife, Erika; many nieces and nephews, including Anne Perry and David Vincent.

My late parents, Bob Berkhemer, Topper Berkhemer and my mother Claire (Casey) Myers Berkhemer—who would have loved to have had a business career, but lived a generation too early; and my Aunt Lola Patton, who owned a small shoe manufacturing company in Columbus, Ohio—she was the first woman business owner I ever knew.

And a special tribute to our friends whose lives were tragically taken by cancer far too early: Mary Jane Hewett, Lynne Doll, Patty Fox, and Roseanna Purzycki. My thanks to Denise Fletcher in New York, founding OCNA board member who introduced me to the Ovarian Cancer National Alliance in Washington, D.C.

And finally, thanks to my handsome and intelligent voyagemate since 1985, my husband, Cris Credaire.

—Betsy Berkhemer-Credaire

INDEX

Ovarian Cancer National Alliance
is the foremost advocacy organization for women with ovarian cancer and
represents tens of thousands of women with ovarian cancer in the United States.

The Alliance works closely with the federal government to increase funding
for research to develop an early detection test, life-saving treatment protocols,
and educational campaigns.

The Alliance advocates to raise awareness of the risks, signs, and symptoms
of this disease, and educates medical schools and general practitioners
that correct diagnosis must occur early enough for treatment to be effective.

The Alliance is a vital source for the latest research on ovarian cancer and
firsthand insight into how this disease affects women's lives.

September is National Ovarian Cancer Awareness Month.

The author will donate a portion of the proceeds from
The Board Game
to
Ovarian Cancer National Alliance
www.ovariancancer.org